John Howard Crawford

The brotherhood of mankind

A study towards a Christian philosophy of history

John Howard Crawford

The brotherhood of mankind
A study towards a Christian philosophy of history

ISBN/EAN: 9783337238315

Printed in Europe, USA, Canada, Australia, Japan

Cover: Foto ©Lupo / pixelio.de

More available books at **www.hansebooks.com**

THE
BROTHERHOOD OF MANKIND

A STUDY TOWARDS A CHRISTIAN
PHILOSOPHY OF HISTORY

BY THE
REV. JOHN HOWARD CRAWFORD, M.A.

EDINBURGH
T. & T. CLARK, 38 GEORGE STREET
1895

TO

ROBERT FLINT, D.D., LL.D.,

*the Historian of the Philosophy of History,
this study in that Philosophy is inscribed
by his friend and some time pupil,*

THE AUTHOR.

PREFACE

THE object of this book is to show that the end towards which mankind are progressing is a united brotherhood.

This goal of mankind is the key to human history, which unfolds a steady progress towards its realisation.

We approach the question from several aspects.

As a matter of historical investigation, we trace the growth of the idea of a united humanity as revealed in the progress of mankind, showing how all life tends to exhibit an advance towards it.

As a theological inquiry, we endeavour to identify it with the teaching of Christ and the general growth of the Church. It appears as the central spirit of Christianity. It underlies all the doctrines of the Church, and unfolds the earthly meaning of the Incarnation. And although in this book we do not consider the life beyond, we may add that it supplies the key to all eschatology.

The relation which the progress of mankind towards unity bears to morality and knowledge has also a place in our theory. It is possible here only to give a general view of so wide a subject; but we hope, as opportunity offers in the future, to elucidate more fully some of the more important aspects of the great principle which underlies all human life.

The whole of humanity is a unity, and is subject to the same law of growth. The Manichæan theory which represents the natural tendency of mankind as towards social disintegration, which religion steps in to counteract, is not confirmed by an examination of history. We read in the movement of secular thought and action the same great law of association, ever tending to a brotherhood of love, which Christianity unfolds to us. Literature, art, politics, and commerce show its operation as well as religion. That this law is the inner secret of the whole history of the human race in all its activities, we believe; and the destiny of man will be accomplished when that perfect unity is attained. Not that perfection may be taken in its absolute sense, for that is not possible for man; but a nearer and nearer approach may be made towards complete human brotherhood.

That the unity of mankind, as Church and State, will one day be accomplished, history and the Christian faith agree in hoping for.

But, since this is the great aim towards which men are destined, is it not our duty to aid it by all means in our power?

We take no such dark view of our present social state as some passionate hearts among social thinkers seem to brood over; but we make some inquiry into the actual conditions of life among us, trusting we may do something to remove obstacles to that free and united brotherhood of man in which God has placed the perfection of humanity. The eloquent words of Lamennais express our hopes for the future: "When each of you, loving all men as brothers, shall act to each other like brothers; when each of you, seeking his own well-being in the wellbeing of all, shall identify his life with the life of all, and his interest with the interest of all; when each shall be ever ready to sacrifice himself for all the members of the Common Family, who are equally ready to sacrifice themselves for him,—most of the evils which now weigh upon the human race will disappear, as the gathering mists of the horizon flee at sunrise, and the will of God will be fulfilled. For it is His will that love shall unite the shattered members of humanity and organise them into a single whole, so that humanity may be one, even as He is One."

I have to thank my brother-in-law, the Rev. J. A. MacCulloch, Acting Vice-Principal of the Theological College of the Episcopal Church of Scotland, for revising the proofs, and making the index, of this book.

CONTENTS

	PAGE
PREFACE	v

INTRODUCTION

CHAP.
I. THE DEVELOPMENT OF CHRISTIANITY IN HUMAN THOUGHT 1

II. TIME THE INTERPRETER 17

III. THE ETHICAL PURPOSE OF DEVELOPMENT 27

THE BROTHERHOOD OF MANKIND

IV. BROTHERHOOD BEFORE CHRIST 38

V. THE UNITY OF MAN 52

VI. JESUS THE CARPENTER 65

VII. THE THEOLOGY OF JESUS 80

VIII. THE ETHICAL PRINCIPLE OF JESUS 96

IX. THE AUTHORITY OF JESUS 115

X. BROTHERHOOD IN THE EPISTLES 128

XI. INDIVIDUALISM IN THE LIFE OF THE CHURCH 139

XII. THE FAMILY, ITS PAST AND FUTURE 154

XIII. THE SACRAMENTS 171

XIV. ENTRANCE INTO THE LIFE OF BROTHERHOOD, AND PROGRESS THEREIN 184

CHAP.	PAGE
XV. The Christian Personality .	198
XVI. Brotherhood in the Early Church . .	206
XVII. Brotherhood in the Middle Ages, with a View of the Relation of Christianity to Childhood .	224
XVIII. Brotherhood since the Reformation . .	242
XIX. Social and Political Progress . . .	259
XX. The Service of Literature and Art . .	271
XXI. The Natural Growth of Altruism . .	295
XXII. Christianity and Patriotism	310
XXIII. The Opposition of Scepticism	321
XXIV. Other Forces which are against Brotherhood .	334
XXV. The Kingdom of God and the Church . .	345
XXVI. The Future . . .	360

THE
BROTHERHOOD OF MANKIND

CHAPTER I

THE DEVELOPMENT OF CHRISTIANITY IN HUMAN THOUGHT

MEN have always desired to know the inner meaning of Christianity, to express its central thought. It is gathered from many sources, and embraces many spheres of life; but there must be a spiritual principle round which all its manifestations cluster, and an end to which they all tend. The efforts of all thinkers help to unfold this central thought, to get nearer and nearer the heart of the divine truth. It is too great a task for one man unaided to try. He might as well attempt to know the whole of the laws of nature. But as the scientific thinker begins where his predecessor left off, so has the theologian the benefit of every previous worker's labour. And he has still more the help of the course of time, which, as it unrolls itself, also lays bare the meaning and purpose of the Christian faith. The history of the Church is a long commentary on the teaching of Christ.

Nor must we confine ourselves to the history of the Church, for the history of the world is also a guide to the inquirer as to the inner principle and final goal of Christianity. The divine purpose reveals itself in the history of mankind, though we can but imperfectly discern it. Whatever it be, it must be the same goal as that to which the Christian religion tends. History and religion have the same inner principle, and must unfold the same destiny for mankind.

It is not given to any age to express the full truth of the Christian doctrine, or reach the perfection of the Christian life. The history of the Church reveals an ever-expanding interpretation of the oracles of God. The old analogy of the tree of existence, Ygdrassil, which was daily watered by the Nornen from the fountain at its root, is a true figure of the progressive life of Christianity. To narrow the living force into a fixed system is an impossibility. For the life is eternal and divine in its nature, and any system is but a child of time and the mind of man. The intelligence of man itself expands; and shall his understanding of divine truth not grow with his ever-increasing capacity? To doubt the fact that our knowledge of Christianity in its doctrines and practice is enlarged with the progress of other attainments, is to doubt the constant presence of God in the world. Shall we go forward in all things except the highest? What a mockery of the onward march of the human race is it to tell us that in religion alone there is no hope of advancement!

We know as a fact that Christian doctrine has developed; we have learned that the very canon of the

New Testament was a growth of centuries; we see that the outward form of the Church has been subject to the law of change: and how then can we say that the fulness of Christianity was reached at any one time? St. Paul himself looks forward to advancing knowledge and fuller faith. "For we know in part, and we prophesy in part. But when that which is perfect is come, then that which is in part shall be done away."

If the Christian religion were so fixed in a final, permanent, and unchangeable form of human conception, where and when was it fixed? If at any time the mind of man grasped its divine perfection, its form must have been unchanging in all circumstances and for all ages. The Sacred Scriptures themselves are the growth of several generations, and we can trace the progress of their various writers. They give us no formal creed, but leave it to the elucidation of successive ages. God spoke "at sundry times and in divers manners" in days gone by, and the same law of advancement still rules our being. The explanations of the mental life of man and the material life of nature, which satisfied Origen and his contemporaries, fail to meet the needs of our present-day knowledge. And since they are in part our instrument for understanding what God has told us, our view of divine truth must also expand with our keener means of insight. Every increase of attainment which man receives sheds light on his character, duty, and destiny, and enables us to interpret more fully the will of God concerning him.

The view which some hold, that our interpretation of divine truth may be confined within a system which remains permanent and immutable, is not consistent with the ever present power of God in the world of men's thoughts. It is a relic of older ways of thinking, when God was regarded as apart from the universe, and as little nearer men than the deities of the Epicureans. Some have endeavoured to find in this a Latin mode of thought as distinguished from a Greek. They have traced it to St. Augustine, but it is also in Plato's *Timæus*, and is perhaps more a mood of thought than a real belief.

The truer doctrine which St. Athanasius and his forerunners, Clement of Alexandria and Origen, taught, that God is always present in all His work, and manifests Himself in the laws of nature and the mind of man, is more and more being received in our day. While the faith, as it is embodied in the Apostles' Creed, is simply a statement of facts, which must ever remain the *foundation* of our holy religion, the relations of these facts to life may be variously expounded, and with increasing accuracy, as knowledge advances.

The development we assert, it will be observed, is a growth in ability to *interpret* divine truth. This differs somewhat from the Roman view, which is maintained in theory by such theologians as Newman and Möhler, and in practice by the dogmatic additions which the Pope makes to the creed of the Church over which he rules. These additions imply a power of constructing new foundations, of declaring the existence of new facts, of practically making fresh revelations to mankind. Both the Roman and Protestant Churches hold that the Church is divinely guided, but they differ as to the results of that guidance.

The Protestants claim no more than a liberty to interpret the divine truth, in which interpretation they must, by the very nature of things, make progress. The Roman Church holds that it can add to the actual store, not only of spiritual fact, but of principles of divine authority. The attachment of Protestants to their systems has, however, made little difference in practical result between them and Rome. To make human thought an absolute standard for religious guidance, as Protestants do with their elaborate Confessions, is to take the same standpoint as the Pope himself. Both alike exclude the power of advancement; and if any is better than the other, it is the Pope, who declares himself, by the mere history of his Church, ever open to new light. This is happily expressed by Steele, who does not forget his humour in his theology.[1] "We cannot but esteem the advantage to be exceedingly on our side, because we have all the benefits of Infallibility, without the absurdity of pretending to it. Many of the quick-sighted and sagacious persons have not been able to discover any other difference between us, as to the main principle of all Doctrine, Government, Worship, and Discipline, but this one, viz., that you *cannot* err in anything you determine, and we never *do*. That is, in other words, that you are infallible, and we are always in the right."

It was the form of thought in days not long gone, to reduce all science to a series of propositions often as devoid of actuality as a map of a landscape. Political

[1] In the Dedication to the Pope prefixed to *An Account of the Roman Catholic Religion*, which Dedication, however, some think was not Steele's own.

economy could be reasoned out from a few general principles, to which facts must agree or be ignored; and so was it with theology. If these had been mere sciences of the study, if they had dwelt in the retirement of thought, the world might not have felt the error so deeply. But the system-maker came forth from his books and parchments, and set up his idols in the market-place for men to worship. Many a dark page in the history of mankind is due to the baleful influence of the disbeliever in development in the spheres of economics and religion.

When Lord Macaulay wrote that neither natural nor revealed theology is progressive, there were more people to agree with him than he would now find. His adherents are rather to be seen in sceptical ranks than among devout men. He says: " All divine truth is, according to the doctrine of the Protestant Churches, recorded in certain books. It is equally open to all who in any age can read those books; nor can all the discoveries of all the philosophers in the world add a single verse to any of those books. It is plain, therefore, that in divinity there cannot be a progress analogous to that which is constantly taking place in pharmacy, geology, and navigation. A Christian of the fifth century with a Bible is neither better nor worse situated than is a Christian of the nineteenth century with a Bible, candour and acuteness being, of course, supposed equal."[1] We find stronger language used by Dr. Draper in his *History of the Conflict between Religion and Science*, where he tells us that a religion based on divine revelation "must repudiate all

[1] Essay on Ranke's *History of the Popes*.

improvement in itself, and view with disdain that arising from the progressive intellectual development of man." And Mr. F. R. Conder, with perhaps a better grasp of the modern conditions of the problem, says: "The theological doctrine of development occupies the same place in religious theory that evolution holds among the disciples of Darwin. A man can be developed out of a child, but A cannot be developed out of Not A, when *not* implies, not absence, but negation."

Similarly, a certain school of theologians hold opinions adverse to a theory of religious growth, and aver that the Confessions of the Reformed Churches, to which they adhere, such as the Thirty-nine Articles or the Westminster Confession, teach a permanent and unchanging systematisation of divine truth. Such a view is not fairly drawn from these documents, and the history of thought in the Churches is a sufficient refutation of it. The old Scots Confession of 1560 prefaces its Declaration of Faith by an admission of the possibility of error, and the promise of amendment on fuller knowledge.[1]

Now, assuming Lord Macaulay to have stated the truth when he said that the whole of divine truth was contained in certain books, he could have learned, even at the time when he wrote, that it was possible, by increased knowledge of these books, to alter the whole conception of biblical theology, and by placing these

[1] " Protesting that gif any man will note in this oure Confessioun any article or sentence repugning to Godis holie word, that it wald pleis him of his gentilnes, and for Christiane cherites saik, to admoneise us of the samyn in writ; and We of our honour do promeis unto him satisfactioun, or ellis reformatioun of that quhilk he sall prove to be amyss."—Knox's *Works*, ed. Laing, ii. 96.

books in their true relation, to advance theology as much as astronomy was made to progress when it was discovered that the sun, and not the earth, was the centre of our system.

I do not stay to point out the fallacy which underlies the theory that the individual Christian can understand the whole counsel of God, which ignores the whole interpretation which the general thought of the Church, and the history of the world, give to the Sacred Scriptures; for of that I shall afterwards speak. But who can believe that the Spirit of God leaves the Church destitute of guidance? As men advance in knowledge, so they grow better able to apply divine truth to human life, which supplies itself the best commentary on it. It would be no hard task to show how doctrines and discussions have lost significance with changed times; and how questions, which were unnoticed by our fathers, have become of deep moment to us. But the whole record of the history of the Church is a demonstration of the fact.

The present conditions of man's thought make it impossible for anyone seriously to hold that his theological system is absolute, and, as it were, archetypal in the divine mind. It is probably due to Herder, in modern times, that we have returned to a sense of the unreasonableness of such a belief. He shows how, in the desire to systematise, men have had to *add to Christianity* elements of their own, fleeting fantasies of their time, which faded at the dawn of fuller knowledge.

It was an older thought than Pascal's, though it is

chiefly associated with his name,[1] that mankind may be represented as one living being, who exists throughout the ages, and is ever learning. We can trace the same ideal unity in the Christian Church, which has ever been regarded by the devout heart as a living body united to her divine Head. There are many analogies which are well worth observing between the processes of organic life and the growth of the Church.

We see how doctrines are adapted to the spiritual life of their time, and perish of atrophy, when they are no longer so understood as to be useful. In the Middle Ages the doctrine of a purgatory had tremendous power, as Dante's great poem shows us; but men grew out of it, and the Reformation swept it away.

Obscurantist theologians join with deists like Lord Herbert of Cherbury in thinking such additions to the Church creed were made by priesthoods and statecraft. But how unhistorical is such a way of reading history! Men believed these doctrines because they thought them honest interpretations of the great facts of divine revelation. Their life seemed to them to hang on faith in them; and it appears as if they were urged by some necessity into their belief. While they trusted the dogma, which at last they threw away, it was an organ of life to them; it was a practical, if imperfect, instrument. But it was more: it had within itself the power of an education to lead to a higher and better knowledge, which would teach them to cast it aside. It bore

---

[1] It is found in the early Fathers; and is fuller in William of Auvergne, in Lessing, and others, such as Bishop Temple. It does not occur in the early editions of the *Pensées*.

on its face its temporary character; it was a mere makeshift, while time ripened its purposes.

For, after all, doctrines and worship are but means to a great end, the perfecting of the soul. "Men are not religious merely by the use of them, but by that which is attained by them. They are not religion itself, but productive and preservative and declarative of it."[1] As an organ in the human body, no longer needed, shrinks into a rudimentary suggestion of the past, so it is with the thoughts of men. They come to a time when they "put away childish things," and are conscious of manhood.

There is a time for a truth to have its perfect day; a time when it reaches its consummation, and has its greatest influence on men. Mr. Matthew Arnold gives an instance of this in the religious history of Germany. The two influences which moved the theology of the Church, and tended to reform it, were those of Tauler and Luther. The earlier form of thought was not easily grasped by the people, whereas Luther's came home to their hearts. "The one leavened a group and individuals; the other created the Protestant Churches." The time had not come for Tauler's views, if, indeed, such mysticism could ever find a wide acceptance; but Luther gave men what they needed, and they took his gift with eagerness. Other minds and other ages might receive Tauler's ways of looking at spiritual truth; and, indeed, Mr. Arnold suggests that our own age might be ready to receive them.

Men grow and progress in line with their fellows;

[1] Whichcote on Eph. ii. 22.

they march in crowds, and obey a general impulse, inbreathing the spirit of their time. It is the sum of the thoughts of individuals which makes up that spirit. Whence these thoughts come we ask not; but can we think them wholly due to environment? We accept the fact that each age has a form of thinking, a way of considering the question which religion offers, a method of using the gifts which the divine Spirit bestows upon men. The average of human thought and morals at any one time is a real fact. The writer on morals cannot escape from its compelling power. When Kant announces his categorical imperative,—" Act only on that principle which thou canst will as law universal," —he implies the underlying principle that a man cannot separate himself from his fellow-men in the march of knowledge, but must keep pace with them.[1] The same truth is also seen in the argument for Theism *e consensu gentium*. We learn how to all men, in presence of the same facts, the same thoughts arise, and we cannot shut out from our acknowledgment the universal need, and the universal supply of that need, in the worship of divine beings.

No one can doubt that every age and people has its mental character, which reveals itself in the form by which it receives and applies the truths of Christianity.

[1] De Wette shows this; and Mr. Bradley, in his *Ethical Studies*, says that a man who seeks to have a higher morality than that of his world, is on the threshold of immorality. We may add that some such specious belief led to the irregularities of life with which such poets as Goethe and Shelley, such novelists as George Eliot and George Sand, such theologians as Hamann and Swedenborg, shocked the moral sense of men.

The river of truth contains the same water through all its course, but it flows through varied scenes. Sometimes it glides softly; and at crises in human history it rushes in a foaming torrent. Over every mile of its course there are different reflexions: at one time it is open to the blue heaven, and mirroring its serene brightness, while at another it is deeply shadowed over by interlacing trees through which the light pierces in struggling and fitful rays.

Amid all the changes of doctrinal thought there abides an essential unity. True growth shows both the abiding element, which links the present with the past, and the advancing element, which joins it with the future. There is therefore both rest and change at every moment in the history of the Church. The unity may be found in the *idea* of the Church (to speak the language of Plato), what Hermas and Clement of Alexandria call the Heavenly Church, to which the earthly embodiment ever comes nearer an exact similitude. The earthly elements change and decay, they blossom and wither; but the life of the Church ever becomes fuller and richer, and ever tends onwards to the great purpose before it. Ever imperfect on earth, the Church is ever striving toward divine perfection. " It is vain to look for aught but a limited power of insight from man as he is constituted at present; just as an infant has but a limited faculty of seeing; but the main lines are already there, and as the vision ever broadens, so does the knowledge of religion become fuller." [1]

These main lines remain the centres from which other

[1] Steudel's *Lectures on Old Testament Theology*.

truths radiate, till the circle of knowledge comes nearer and nearer to completion. Hence present Christianity is so related to the past as to retain a recollection of it, which ever governs its thought and action. As Professor Clifford says: "It is the peculiarity of living things, not merely that they change under the influence of surrounding circumstances, but that any change which takes place in them is not lost, but retained, and, as it were, built into the organism to serve as the foundation for future actions. If you cause any distortion in the growth of a tree, and make it crooked, whatever you do afterwards to make the tree straight, the mark of your distortion is there; it is absolutely indelible; it has become part of the tree's nature."

It is practically impossible for any age to cut itself off from the past and make an entirely new beginning. The theory of Protestant Church life, which seems to find its origin in the Reformation, and takes no heed of the long centuries before, is barely coherent, far less probable. There is no fact more certain than that the life of the Church is a unity, a living unity, animated by a spirit of growth and progress. Every Christian shares in the life of the Church, and is shaped by it. Macaulay's fifth century Christian and his nineteenth century successor have many points in common, but their life-education has been in widely different schools; and the language of their soul is not the same. An individualist interpretation of divine truth is an impossibility, however men may feel sure they are free. We are children of our time, and are borne on the currents of the thought around us.

The efficacy of doctrines depends on the fact that they are real to the age that conceives them; that they are felt to be a sincere interpretation of divine truth. Men can only speak as they know; they can only use their own language; and if a doctrine is unintelligible, it is useless. Nay, if it comes from outside, if it is not the effort of the times to realise the truth, it is without meaning to those who hear it. Our Saviour took not on Him the nature of angels; He came as man. Divine truth speaks in human language when it speaks to men.

The law of development is truly regarded, therefore, as *growth in interpreting power*. The basis on which it works is ever the same: "Jesus Christ, the same yesterday, to-day, and for ever." The foundation is immutable, though the superstructure is a creation of time, and subject to its laws. I do not say that our knowledge may not bring to light truths which Jesus and His apostles taught, but which other ages have not seen; for I believe that we do recover forgotten elements in their teaching. But as time goes on, we also come to understand them better. Revelation is an unveiling of truth—truth hidden in the heart of God, and made known to man; and we come to be better able to read the scroll which is opened to our view, with every successive generation. The giving of revelation is but the starting-point of the new world which opens to the soul of man.

Such a view excludes the possibility that our beliefs are but the toiling of our reason, which, like a blind Samson, urges us on some devious way; are but the poetic imagination of our brain, and have no reality out-

side the mind that thinks them, and beyond the brief
season of their existence. When Simmias asked "a word
from God" to confirm the speculations of Socrates, he
expressed what all men feel; and we would have our
desire still unsatisfied, were we told that there was
nothing in our religion but the gradual growth of the
thoughts of man. It is because we are sure of the divine
seed, and have seen it sown, that we know the fruits that
we harvest. Nay more, it is because we are assured of
the divine end of all things, that we are able to understand them in the feeble measure that we do. As
Hamann says: "The future determines the present, and
the present determines the past."

The devout mind is not content, therefore, to accept
the mere statement of the law of development as summing
up the history of the Church. What is the power, we
are compelled to ask, which is ever present to animate
the ever living, ever growing Church? This brings us to
the clearer theological statement of our position.

Our Saviour, the divine Logos, appeared on earth and
revealed to us the nature of God and the complete
destiny of man. He did this, not only by His life on
earth, but by the perpetuation of that life through the
Church and in the world. We could only faintly trace
the progress of mankind by toilsome effort, had not
Christ revealed to us in one supreme moment the great
purpose of God. It is as if for the time we shared the
eternity of God, which knows not the limitations of time
and its slow process. But our mind cannot, after all,
receive this revelation in its fulness: it requires ages to
interpret it. It unfolds itself with the lapse of centuries,

and every year discovers some new ray of light hitherto wrapped in darkness.

It is by the developing life of the Church in the world that alone we can come fully to understand the whole truth of Christianity, which is ever living and active, and not formal and theoretical. When Jesus said, "Lo, I am with you alway, even unto the end of the world," we must understand the passage in its full meaning. The life of the Church is divine in its source, its progress, and its destiny.

The ordinary forces of our human life must not be left out of our consideration of the development of Christianity. The history of the world is a vast commentary on the life of Christ. Nor are the truly Christian energies which give life to mankind separated from the currents of our common existence. The progress of civilisation, the increase of secular knowledge, the influences of art and industry, the spreading of the peoples of the earth over its surface, the growth of political and social institutions, and the thousand other facts of human history, have all their tribute both given to and received from Christianity. They give the Christian religion forms of thought and modes of application, expand its meaning, and are brought into various relations with it. Men begin to see how the Christian life includes all science, all morals, all politics, all art, and all literature. It was the dream of Comte to include everything human within the scope of his philosophy: what he could not attain, Christianity has accomplished.

CHAPTER II

TIME THE INTERPRETER

THE development of Christianity is, as we have seen, an advance towards better interpretation of divine truth. Strictly speaking, a creed, such as that called the Apostles', does not fall within the description of interpretation, for it is really statement of *facts*. To doubt these facts was to the early Christian the same as to doubt the sunrise. But as they were facts which to believe needed a certain knowledge and a special condition of soul, the possession of the creed was one of the last of the privileges of those who were admitted to the Church. Probably it was a wise plan, and our modern methods might take a hint from it. At all events, it is well to make it clear that the Church, when it formed the creeds into connected statement, regarded them as the foundation truths of Christianity, and did not think of them as mere theologisings of men.

What is to be the canon by which we are to unfold the meaning of these truths? The answer to this question determines the whole character of our theological thought.

Briefly, we may say that the life of the Church and the history of mankind are the true interpreters of divine truth. The pages of history are but a successive unfolding of the divine purpose. As we have seen, that purpose is fully revealed in Christ; but the progressive wisdom of mankind, the sequence of events in human history, alone can make the divine end fully clear to men.

The historical method is the only way in which we can come to see the development of Christianity in the life of mankind. By observing the movement through the centuries of its thought and activity, we can discover its essential ideas, and trace its future purpose. As the astronomer who knows a part of the orbit of a planet can follow it through its whole course and predict its future position, so the historian can trace the march of the Church through time, and deduce therefrom its steps yet untrod.

The method which begins à priori is no longer held in such honour as once it was. When men's materials were slender, there was a temptation to resort to it, as no other way was open; and now, when the facts we must take account of are overwhelming in their bulk, there may again be an inducement to return to the à priori method. But where is the need of hypothesis when such a vast accumulation of experiment is embedded in history and in present civilisation? We see what Christianity has been; we see its present conditions and tendencies; and we can form some induction as to its inner principles and its future destiny.

It is not enough to examine individual consciousness, and listen to its testimony. Not enough is it to analyse the highest forms of piety, and tell their internal contents. Such a process, basing itself on the subjective feeling and knowledge, as in the theory of Rothe, does not meet the claims of the inquirer into the history and future of Christianity.

In our investigations we must follow the corresponding methods in mental science, where the historical and anthropological standpoints have their share in the survey of morals and psychology. It is from the point of vantage of an observer who has eighteen centuries to look back on that we view the Christian Church. Though the future may be wrapped in clouds which refuse to open before us, the past is within our ken.

Our course of inquiry limits itself to this world and the possibilities of this mortal life; for the other lies outside the limits of our reasoning powers. "Eye hath not seen, nor ear heard, neither have entered into the heart of man, the things which God hath prepared for them that love Him."[1]

We humbly desist from a task which is by no means laid on man, the duty of inquiring into the future conditions of existence beyond the bounds of our mortal life. Nay, we are rather dissuaded from it by the words of the Master, and asked to lean our faith on His sole word, meanwhile ceasing our vain speculations.

Confining ourselves, therefore, to the actual operations of the Christian religion among mankind, we are relieved of the burden of much dogmatic discussion. Time is the best eclectic philosopher. In its course the useless and untrue dogmas drop out of sight, and the true and serviceable remain. Through the long sifting process of

[1] 1 Cor. ii. 9.

the centuries all the thoughts of men must pass, but the transient moods vanish into oblivion, while the permanent forms abide. Coleridge, with many other philosophers before and after him, expressed a desire for such a system as " would at once explain and collect the fragments of truth scattered through systems apparently the most incongruous. The truth," he goes on to say,[1] "is diffused more widely than is commonly believed; but it is often painted, and oftener masked, and is sometimes mutilated, and sometimes, alas! in close alliance with mischievous errors. There is," he says, " one perspective central point which shows regularity and a coincidence of all the parts in the very object, which from every other point of view appear confused and distorted. The spirit of sectarianism has been hitherto our fault, and the cause of our failures."

Such a point of view is afforded us by the process of time. The natural selection, which must, and which does, act through the course of ages, enables us to see the best of each system, and the real influence of all. Nay more, our very thought, by the power of heredity, is conditioned by elements from all the varied movements of the past, and our intelligence is a composite of the mental energies of our ancestors.

Such a survey enables us to see the relative importance and usefulness of various doctrines. We are able to have a true perspective of the forms of Church thinking; and are able to rise above the theory that attaches as much value to abstruse minutiæ as to the cardinal beliefs of religion. It is, indeed, a truth of the

[1] *Biographia Literaria*, chap. xii.

Sacred Scriptures that doctrines are only a means to an end, as St. Paul says, "that the man of God may be perfect, thoroughly furnished unto all good works."[1] Dogma has been made an end in itself, as if men existed for the expression of belief, and not for its practical issues. The opening of the classical writings to the study of men at the Reformation put to flight so dark a shadow over life. The lofty heights which were reached by the best men of the ancient world enlarged the sense of life to those who for the first time saw the clouds dispersed that had concealed the summits, and made them impatient of their ecclesiastical confinement.

It was the Reformation which ensured for men the possession of a truer ideal of Christianity, which had been lost or forgotten through the preceding ages. The doctrines and worship of the Church exist for the purpose of making men holy; religion has its end in morals. Without such a purpose it descends to mere ritual. But in order that the moral ideal may reach its triumph, it must be enforced by religion. In God alone can man find the harmony of his soul and of the world; and on a foundation of Christianity alone can the social fabric be built and held together.

It is doubtful whether the true view of dogma and worship as instruments is yet fully realised in the Church among theologians, yet the most careless observer cannot but note how it has permeated the lay mind. The progress of secular knowledge, which awakened the leaders of the Reformation to grasp the truth, has aided to spread it through all men; and the general mass of

[1] 2 Tim. iii. 16.

men have probably sounder thoughts on this matter than many professed theologians. It is the knowledge of the history of the Church which enables us to feel firm ground beneath our feet here. We see how dogmas which appear of cardinal value to the makers of theological systems, are rudely brushed past in the march of mankind. Nor think that it is the individual reason which has so acted; a higher power lies behind. The instincts of man are in themselves a revelation. When the strings of the wide harp of human thought sound in a long unison, we feel that they are touched, not by the capricious will of men, but by the finger of God. As Cousin says,[1] and with reservations it is true: "History is the manifestation of God's supervision of humanity: the judgments of history are the judgments of God Himself."

The doctrines which bulk most largely in the eye of the theologian, have often least influence on the world; nay, the world of Christian thought as a whole, the untechnical judgment of the people, often reverses the decision of theological experts. A remarkable instance of this may be found in the Councils of Carthage held in the third century, which declared the baptism of heretics to be invalid. The dogma is, from a Church point of view, of great importance, for baptism is the condition of entrance to the Church; and yet the mere drift of popular opinion, which ignored the decisions of the Councils, was so strong as to render them null, and, like a court of appeal, to reverse them. The currents of popular thought have an almost irresistible power in

[1] *History of Philosophy*, p. 159.

theological discussion, and though at any one point of history a hasty decision as to the real value of any such current cannot be given, time shows where the truth lies. Talleyrand once said that there is one who has more intellect than Voltaire or Napoleon: it is the body of the people. M. Guizot, quoting this, adds to the weighing of opinion of men at any one time a consideration of the progressive and collective reason of humanity, saying: "There is a deeper observer than Bacon, a greater thinker than Kant: it is mankind." Thus, at all events, the popular voice generally speaks authoritatively as to the value to men which results from any dogma; for the dogma is either sown as a seed, and we see the fruits, and know them; or else it is borne away by the wind, and passes into oblivion.

The doctrine of the Trinity is an essential point of the Christian system, and one which marks it out as distinct from the Jewish theology. At one time such importance did the Church attach to the correct promulgation of the dogma, that the whole spirit of the people was raised in its favour; and, notwithstanding the subtleties of theologians, the general mind of the Church was determined to vindicate the orthodox view, which the Council of Nicæa declared. And yet it soon faded out of sight, because no practical issues were connected with it, and gave place in the Middle Ages to the worship of the Virgin Mary.[1] To the ordinary uneducated Christian of the mediæval Church, the

---

[1] That this was connected with the Apollinarianism which has so often accompanied views which seem orthodox, is probably true. See Plumptre's *Boyle Lectures*, p. 372.

Trinity was practically expressed by the Father, the Son, and the Virgin,[1] whom he regarded for all purposes of devotion and influence on the events of this world as equal.

It was not till Luther's dogma of justification by faith showed the various agency of the Father, the Son, and the Holy Ghost, that the popular grasp of the Trinity was restored. Again, when that view of justification became obscured, so also a mist enfolded the doctrine of the Trinity, and it vanished from the spiritual vision of great numbers of mankind. Its further course, in the minds and faith of men, would still more serve to show that doctrines exist for moral purposes; and when they are taught as mere abstract formulae so as to lose touch with the real life of mankind, they fade into mere memories.

Of necessity, the thought of men seeks the truth by a process of trial and error, as in most experimental acts. It seems as if we must believe for a time the wrong, so as to know its falsehood, and cling more closely to the right. The view that sin is a needful element in the discipline of our life, though often crudely enough stated, is not without its evidence as a fact of human experience. To feel a due abhorrence of evil, we must have been under its power; and then we strive the more to hold fast that which is good.

It is history alone which can give us the result of the experiments of man in theological thought, and appraise

---

[1] This was Mahomet's idea of the Christian Trinity, which he derived from the practice of a sect of Arabian Christians in worshipping the Virgin.—Monier Williams.

their true worth. Yet we must not think that Church history is a mere record of controversies. The historians have too much directed their attention to this series of facts, and often unintelligently enough. Wiser thought would have endeavoured to see in the issue of events a reconciling element. In the great controversy as to the Trinity, it is clear that both sides were aiming at asserting the close union of Christ and mankind, and that, though the Church was saved from polytheism by the triumph of Athanasius, it was also preserved from a vague theism by the efforts of Arius and his successors.

It is really only by observing the moral and practical issues that we can come to true conclusions. The living humanity who constituted the real Church are more worthy of study than the dry bones of discussions, many of which have lost all bearing on our modern times, even if they ever had any influence on their own. We should treat the early Fathers as literature, speaking the hopes, the fears, the joys of the hearts from which they came, and not as mere herbaria for dried specimens of theological opinion. The *Confessions* of St. Augustine, and the career of St. Athanasius, have a value to the historian far above the accurate statement of predestination or of homoousianism. Then as now, Christianity, with its feverish zeal in seeking for the divine truth, its perpetual interest in divine worship, which culminated in the sublime and elaborate liturgy, and its growing complications of hierarchical government, sought to direct the lives of men into harmony with each other and with God.

In the present day, theologians of one school attach

primary importance to the principle of apostolic succession through bishops, and hold that the very existence of the Church hangs on the presence of Episcopacy. Theologians of another school oppose such a theory with all their energy, and even with bitterness. Apparently the world goes on at present heedless of the controversy. Men see that the influence of the Church in the moral progress of the world is the cardinal consideration in religion, and do not seem to see any relation of the apostolic succession to that influence. Their minds are in suspense on the subject in a world of sin and sorrow. But let them be convinced that this question involves practical issues; that it holds inwrapped in it a living faith in the unity and brotherhood of the Church; that it points to solutions of Church problems which bear on social life,—and their attention and sympathy would be aroused. It is the practical side of Christianity which after all is our touchstone.

That the mission of Jesus to this world was to interpret to mankind the true goal to which they were marching forward, we shall try to show; and that He enabled them to see it clearly before them, and journey steadfastly towards it. He was the Way for mankind; and the history of the world explains in what sense this was true. Both the history of the Church and the history of the world show the definite ends which the progress of mankind has in view.

CHAPTER III

THE ETHICAL PURPOSE OF DEVELOPMENT

THE ideal perfection of mankind is revealed in Jesus, who expresses to us the goal to which the human race must strive : a unity among men, and that unity finding its eternal completion in union with God. The life of the Church and the progress of mankind exhibit the development of this great purpose. We see it unfolding itself in the understanding of men, who are able more and more to know, as time goes on, the divine end of humanity. But we have more than a progress in human *thought*; before us lies the whole course of events of human *history*, which is likewise inspired by the same onward tendency.

The development of theology, accordingly, shows this ethical end becoming more and more distinct, both in the thoughts and acts of the Church. All doctrine and worship advance for moral ends, with the single goal of the unity and perfection of mankind in view.

There are, as we have seen, two kinds of theological statement: such teaching as we find in the Apostles' Creed, which is regarded as pure matter of faith ; and the interpretation of these facts, which is the progressive effort of man's mental and spiritual powers.

Although men apply their reason to the facts in the creed, their thought does not always rise out of them, while it unfolds them more fully. In the very effort to interpret them, age after age returns to the same standpoint after a long journey. In the nature of the case this must be so, when we are thinking of matters that are outside the scope of our reason, as at present we are made. When Mr. Mill said, in his *Essays on Religion*, " that the indulgence of a hope with regard to the universe and the destiny of man after death, while we recognise as a clear truth that we have no ground for more than a hope, is legitimately and philosophically defensible," his position comes very close to that of the devout thinker. The pious heart, indeed, has more than a hope, but its assurance is not based on rational grounds, but on trust in the word of Jesus. At present these questions are beyond the capacity of reason to establish, though there is no ground for saying that they will ever be inaccessible to its efforts. As Mr. John Fiske says: " The belief in a future life is without scientific support; but at the same time it is placed beyond the need of scientific support, and beyond the range of scientific criticism."

It is thus characteristic of many of our intellectual efforts after divine truth, that they move in a circle. The modern world advances beyond the mediæval, it may be, but it only returns to the speculations of the Fathers. As Sir Thomas Browne says: " For as though there were metempsychoses, and the soul of one man passed into another; opinions do find, after certain revolutions, men and minds like those that first begat them."

But this is not true of all doctrines, and it is never the case with those which touch the moral life of man, or the unity and brotherhood of the human race. When any real step is to be taken forward which will open up the way of men to their great goal, it is marvellous with what power the doctrinal movement progresses.

The doctrine of the Trinity in its orthodox form was won at Nicæa, not so much by the energy of technical theologians, as by the general enthusiasm of the whole Church. For men seem to have felt that the teaching of Arius would deprive them of assurance in the real presence of God among men, unifying and purifying them. They saw, more clearly than we now can fathom, that to deny the divine being of the Son was to return to the old external view of God as dwelling apart from men, and to lose that moral life of love and union which the divine Spirit could alone impart. It was no mere subtlety of theology which was at stake, but the very existence of Christianity as something more than a philosophical system. A perception of far-reaching issues moved the heart of men; an unconscious perception it may have been, a feeling after rather than a grasping the realities which were in jeopardy; but it was an irresistible movement, and a permanent victory of the great truth that "God is with us."

The developing movement of Christianity has been ethical in its aim and results. It is the effort of men to apply divine truth to human life which makes them examine into it. Mere theoretical reasoning dies with the mind that conceives it, or remains the curious inquiry of leisurely thinkers. But questions which involve practical issues take root in the heart of mankind; and to the observer, at such a distance as we now stand from the past, the moral end is apparent. I do not say that such a conscious purpose has been present to the minds of those who were pioneers of doctrinal progress, or to those who crowned any stage of it with completeness, but the divine power that rules all men has guided them into the truth, though they knew not how great was to be the fruit of their labours.

The old view, that is not without its adherents in our time, among the cruder scepticism of ignorance, which attributed the rise of dogma to the design of priesthoods to aggrandise themselves, is manifestly without any historical ground. It gave occasion, in its day, for many a tirade against priestcraft, and the echoes of such denunciations still abide with us. Dean Stanley says, speaking of Aaron's dedication of the golden calf: "And not then only, but again and again in the history of the Jewish and of the Christian Church, has the same temptation returned. The Priest has set up what the Prophet has destroyed." Similarly, Sir Edwin Arnold, in the preface to his poem, "The Light of Asia," tells us that "the extravagances which disfigure the record and practice of Buddhism are to be referred to that inevitable degradation which priesthoods always inflict on great ideas committed to their charge."

The little truth that is in these statements lies in the fact that men pursue in detail, often profitless, the special lifework they undertake. The theologian wastes his time on useless subtleties, the poet on pedantic refinements, the priest on trivialities in ritual; but they do not necessarily lose sight of the great principle of their work. It is a far wider and deeper influence than the vagaries of individuals which governs the adaptation and accretion of dogma.

Doctrines may be promulgated by priests, but they are the best thought that the spirit of their time can give to the question they treat of. We read in Plutarch that when Solon was asked if the code of laws he had given to the people of Athens was the best possible, he answered that it was the best that the people would have accepted. The same thought is found in the teaching of Jesus and the apostles. When speaking of divorce to the Pharisees, who asked Him if it were lawful, He replied: "For the hardness of your heart Moses wrote you this precept." There must be a capacity to receive and understand a law which is laid on any body of men, and a certain preparedness of will before they can obey it. Otherwise the result of absolute commandment is a heedless reaction which goes far beyond mere refusal to obey, and often carries away moral safeguards already attained. The records of modern missionary labour show the necessity of gradual development in questions of practice. Here the strong words of Jesus sometimes find application in our experience. "Give not that which is holy to the dogs, neither cast ye your pearls before swine, lest they trample them under their feet, and turn again and rend you." Men do not reach heights of moral excellence by a leap, but by slow and toilsome steps. They unconsciously adapt the truths they hear to their own power of realising them.

The doctrine of purgatory was, in all probability, the child of philosophic thought, but it became a part of the Christian religion for many centuries, in answer to a felt ethical need. The moral sense of the ancient and mediæval world could not grasp the dogma which is now found in orthodox Protestantism, of an immediate passage into paradise or hell. All the discipline of this life leaves us by no means perfect at its close; and the ordinary feeling of mankind desired something more to fit them for eternal joys. Such things were beyond their deserts, they thought; and so also they may have regarded eternal woe.[1] The natural revolt against forms of a possible Antinomianism, which lies dormant in orthodoxy, led to the growth of a belief in purgatory. Whether the moral effects of such a doctrine were all that was needed, it is hard to say; but it is clear that it grew out of the requirements of the conscience of man. Men saw that they could not have the communion with the saints which was presented as the doctrinal form of human unity, and the best hope of mankind for the future, without being themselves pure; and to express the belief that neither could they see God without holiness, nor could they be in perfect harmony with man, they shaped their thoughts into the doctrine of purgatory. And now, when our religion seems in danger of becoming wholly formal, and when men reflect on the strange adjustments of reward and pain in this world of ours, the thoughts of man move round this theory of probation in the world to come. The assumed ethical need brings again the dogma into the circle of present

[1] See this treated by Comte, *Philosophie Positive*, v.

discussion. But how little it meets the wants of our age, is shown by the almost total absence of response from any but professed theologians.

The worship of the Virgin Mary has been explained as a transfer of heathenism into the Christian faith. The Queen of Heaven in the pagan pantheon finds her representative in the "Mother of God." But the heart of man must have craved for her presence, or Mary would have been as little honoured as she is among most Protestants. The religious consciousness of man is not an Athens, where the altars of many strange gods are erected; and a mere eclecticism of classic tradition and Christian creed will not explain the remarkable and widespread worship of the Virgin, which, as a *note* of mediæval Christianity, as also of modern Romanism, needs further inquiry.

It arose at a time when the world was in danger of losing its deepest reverence for these mysteries of our being by the spread of the celibate life, and some sanction of family life was required to anchor the heart. The devotion which a knight paid to his lady love, which a son gave to his mother, found a substitute in the loyalty to Mary which brooded in the solitary monk's heart, whither earthly passions were denied an entrance. While the rise of monasticism was one of the main causes of the growth of Mariolatry, in that the monk, shut out from sweet thoughts of earthly womanhood, fixed his soul on the motherhood of the Virgin, that worship maintained itself because of the longing to consecrate the family life by the holy influence of devotion. In rude, unsettled times, when life was brought down to its barest elements, such a worship infused refining thought into hard hearts. Art helped to strengthen the practice, for it could realise the dream of piety. The spiritual influence of Giotto, Cimabue, Botticelli, Fra Angelico, must have been a power in the world they lived in. From the mere abstract formulæ which the Byzantine artists gave as representing divine things, we pass into a time when the life of man seems to reach an ideal purity in the pictures of the pre-Raphaelites.

To vindicate the unity of the family as the great preparation for the unity of the race, the thought of motherhood was worshipped in Mary. It needed a strong force to fight against the ascetic theory of life, which endeavoured to detach men from their true relationships, and place them in an artificial setting. Had religion taken entirely the ascetic form, and withdrawn its sanction from family life, it must have failed to reach the first step on its onward journey. Men would have been hopelessly sundered into natural and religious, and the natural instincts of man would have overpowered what religious influence was left. But the reverence paid to the mother of Jesus ever reminded the world that the most sacred associations clung to the facts of human kinship; that a radiance of heaven shone on family life, and that its love and tenderness were in their origin divine.

The Reformation was one of the great crises of human history. Some men of our time are inclined to underrate its supreme importance; but a wise observer sees in it a movement which more nearly resembled the rise of Christianity from Judaism, than any ordinary doctrinal progress. The appeal which Luther made to the sole authority of Jesus altered the whole course of religious thought, and gave a fresh impulse to religious growth.

The fact that the Reformation broke with the old theology, and disturbed the continuity of the Church's worship, without staying the current of her life, proves that the development of Christianity, of which it was an important manifestation, is on ethical lines. Luther endeavoured to gain for mankind the sense of individual life which had been extinguished in the religious sphere, that he might prepare men for a Church which should express the brotherhood of men who had yielded their individualism as a gift on the altar of love. In later days, Schleiermacher did the same office to mankind, and each has been widely fruitful of result. Both great teachers made an effort to realise the brotherhood of men in Christ; both revolted from a world in which that great truth was lost. And we may see, too, how the history of the world illustrates and develops the doctrine of Christianity, for Luther and Schleiermacher found their motive power in the secular progress of mankind. The revival of learning gave to men a wider sense of the universal love of God, and made them turn from narrow ecclesiasticism and feudalism to the thought of the republic of mankind in all ages and all lands. Luther's preaching of individual faith had this fertile soil to spring up in, and the Reformation was the result. Before Schleiermacher's age there passed the awful tragedy of the French Revolution, with its baptism of blood, and its gospel of fraternity. To men who saw such portents, the voice of a Christianity which proclaimed itself social in its aim, was as the still small voice after the thunder and the storm.

Let us now see what point we have arrived at in our view of doctrinal development. The source of Christianity is the life and teaching of Jesus. Not only has the Church gathered strength to interpret the documents where these are told us, but she also has placed them in ever truer relation to mankind. This she does by the divine presence, which is never withheld from her. But that divine presence is also manifested in the movement of history, which itself is an interpretation of the mission of Jesus, and ever tends to fulfil it. That movement includes the progress of human thought in the philosophy of morals and religion, in biological and sociological science, which, though taking their journey independent of Christianity, are in reality interpreters of it, and travel alongside of the Christian faith.

The main interest of doctrinal development is in observing the ethical result of Christ's life and teaching in the progress of man. We can gather the divine purpose of the Christian religion from its past history; and all our science comes to our aid in explaining and confirming that purpose. The sublime end which Christ had in view was the union of all humanity; and history tells us that the world is marching on to that great conclusion. The study of that purpose is the noblest which man can undertake, and affords most stimulus to practical life. Many philosophical studies are by their nature removed from the sphere of action, and prison the student in an abstract region; but the observation of this great ethical development moves him to take part in it, and urge it on. However little his effort may be worth, it always helps to swell the great and ever-rising tide of love and union which must one day bear all men into universal brotherhood.

CHAPTER IV

BROTHERHOOD BEFORE CHRIST

JESUS came to this world to establish and perfect the brotherhood of man. The human race was at His coming a collection of separate atoms, divided from each other by many causes. His life and love were given in order that they all might be brought into one great unity. The sum of the processes by which that unity was to be attained is the Christian religion, embodied in the Christian Church. The operations and efforts of the Church will continue till the human race are brought into a perfect unity, when the ideal of the creation of man will be reached and made permanent.

In the above words we have stated our purpose, which we shall now go on to unfold more fully.

The development of the principle of brotherhood was slow and gradual. There are no truths to which man's ascent has not been toilsome; and yet, when they appear above the horizon, they come suddenly revealed, like the sunrise in the tropical seas. The twilight of morn is faint and struggling, till it is all at once turned into splendour by the approach of the sun.

In all nations there was a certain advance made age by age into the knowledge and practice of the brotherhood of man. Yet that advance was by no means rapid, and was rather a theory for the few nobler spirits than a practical belief of the multitude.

Jesus Himself was come of the Jewish nation, which has ever held itself a peculiar people. The more closely they held by each other, the wider they were separated from the rest of mankind. Their law and custom bound them with strong ties to each other, but it was in a league of defence against the Gentiles, among whom their neighbours the Samaritans were included. This feeling we read of in the New Testament, sometimes apparently to be deferred to, as in the injunction to the disciples, "Go not into the way of the Gentiles, and into any city of the Samaritans enter ye not"; and sometimes to be reproved, as in the parable of the Good Samaritan.

In the Old Testament a wider thought had visited the nobler hearts of ancient Judaism. In the second Isaiah we find a vision which extends beyond the bounds of Israel, and which stretches forth to all mankind. The magnificent strains of triumph which greet the opening dawn of the great doctrine of a united human race, are worthy of so lofty a theme. The gates of Judaism were to be thrown open, and the Gentiles were to enter a city, no longer of David, but of mankind. The acceptable year of the Lord was to appear; and as the earth brought forth her tender sprouts in spring, so the first signs of brotherhood were to be the heralds of its universal reign.

But how slow were the Jews to enter into this lofty prophecy; and it is, indeed, doubtful if they ever realised its full force even as an anticipation. Their old ways are still with them, notwithstanding the swelling tides of modern thought. We are assured by the Abbé Chiarini that the law enjoined—if not explicitly, yet as inwrapped in the other precept—that men should hate and injure those outside of their brotherhood, as well as love and benefit those within it. The same writer, indeed, draws a distinction between the teaching of the older Judaism, and the later, of the Mishna; but while there are many differences, the essential exclusiveness of the Jew is maintained throughout all his history. The earlier Jews may not have thought that immortality was confined to their race, but they had no clear view of immortality; and when they came to regard it as one of the possible privileges which God gives, they claimed it, as they did the other blessings of the covenant, for their special possession. Doubtless there were some who were better than their creed, as always happens; for we read in the Talmud: "It is our duty to maintain the heathen poor with those of our own nation. We must visit their sick, and relieve them, and bury their dead." "The pious men of the heathen," said Rabbi Joshua, "will have their portion in the next world. Be kind and friendly to all, even to the heathen." Such statements do not affect the general fact of national exclusiveness, but they enable us to receive with more readiness the Chief Rabbi (Dr. Adler's) assurance that the Jews of the present day believe in the brotherhood of man.

In Greece the same national exclusiveness was found, though it would be hard to say that it was a stronger feeling than the French have to the Germans. The nobler minds among them were led through the pursuit of truth or beauty to a wider thought of humanity. In all ages the pursuit of knowledge or of art has so enlarged the heart of men, that they overleap the bounds of their hereditary prejudices. The wandering bard or minstrel has in all times enjoyed immunity, even among hostile peoples, so great is man's reverence for the divine arts. But though the feeling of unbrotherliness may be laid aside by the populace for a little, it abides with them, and constitutes one of the most powerful forces in human history down to this day. Let us not even be deceived by Greek ideals of democracy, for the Demos was but a limited number of free citizens. At their feet were the provinces, whom they ruled with an iron despotism. And yet some of their best thinkers rose above the narrow thoughts of their nation. In Xenophon's *Cyropædeia* we read that Cyrus, when dying, charged his sons to have regard to the good of the whole human race. And the Stoic philosophers, who reflected on the dignity of man, and his independence of outward surroundings, naturally arrived at a point from which they did not concern themselves with such an accident as being born in a particular country. And the nobler teaching, which St. Paul refers to in his discourse at Athens, that men are the offspring of God, which is found in Kleanthes and other poets, is used by Epictetus [1] as a proof of the brotherhood of man. We find both in Cicero and Epictetus, that Socrates, when he was asked what country he belonged to, replied that he was a

[1] Bk. i. 13.

citizen of the world.[1] The famous line which Terence translated from Menander, that all things human were within his sympathies, represented rather a Greek than a Roman view of life, though the same cause, extension of empire and intercourse with foreign peoples, broke down the barriers of exclusiveness to both nations. An ancient writer attributes to Alexander the Great the desire that all should regard the whole world as their common country. The same benevolent motive has been claimed by other conquerors, and finds expression in the " Idées Napoléoniennes," which aims at developing the first Napoleon's policy; but it is so plainly an afterthought, that it is surprising that panegyrists should still bring it forward for their heroes. If the world is a brotherhood, whence comes the right of conquest?

The Roman people, from their intercourse with Greece, were permeated with its best thoughts, and accordingly what advancement Greek philosophy had made was also shared by Rome. The mere association with so many nations as Roman conquest brought into the empire, gave the death-blow to an exclusive national feeling. The evidences of civilisation in Greece and Egypt were so many reminders to the Romans that the world was wider than the bounds of Latium. The history of their people, from the earliest times, is marked by a large foreign influence. That foreign influence was so marked, that there is no parallel to it except in the modern phases of government in the United States, and specially in some of the separate States. The result of this infusion of aliens into Rome was the formation

[1] Epictetus, i. 9; Cicero, *Tuscul.* v. 37.

of a *law of nations*, which was based on a kind of assumption of equality of all men. But, as an actual fact, it was the offspring of jealousy which was unwilling to admit foreigners to the privileges of the Civil Law. The ideas of the *law of nations* were strengthened by the movements of philosophy, specially that of Zeno and Chrysippus, which brought into thought, conditions like those which the *law of nations* realised in politics. The idea of equity, of a fraternal justice, penetrated the Roman Empire, and prepared the way for a true view of human brotherhood. National jealousy died away, and class distinctions took its place. Professor Flint's statement is substantially right, that "the Roman mind recognised that there was One Law, embracing all nations and all times, which no senate or people had created or could annul, and which enjoined universal justice and universal benevolence. That men are not merely citizens—that every man is debtor to every other—that they have a common nature, and, in consequence, reciprocal rights and obligations—were well-known truths in the time of Cicero, and commonplaces in the times of even the earliest emperors. . . . Christianity is often represented as having exclusively originated and promulgated truths which were, intellectually at least, undoubtedly recognised in pagan Rome."[1] The words of Cicero are worth remembering, so full are they of that spirit of fraternity which has too often been regarded as wholly modern. In his treatise, *De Legibus*, such passages occur as the following:—"The whole of the world should be con-

[1] *Philosophy of History in Europe*, 1st ed. p. 51. See also Lecky, *History of European Morals*, i. chap. 2

sidered one State, the common home of gods and men." "By nature we incline to love men, which fact is the foundation of law." "A wise man does not regard himself as the inhabitant of any one place, but as a citizen of the whole world, counting it but one city."[1] In his treatise, *De Officiis*, as is natural, the statements are even clearer in declaring the universal brotherhood of man. The tolerant Cicero, however, had nothing but scorn and hatred for the Jews, whom he calls a race born for slavery;[2] and his scorn is shared by the genial Horace and the philosophic Seneca. And, doubtless, the popular feeling echoed such sentiments, not to Jews only, but to all foreigners, with as much cordiality as, in days gone by, the English people hated the French. The spirit of selfish nationalism could not but have possessed the Roman people, notwithstanding their cosmopolitan tendencies. It finds expression in the Satires of Juvenal, who laments this national equality; and doubtless he expressed the feeling of his age.[3]

Among nomadic peoples the tribal exclusiveness is modified by the laws of hospitality. These laws are a necessity of a scattered population, for without some sacred sanction given to the duty of kindly treating a wayfarer or a stranger, mankind would return to a state of mutual suspicion, and to the ferocious solitude of wild beasts. When men can go from place to place in safety, they carry knowledge with them, and trade becomes possible. The laws of hospitality are a guarantee of

---

[1] *De Legibus*, Bk. i.
[2] *De Prov. Cons.* 5. Judæis et Syris nationibus natis servituti.
[3] See *Ecce Homo*, xii.

some measure of progress in arts and morality. We read in Tacitus how the ancient Germans gave as kindly a welcome to strangers in their homes as they met them fiercely in the field of fight. And the *Edda* gives us a like picture of the northern Teutons. Such verses as these occur more than once :—

> "Never treat with scorn or with wanton slight
> The wayfaring stranger or guest."
> "Hail to the giver! the guest has come!
> Where shall he have his seat?"[1]

A similar condition of things is found among the early Eranians, where one of the articles of the Avestan creed is a promise "to householders that they may roam at will and abide unmolested wherever upon the earth they may be dwelling with their herds."[2] Zoroaster, indeed, imbued his followers with a deep hatred against the Turanian nomads, who descended on the Eranians like Highland caterans, regardless of every law but the right of the strongest. But the national boundaries could be enlarged to receive proselytes to the Avestan creed, as we read in its early precepts. And it was a tradition of the Persian monarchs, which Cyrus, Cambyses, and Darius carried out, to tolerate, and even to reverence, foreign religions. The one power, as we shall see, which mitigates national jealousy is not mingling through conquest, which in Rome failed to cure it, but the recognition of the powers above men. From heaven always comes peace on earth and goodwill among men.

The most singular state of things occurs in India,

[1] Translated by Karl Blind in *The Ethic Ideas of the Edda.*
[2] Ragozin's *Media*, p. 111.

where the people are broken up into several parts. In Hinduism the system of caste at once shuts out the idea of brotherhood. Each caste is a walled fortress, where intercourse is free enough within, but cannot pass the gates. It must not, indeed, be thought that the distinction is regarded as a disgrace by the lower castes, however much the upper castes may pride themselves on their superiority. "The Mangs, whose poverty and squalor are unrivalled, would indignantly refuse a Brahmin who might offer himself in marriage. The Chenchwars carry their contempt for all castes and tribes but their own to such an extent, that they declare they live in the jungle for the sake of health, because there the smells of other men cannot reach them." Exclusiveness is here carried to its utmost, and whatever the relative rank in their own, or in each other's eyes, of the various castes, their position is utterly inconsistent with brotherhood.

Buddhism disapproved of the caste system, and declared all men equal so far as religious privileges were concerned. Its admirable ethical system, which prescribes universal benevolence, and which really is put into practice by its adherents, cannot fail to beget kindly and social feelings towards all men. The presentation of Buddhism which Sir Edwin Arnold gives in his *Light of Asia*, is such as to impress the reader that the Buddhists have little to learn in the way of brotherly feeling. But it is the sympathy of slaves bound to a hopeless chain, where services are given and received in dull apathy. To take religion as an opiate, that we may spend life in a trance, is to give up the right to live. Such a view of existence makes one long for the fierce competition of our modern paganised Christianity, or the more strenuous days of the older polytheisms; for anything rather than this intoxicating draught of death itself.

Modern Hinduism, as represented by the Brahmo Somaj, has for one of the articles of its creed: "Knowing God to be the common Father, thou shalt love every man as thy brother, and every woman as thy sister." But the Brahmo Somaj borrowed its principal tenets from Christianity, and, like the faith from which it originated, it does not permit *caste* within its borders.

There is, notwithstanding all the peculiar institutions of Oriental peoples, a certain national brotherliness, which is a legacy of primitive times, and which is not found in our more elaborate civilisations. It is this feeling which made an Eastern country the first home of the great principle of brotherhood.

Even the Chinese, who seem to have been separated from the rest of mankind for long ages, and to have been walled off from the world without them, are said to be not unacquainted with the principle of benevolence to all as a law of life. In the Chinese classics we read several exhortations to mutual love as a duty; and the strictly ethical character of Confucius' teaching gives it a strong likeness to modern positivism, which has an enlightened altruism for its practical form. In such a saying of Confucius as this,—"The good man loves all men; all within the four seas are his brothers,"—we have as clear a statement of the universal principle that Christ came to teach, as may be found in our own literature.

There is a darker side to the picture of human life than any that the mere sundering of nations can show. The presence of slavery in the ancient world made a mock of the lofty philosophies and the cosmopolitan laws of Greece and Rome. The artisans themselves were regarded as little better than slaves, though they were free from the awful tortures which the ancients inflicted so recklessly on their bondsmen. In Egypt, the splendid luxury of the Pharaohs had its bloody fringe of oppression and cruelty. The toilers in all that is useful in life, by whom the world is kept going on its way, and whose worth only now we are getting to know, were treated with contempt. What rights had the "stinking masses," "craven labourers," to aught but toil and death?[1]

And the lot of the slaves was yet worse. The lash of the taskmaster, amid famine and heavy labour in the cruel sun, was all that life yielded them, and their only happiness was the uneasy sleep which gave them a night's respite from the day's bitterness, till they won the prize of death. All the life of Egypt lies open to us in the monuments, and such is the tale they tell. Of the horror of Greek and Roman slavery we need not speak; it is embalmed for us in the writings of classical times. All labour but that of the fields was counted ignoble, and the traditions of that scorn are still with us. The knowledge of the past may have kept it in our minds, but it seems a relic of the days when all men were shepherds and farmers, and the Aryan people dwelt on the great European plain.

The philosophers might talk (as Zeno is recorded to

[1] Brugsch's *Geschichte Aegyptens unter den Pharaonen*, p. 21.

have said that all men were equal, and that the only difference between them was in their measure of virtue) and the poets might dream of equal justice, which sometimes might in common life be given to aliens, but charity was unknown. Kindness to the poor and the aged was better known among the barbarian Germans, or the wandering tribes of Asia, than to the Greeks or Romans. These possessed neither the spirit of benevolence nor had any systematic way of relieving suffering. Their chief thought was to keep it out of sight. The same spirit exists in the heart of modern luxury as it did in the days before the French Revolution, in spite of Christian influences. But it only lurks in a corner; it does not vaunt itself in open day as it did in the old world.

That Jesus came to a world which had little knowledge of the principle of brotherhood, is a commonplace of literature, and needs not to be further enforced. But it is also true that throughout the ancient world the sanctions of religion and the teachings of philosophy were often on the side of kindness and benevolence. But these feelings were not the coin of everyday exchange, but rare pieces in the cabinet of the collector. The world has taken long strides forward since then, and yet we are not even now familiar with the spirit of love as the moving power among men. But we cannot neglect these premonitions of the fuller knowledge which Christ gave us: we are bound to remember that all the world belongs to God, and has been always His. "The earth is the Lord's, and the fulness thereof." Any harvest of truth which was reaped in days before our Saviour, was due to the divine sowing. This great truth has not always been remembered, though some of the earlier Fathers freely acknowledge it. It is one which modern thought grudges to the Christian system. A writer,[1] who speaks always with a voice of authority, assures us that "theology is bound to pass by in disdain or silence all that was great and beautiful in the vast ages which believed in many gods; the polytheisms and the theocracies; the heroic growth of Rome; the thought and grace of Hellas; the complex civilisation of Egypt; all that the Assyrian, Persian, Indian, or Chinese teachers or prophets ever gave to the countless myriads who rose into civilised life beneath their care. All this theology is bound, as theology, to ignore, if not to condemn." But who gave this critic the right to mark out the bounds of theological inquiry, or set the limits of theological science? True theology is concerned with all that concerns the efforts of man towards religion; and St. Paul has shown, as in his speech at Athens, that it comes within our scope. There have been few theologians since St. Paul's day who would accept the narrow limits in which their jealous opponents would confine them. We must therefore do justice to all the anticipations in ancient thought of the great future of our race, for these thoughts have rendered the acceptance of the gospel more ready among men. These natural instincts of our race often appear long before there is any hope of realising them; they are barely understood by those who publish them; but they show the guidance of Providence in the hearts of men, and point the onward way.

[1] Mr. Frederic Harrison in the *Nineteenth Century*, 1880, p. 528.

Though we have dwelt more on the opposition to the principle of brotherhood than on its manifestations, as was necessary to give a true historical picture of what, indeed, has often been described before; yet there is no doubt that our attention should be also given to the foregleams of this glorious dawn of the Sun of Righteousness, which are seen in the sages of ancient times. It was a beautiful thought of the reformer Zwingli, that God had His chosen among the heathen as well as the people who saw the great Light; and that heaven is shared by Socrates, Plato, Cato, Seneca, and the other good men of former times.[1] We see the debt we owe to the Reformation, when we remember that Dante places in hell, in the first circle, it is true, but still in the place of pain, "the master of scientific men," Aristotle,[2] Socrates, Plato, and the other sages of antiquity. The old theory of the Fathers, from Justin Martyr downwards, that the divine Logos moved the hearts of men to knowledge even before He taught them on earth, has such truth that we are grateful to Zwingli for recovering it; and we must not let it altogether perish, though the form in which we believe it may be changed. St. Augustine himself tells us that any follower of Plato might become a Christian,[3] "with only a slight change of opinions and expressions"; and we should rejoice to know that the human soul is in many ways Christian by nature, as Tertullian called it, and that its higher thoughts tend in all times to reach the divine ideal of love and brotherhood.

[1] *Expositio Christianæ Fidei.*   [2] *Inferno*, iv. 131.
[3] *De Vera Religione*, cap. 4: "et paucis mutatis verbis atque sententiis Christiani fierent (Platonici sc.)."

CHAPTER V

THE UNITY OF MAN

MODERN anthropology has gone further than the facts of human history lead us in considering the separation of mankind, and told us that not only were men divided in national life and habits, and at variance by reason of jealous exclusiveness, for which they claimed a sanction from the gods, but that the human race was broken up into hostile sections, because it embraces families which are of diverse origin, and really comprises distinct species.

Our science long followed the teaching of the biblical narrative, and assumed that men were derived from a single pair. Men of the eminence of Dr. Prichard and M. de Quatrefages came to the same conclusion, from an examination of the facts that scientific anthropology had collected. But a change has come over the teaching of those who have devoted special attention to this subject. We are now assured that men are so diverse, that no hypothesis can really meet the facts but the assuming them to come from distinct parentage.

This is, indeed, no new theory, for it is found in the mythology of the ancient peoples. The Greeks thought that every tribe descended from a common ancestor, who either sprung from the gods or was a direct product of the earth. Each of these mythical parents was a separate creation, having no relation to the originator of the neighbouring tribe. The aboriginal inhabitants of every country were supposed each to have so come into being from the mother earth, which was the begetter of all things. This belief in separate origins undoubtedly strengthened the exclusive spirit which the ancient peoples manifested to each other. But its evidently legendary character deprived it of any claim to regard, as even shadowing forth a fact in human history. So far from a tribe deriving its name from an eponymous ancestor, we know that he is an afterthought, and the name of the tribe has been given to an imaginary being, for whom some lofty or singular origin is supposed. And still, though it was a mere fiction of the myth-making fancy of man, it had great effect in keeping men apart, and fostering national jealousies and hostilities.

The differences between the great races of men are very marked, and are such, in the estimation of some men, as to lead us to conclude that they arose from ancestors whose features were specifically different.

Agassiz thought that men came into being in eight different centres upon the earth, without relation to each other; and these centres, he points out, are distinguished by their plant and animal species as well as by their variety of men. The more common opinion, however, takes note of the variations by which species originate, and does not need to suppose so many distinct ancestors. Such anthropologists as Broca and Topinard represent man as going backward into time, not to a single centre, but by lines which are sometimes parallel, sometimes intersecting. They take account of many circumstances which cause variation, but refuse to admit the need for supposing that only one species was the ancestor of all mankind. One would think that the surroundings of man and the natural varieties that occur even still among men, would account for the different races of mankind, more especially as geology gives us tens, perhaps hundreds of thousands, of years for the period of man's dwelling on earth. But the question is one on which opinion is too much divided for any-one to be able to form a decided conclusion, though the candid observer will ask much more evidence than has been shown, if he is to disbelieve that unity of man which is almost a postulate of human life and history.

The growth of race peculiarities needs not, moreover, so drastic an explanation as to suppose separate species of man. Are not the present facts of human life enough to explain the national divisions without any such hypothesis? The nation is but a large tribe; the tribe but a larger family; and the family tends to isolation from others as much as to union among its own members. The primitive communism was a league of mutual labour and defence, when all men shared in the work and had a common harvest of their toil, and isolated themselves from their neighbouring community. Even in the time of the great Hordes, if such a time ever existed, when men lived in a rude promiscuity, and relationship was hardly realised, the men of one tribe or totem had a natural antagonism to the men of another. The mere accidents of life and of the struggle for existence would be enough to beget an exclusive and hostile spirit.

It seems to be little else than an ill-grounded hypothesis that man emerged into an earnest of his present bodily and mental condition and powers from some lower form, and that this happened at various parts of the earth, as Haeckel imagines the long-headed men of Europe and Africa may be derived from the long-headed chimpanzee and gorilla of these regions, and the broad-headed Asiatics may descend from the broad-headed orangs of Borneo and Sumatra. But suppose that the species of men have fundamental differences, arising from the fact that the primal ancestors, who emerged from the vast sea of the lower animal life, were also marked by strong distinctions. Let all this be granted; it is clear to the most casual observer, that the march of the human race is towards unity.

We do not think any evidence at all strong enough has been brought forward to establish the theory that man has diverse origins; but still less is it clear that man has diverse natures. The present varieties of mankind possess many outward differences, but their mental nature and possibilities seem similar in character. To imagine the early river-drift men to have been necessarily inferior in brain-power to the average of their successors, is to make a gratuitous assumption, for the originators of all arts must have made a huge mental effort to produce their work. The first discoverer of fire, the first maker of musical sound, were geniuses of no common rank, for the step they took is a vaster one than subsequent advances can show. There is every reason to hold that men are alike in nature, and it is a profound thought which makes M. de Quatrefages draw attention to his religious character as marking man out to a separate place in the zoological series—the human kingdom.[1]

The tendencies which make for unity in the present day are numerous. The blending by intermarriage, the connection by intellectual sympathy, the union in common activities, have all aided in the past to obliterate the distinctions of mankind. The cosmopolitan cities of the ancient world, such as Rome, showed, in a much less degree, that intercommunication which the whole world now manifests. The causes which unite are destined in the future to have still greater influence. The needs of commerce and the facilities of travel have already made the world one great people. Some lands are getting too crowded to give support to their teeming people, who must set out to seek other worlds to conquer. Colonisation breaks down the barriers between nations, and the knowledge of one becomes the possession of all, so that we gradually advance in the scale of being. Still more do the thousand daily communications of civilised life bring people practically to think and act alike. Men tell us there is a lack of originality in mankind; but what could be expected from the uniformity of education, of occupation, of recreation,

[1] In this he follows Schleiermacher and Jean Paul, who both teach us that the distinguishing feature of man which alone separates him from the brutes is his *religiousness*.

which our life gives us ? It has come to this, that we almost think the same thought at the same moment, and our whole mental nature becomes more and more sympathetic with that of our neighbours.

Such are some of the facts which point to an ever-increasing kinship of the human race, which may have been one in the past, but is certainly going forward to future unity.

If men were as far sundered by various origins as the anthropologists say, they have made immense strides towards a general resemblance and brotherhood. The truth which St. Paul tells us, that Jesus came in the fulness of time, even receives further force from these theories. Onward moves the great purpose of God for mankind; onward sweeps the great force which is bringing men closer and closer together, till, when the race has achieved a certain measure of unity, and a certain approximation of intellectual and moral endowment, the great event which crowns the history of man appears, and the divine incarnation takes place.

If the theories of the anthropologists are true, there have been times when the man of one race could have been but an imperfect representative of all; it was only the lapse of ages that could obliterate the distinctions and bring the consciousness of mankind to one form. But, on the other hand, if we are to regard Christ as the ideal man, to whom the race may tend by varying degrees to approach, there seems no difficulty in holding that the approaches might be made from different starting-points. We hold that the unity of the human race is the theory most reconcilable with all the facts, but it is worth while pausing a moment to observe that the beliefs in the gradual ascent of man, and his diverse origin, do not seem incompatible with the appearance on earth of the divine Son in the garment of humanity.

To those who doubt these theories, the form of the argument little alters. The differences of man are wide; and if these differences have been caused by a departure from the original unity, as we are taught in the Scriptures of the Old Testament, they are none the less real. It is a fact of deep meaning when we are told that the original separation which set Cain wandering was caused by a violent rupture of the tie of brotherhood; by triumph of the individualistic spirit of evil. The glimpse of the unbridled fierceness of primitive man which we have in the song of Lamech,[1] tells us how soon the spirit of man rejoiced in his unbrotherliness. It is probably the most ancient poetical fragment we have, and may carry us back to the days when men dwelt in caves in the ruder stone age; but it shows how completely and how soon man learned the lesson of hatred and war.

The ascent of man is one of the commonly received theories of science, and all history goes to prove that man has gradually advanced from ruder times to his present civilisation; but the question remains if this ascent was not from the ruins of a past which was pure and good. There is much to establish the view that man shows signs in his history and mental and moral condition of a fall from some better condition. We need not go so far as Schelling, and believe that there was a primitive revelation of knowledge and morals and religion of a

[1] Gen. iv. 23, 24.

high and complete character. Nor need we suppose, with Julius Müller, who gives us a Christian Platonism, that we carry with us the memory of some pre-existent form. It is enough to believe that the nature of man was at one time morally sound, that love and brotherhood were the law of life. His knowledge might be small, his attainments in the arts childish, and indeed the Old Testament represents the arts of life arising after the separation through hatred and murder; but the unity of family life was at first undisturbed. From that unity he fell, and after long centuries he is still striving to regain it.

He who has an open eye for truth may find in the early relations of mankind a promise of something higher. Under their diversity, since there is a diversity, however caused, there lay buried an ideal of unity, a germinal power which compelled man to rise out of his isolation and division into a complete whole. Through all the ages this power has been working, and is still working toward perfection. It is the divine seal on the soul of mankind, which cannot be effaced. As the fruit-bearing tree surely comes from the seed which is planted, so the final perfect unity of mankind is assured by the original divine impulse which urges it ever on.

Whether this unity is a lost ideal, which we are now toiling after that we may regain, is perhaps not a practical question. But it is a vision not without encouragement to think that the perfect divine ideal, as it rested in the heart of God, had and has a real existence, which, though veiled in the struggling darkness of our mortal world, has a noontide yet to come.

The anthropological history of man shows, as we have seen, a gradual development from individualism; and certain savages, such as the Australian, are still in a condition of primitive isolation. One of the most interesting fields where this can be studied is in the negroes of the United States. It seems pretty well agreed that the negro has little power of association. He cannot so keep in check his individual impulse as to allow it to be controlled by any collective purpose. He is barely able to enter into joint action or social partnership, and his sense of family obligations or personal purity is said to be low. One of the great safeguards of Southern society before and after slavery was this incapacity for any kind of co-operation, which rendered insurrection an impossibility. Whether this is the result of slavery altogether, or is a characteristic slaves had in common with their kindred in Africa, is a moot point. The truth probably combines both; but this is certain, that the individualistic tendency of slavery, which dissociated a man from family life, and made him, as Aristotle calls him, a mere living tool, could not but bring about such a result.

And many of the socialistic movements of our day aim at little else than an organised slavery, which would entirely destroy the brotherly spirit. Among slaves little sympathy is known, little brotherly feeling, and a general callous indifference is the ruling sentiment which they have towards mankind. Such a state of things would result from the success of some plans for reconstructing society which have been proposed. They might produce their own cure by the excess of individualism, but would more likely bring man in a gradual descent to a selfish torpor which would annihilate the higher affections and nobler impulses of life. Freedom is an essential element in brotherhood, freedom in the exercise of will and command of action. The present disorderly state of Hayti is a proof that even when the freedom is won, men only slowly rise above the habits and traditions of the past, and slowly do we recover any ground which we have lost. The ascent of man is at all times a toilsome process; but if at any time he loses his natural impulse upwards, it seems almost impossible for him to regain it. As a wound which might heal if treated with care loses all restorative power with a fresh injury, so it is with the progress of man when it is paralysed by a backward fall.

The mental difference of mankind need not form a serious difficulty to a belief in its unity. In every individual man there are various stages of acquirement, and among the people of any one race the same variety is found. We only come slowly into consciousness, which is in all its forms a growth. The consciousness of individuality is in a true sense a late acquirement, but by degrees we come to have the family consciousness and the tribal consciousness, which more and more relate themselves to a conception of individual existence. Out of these emerge the general sense of a human kinship, in which we may discern the development of an organic consciousness of humanity. Savages do not possess this, for they think that the missionaries and travellers are of another race, whether divine or devilish. But the civilised man has no doubt of his actual unity with the darkest savage. As Edmond About says, writing to his own countrymen: " Let me suppose that business takes you to the heart of Africa. You are among the Gallas, the most barbarous of the negro tribes. Suddenly, at a turn of the road, a white face appears. Your heart beats; you run. What joy! It is a Prussian of Königsberg. He is a Protestant, you are a Catholic; his flag is not the same colour as yours; his fellow-citizens are perhaps engaged in sabring yours on the Rhine! But what matters it? Your provisions, your arms, your purse, are at his service. Is he not a citizen of Europe, a member of the great European society? The first who attacks him will have to reckon with you.

"But if, three months after, in some wilderness, in the midst of serpents, crocodiles, and jaguars, you meet a Galla; that glossy skin, those tangled locks, fill you only with confidence and joy. He is black, he is a heathen, and he eats raw flesh; but he is a man like yourself, a member of the great human society You have need of each other in the fight against death."[1]

But it must be kept in mind that the original unity of man, if proved, is rather a theoretical than a practical triumph. For that unity has been long lost, and mankind is only awaking to the blessing of its future recovery. It is more stimulating to the mind of man to place the golden age in the future, than to dream of it in a long-distant past. The desire of unity may be a native instinct in the mind of man, which lay long dormant, and only had a fitful existence in the light of common day; or it may be due to a new development which realises the future destiny of mankind, and hastens to accomplish it. But the fact is that all the thought and

[1] *Le Progrès*, pp. 72, 73.

action of man are striving to co-operate towards its attainment; and we are bound to believe that all the forces which govern this earth are on the side of this great principle. Not only the commercial activity, but the missionary energy of man, use their utmost efforts to bring about this purpose of unity,—half unconsciously it may be, but not the less surely.

And there are other facts, of which we have not a full interpretation, which seem to point in the same direction. The unity of the human race is in process of slow accomplishment even on physical grounds. We cannot but lament the disappearance of the aboriginal people from countries which have been colonised. The Caribs and Tasmanians have entirely perished; the Australians and Eskimo and American Indian are rapidly diminishing in numbers. Influences of many kinds, some unspeakably sad, are bringing about this result. The fatal progress of new diseases, and the equally fatal infection of new vices, are among the most rapid agencies; while slower but not less certain forces are found in the compulsory change of habits, and the lessening of the natural food supplies by the spread of cultivation. In Africa it is said that certain tribes have become extinct from no known cause, but by gradual diminution in productiveness. The process has been going on ever since man came upon this earth, and the less developed races have had to succumb before the arrival of the more powerful. It is an unhappy and mysterious page in human history, which we can only record and not interpret; but it is a page which is not yet finished. Some theorists suppose that the negro race is destined to people all the world, although there are not many facts to give support to such a view. Others think the future of the world is with the spread of the white peoples; but all is the vaguest speculation. All we can be certain of is, that while the greater families of mankind seem to keep their steadfast position, the lesser varieties are doomed to extinction. We can only record the fact, as we are led to do in our consideration of the subject, but its meaning in providence we do not presume to interpret. We can only say that its tendency is to bring into a gradual identity all the inhabitants of the globe.

We have confined our present survey to the physical unity of man, but there are important aspects of the subject yet to be considered, especially in the growth of the social and altruistic feelings. These deserve thought, and will repay inquiry.

CHAPTER VI

JESUS THE CARPENTER

THE humble birth of Jesus is one of the reproaches which Celsus brings against the Christians in his *True Word* (λόγος ἀληθής), the work which Origen refutes, and which he largely quotes, and thus preserves to us. Some orthodox catechisms, such as those of the Westminster Assembly, account the poverty of the surroundings of Jesus as part of His humiliation. The Fathers, including St. Augustine, attribute to Mary perfect freedom from sin; while the Orthodox Greek Church put her above all created beings; and the Roman Church has held, since 1854, the doctrine that she was born immaculate from all stain of original sin. This removes the birth of Jesus from any shadow in the eyes of those who believe the infallible pope; but the "low condition" seems to strike the minds of Protestants: and the pious Jansenist Quesnel says: "The humble condition of Jesus is an occasion of offence to many. It seems to be unworthy of Him; but it was necessary on our account."

To hold that the birth of Jesus was a part of His humiliation, is in accordance with Scripture, because it was a change from a divine to a human nature, in which He emptied Himself of His glory. But to add that an additional part of the divine humiliation, another drop in the cup of bitterness, was the birth "in a low condition," excites our wonder. Who may bring such paltry earthly distinctions into the lofty temple of God's love? Is a peer higher in the scale of being than a peasant? God forbid that we should introduce these toys of our childhood, these trappings of our vanity, into events of such infinite import. What are such things viewed *sub specie æternitatis*? A little thought will show us that all these earthly differences of rank or circumstance mean very little, and weigh very lightly in the scale of our real value or happiness. If a Diogenes can grasp this truth, what would be its significance to Jesus?

In that elementary view of life which we are forced to take sometimes during life, and always at the approach of death, we recognise no grades of worth except as they are measured by truth and purity. In our ordinary daily existence we are willing to give their due meed of ceremonious respect to those who claim it or who merit it; it is a part of the machinery of the world, and no sensible man refuses it. But we do not blind ourselves to its actual value, and times come to all men when it counts for nothing. The importance of the life and mission of Jesus dwarf it into as utter insignificance as any number divided by infinity.

We can form some judgment on the meaning of Jesus taking the position of a carpenter, from the general course of His teaching and His life, as well as from Jewish feelings and customs. When the disciples were sent out, they were told not to burden themselves with superfluities, and not to be in bondage to any artificial wants, so that they might have the full liberty of their whole being. May we not conclude, therefore, that Jesus chose His calling and rank in life because it was least encumbered? When we speak of rank in life, we must remember, too, that in the Holy Land, in the time of Jesus, such distinctions had less meaning among the Jews than they have in our day.

It seems clear that Jesus chose the calling of a workman because it is nearer the natural condition of things, and touches life to the quick in a way that many callings lack. Riches and rank are great hindrances to our knowing and feeling the realities of life. They waste time in ceremony, and create a host of appetites which are not born with us, and which we are better without. They make us the spoiled children of fortune, and cripple us in many ways. Why should man not use his limbs if he can; why suffer himself to be driven in a carriage while he has health to walk?

We read that, when Socrates was asked, "Who was the richest man?" he replied, "He that is content with least, for the natural wealth of man is to be independent of outward surroundings." The ancient world was made familiar with this view of life from its forming the heart of its Stoic philosophy; but modern life has laid it aside. It is only now and then that men, who seek better things than outward conformity to the world, preach the gospel of simplicity, to which, whether it come from the lips of American transcendentalists or Russian nobles, the most of men listen with a pitying smile.

But Jesus often recurs to the subject. "How hardly

shall they that have riches enter the kingdom." "Blessed are the poor: for theirs is the kingdom of heaven." When the young ruler came to Him, with some measure of sincere love for goodness and of anxiety for truth, what kept him from following the higher impulse of his nature? He could not break with the conventionalities of life; he was enslaved by the poor deception of outward wealth. When wealth and power and dominion came before the heart of Jesus, they came as a temptation of the evil one, which He spurned from Him. To most men they come in like manner to tempt them. It is not because they afford opportunity of pleasure or idleness, or facility for the primrose path that leads to the eternal fire, as because they actually burden the soul, and disturb its balance and blear its sight. They feed the selfishness of the soul, and shut men out from the true fellowship of mankind.

The noble Mazzini found that the love of ease and art, and the cravings which an indulged youth had created, were too strong for many of his young followers to resist. Like the young man who came to Jesus, they went away sorrowful, for they had great possessions. They were traitors to eternal truth and justice, because they had been born to sleep on soft pillows and drink generous wines. Mazzini found that his followers in humbler life were encumbered by no such childish helplessness. Among them were shown indomitable courage, a scorn of comfort and steadfastness of purpose, which proved how free a life the plain man lives, and how much readier is his perception of lofty ideals and divine thoughts.

Christ chose His friends from among working people, and committed His gospel for all the world to a handful of humble fishermen. The common people heard Him gladly; and throughout His earthly life He identified Himself with their simple joys and sorrows. I doubt if we realise how near the life of Jesus comes to simple people who are out of the busy intellectual currents and material progress of our times. We need to go to some more primitive community than our Western civilisation can show, to see its full power. In Russia, a French writer tells us, we may be able to observe its workings among the peasants—*unlearned and ignorant men.* " Every lesson, every parable of the New Testament, fits into the peasant's way of life, and goes to the heart of his desires and his sorrows; the feeble are persecuted; the humble are glorified; a few fishermen turn the world upside down. The reader goes on to the Acts, and sees with wonder the society of his peasant dream, of poor men living in community, helping each other, and ruled by love and justice, without the interference from without of a hard and elaborate mechanical government. He sees a sublime moral code perfectly adapted to simple hearts. The letter is sacred to him, and enough for him; it fits in with his ideas of the universe; he does not need to twist it so as to suit the exigencies of a complex civilisation." [1]

It has been said that Jesus took His station in life out of the depth of His sympathy with the poor. True it is there is a peculiar tenderness among the poor to

[1] M. E. M. de Vogüé in the *Revue des Deux Mondes*, January 1883, pp. 64, 65.

each other, that there is a pathetic beauty about the few enjoyments, that there is a soft light which illumines the self-denying acts of aid and half-uttered consolation, and a heavenly lustre about the bond of communion in toil and sorrow which unites the poor. But we cannot read all this into the life of Jesus as a carpenter.

On the contrary, we see a simple, cheerful, homely life, with all the sweet affection and happy days which peace and contentment bring. There is not much said of privation or suffering through straitened means, but the current of life flows with placid tranquillity. The patronising sympathy and aid which seem the highest attainable form of our Christian benevolence are never once heard of in the New Testament, except, perhaps, from the lips of Judas Iscariot.

Christ meets the working people on their own level with a frank brotherhood which they at once recognise; and the blessings they gain by that receptive impressibility which opens their souls to His loving life and teaching, far outweigh the doubtful advantages which the rich men of Judea possessed in combination with a hardness of heart which made them deaf to the words of Jesus.[1]

[1] A great writer of our time, who, amid much that is evil, has given us not a little that is noble and true, has brought this vividly before the imagination in an allegory, which he entitles *Jesus Christ in Flanders*. In the boat in which Christ is represented as travelling, He takes His place beside the poorer passengers, one of whom makes way for Him. "It was one of these indications of willingness to oblige each other by which poor people who know the happiness of brotherly sympathy, show the openness and naturalness of their hearts," says Balzac, with his keen observation. The allegory further develops the mutual sympathy, and the aid which Jesus is able to give, because the poor trust Him. Balzac, *Romans Philosophiques*, tome 3, 2nd ed.

It was in accordance with the custom of the Jews that their teachers were poor men. The "wise men" who guarded the laws and traditions of the Hebrews were held in high esteem. Many of them were artizans, yet no priest or nobleman was more revered. We read that many of them spoke of the value of labour, and all abhorred idleness. Such sayings as these are handed down. "The tradesman at his work is the equal of the most learned doctor." " He who derives his livelihood from the labour of his hands is as great as he who fears God."[1] The Jews taught every boy a trade, and piety and learning were only honoured when they were joined to bodily work. In modern times this has been taught with but poor success, as far as the winning of followers is concerned, by the founders of Brook Farm, by Mr. Ruskin and Count Tolstoi. The Rabbis, we are assured,[2] deemed it an unworthy act if they were paid in any way for their religious duties, and, like St. Paul, maintained themselves by their own toil. It is strange to find the trade of the Rabbi often mentioned in the Talmud in connection with his teachings, as thus: "It

---

[1] The following additional maxims may be added from Farrar's *St. Paul*, i. 23 : "Learning of any kind, unaccompanied by a trade, ends in nothing, and leads to sin " (Gamaliel). " Labour honours the labourer " (Rabbi Judah). " Not to teach one's son a trade is like teaching him robbery " (Rabbi Judah). Additional instances are given by Chief Rabbi Adler in the *Nineteenth Century* for Dec. 1881, " Recent Phases of Judæophobia." On the other hand, we read in the Jew Leopold Kompert's Jewish story, *Trenderl*, that one of the most obstinate prejudices of the Jews of the present day is that the law of God forbids them to be artizans. The object of the tale is to correct this view.

[2] Dr. Adler, *loc. cit.*

was taught by Rabbi Jochanan, the shoemaker"; "by Jose ben Chalafta, the tanner."

The traditions of Greece were different from those of Judea in the matter of labour. In Athens the free citizens did not think it worthy of them to engage in mechanical toil, which was only fit for slaves. Aristotle excluded tradesmen from equal rights of citizenship in his ideal commonwealth, and mentions that in former times the mechanics were either slaves or foreigners, "for which reason," he adds, "many of them are so now." The same tendency is shown in Plato; and Aristophanes' contempt for workmen, shown in his Comedies, seems to have been appreciated by the Athenians.

A similar state of things was long seen in India, though times have somewhat changed. The handicraftsmen and artizans are all placed in the lowest caste, the Sudras, who were supposed to have sprung from the *foot* of Brahma. As was natural to a people whose chief industry was agriculture, the farmers, herdsmen, and hunters belonged to the class above the Sudras. In our own country, the people of the Celtic parts of it for long looked down on many crafts as unworthy of man, and indeed all occupations of peace which had no relation to war were placed in that class. The same feelings seem to have animated almost all the branches of the human family speaking the Aryan tongues. We find that throughout long periods of history, labour was regarded as ignoble; that the early Greek and Roman heroes despised any calling but war; and that the same feeling animated the Teutonic peoples down to the borderland of modern civilisation. The hard toil of life was done by bondmen, or, as among the North American Indians, by the women. In the existence of slavery is found the reason for this; and even in our own day a like sentiment inspires the planters of the Southern States of America.

The loss to a community of the discipline of regular labour is not easily reckoned, and the restless democracy of Greece needed the balancing influence of settled occupation, in which the day could be spent better than in their ceaseless and useless babble. It was not until the guilds of tradesmen were formed in Europe that the civil condition of society became stable, and the arts of life began to recover from the torpor of the Middle Ages. The Church, as well as the State, benefited by the steadfastness and uprightness which honest toil begets; and the revival of religious life in Europe was in no small degree aided by the labouring classes, whose life, dealing with realities, helped them to look at all questions with a clear vision and direct insight. The value of simplicity began to be more evident to their minds, and their view of active life conditioned their ideas of religious truth. This state of things, however, is even more seen in the East, where the great religious movements have had a close connection with labour and self-denial and simplicity of life.

There is in the East, notwithstanding the Hindu castes, and always has been in the East, a readier recognition of the value of such simple ways than among Western nations. It may be merely the influence of civilisation which makes the difference, or it may be a feature of the races who dwell in more genial climates than ours. The Germans seemed to Tacitus a manlier race than his own, by reason of their plain ways of life, and those who praised the olden times in Rome thought with envy of the simple labours of the heroic Cincinnatus, as in Athens they spoke of the men who fought at Marathon. The golden age, to their mind, appeared as a time when "a few strong instincts and a few plain rules" did "more for mankind than all the pride of intellect and thought."

The pastoral habits of a great part of the population of Eastern countries, and the easier life they led, caused them to keep to the primitive instincts of mankind, daily toil and plain fare. It was of the essence of Buddha's teaching [1] to live simply and avoid all covetousness; and he showed his followers the example of a great renunciation, by giving up his princely state, and teaching mankind that by such sacrifice of self-seeking they may gain a true insight into life.[2]

We must not, however, regard the voluntary choice of the working life and earthly portion of an artizan which our Saviour made as a renunciation. We see in it rather that healthy state of the natural soul of man which craves the open road of life. Too often the teachers of mankind have loved the seclusion of the academic grove,

---

[1] Strauss says, in the *Old and the New Faith*, that Buddhism and Christianity both discourage labour; but in this he has no justification.

[2] "In the Norse legend of our ancestors, Odin dwells in a fisher's hut, and patches a boat. In the Hindu legends, Hari dwells a peasant among peasants. In the Greek legend, Apollo lodges with the shepherds of Admetus; and Jove liked to rusticate among the poor Ethiopians."—Emerson, *Works and Days*.

have held aloof from the great heart of humanity, and have chosen bypaths sheltered and pleasant, whither few have cared to follow them. Socrates lived and taught right in the centre of Athenian life, in the crowded market-place, or in the busy harbour, with open sympathies and a genial heart and simple ways; but Plato retired to his garden, and shunned the multitude, whom he never trusted. There have been more to follow the course Plato took than to imitate Socrates; and though one does not willingly judge, in a critical spirit, the leaders of mankind, we are compelled to ask if there is not a weakness in this. There is a reluctant shrinking from the real world which is eminently unwise in those who seek to guide it. Jesus took the broad highway of life, with its freedom, its sympathy, its reality. The workman is the traveller afoot through time; he breathes the pure air of common life, a true son of man. He is "on the broadest human plane"; as a writer says, "on the level of the great laws and heroic deeds." His emotions are

> "Chiefly those
> Essential and eternal in the heart,
> That 'mid the simpler forms of rural life,
> Exist more simple in their elements,
> And speak a plainer language."

Wealth brings isolation, which develops into selfishness, and a man walls his soul round as he does his park. The workman gets a closer grasp of his kind, comes nearer to his brother man, and learns every day those lessons of mutual aid and tolerance and sympathy on which our life depends.

The mission of Christ was to all mankind, and He would not lose any possibility of bringing Himself nearer the affections of men; He would not exclude any from His sympathies; He was a man, and His heart was free to all. He chose His calling because He felt that it best gave Him the scope for carrying out His great and divine work. Buddha did the same in old time; so, too, did Socrates; and men have seen, even in our own times, the value of a simple life lived in the heart of humanity. Who can tell the amount of religious indifference among the working classes which is due in England to the great social division which often separates their clergy from them? Fortunately, they seek teachers born in their own circumstances, whose influence is strong with them. The heart of England has been kept pure, not so much by the clergy of the Established Church, as by the less observed labours of the obscure ministers of many sects who go in and out and live their lives among the artizans.

There are, indeed, other considerations which enter into the worth of a position where one must labour steadfastly for sustenance. The discipline in which our lawless self must keep itself, if we have to continue in work, is one of the best educations of body and mind. The moral faculties acquire a truthfulness which the selfish lounger in life soon loses, and the sense of justice is strengthened by orderly action, while work by fits and starts, at the bidding of irregular impulse, is apt to make mere passing pleasure the test of conduct rather than an unvarying moral standard. The "exact arts," as Goethe[1]

---
[1] Strenge Kunst, *Wilhelm Meister's wanderjahre*, iii. 12.

calls the handicrafts, imply such a degree of practical usefulness, that they must be sound and true in their workmanship; which fact itself acts on the mind, and begets a love for truth and justice. These influences on the life of man are real, and no mere theoretical fancy; and history confirms them. In modern times the poets have drawn our attention to such moral forces, and the teaching of Wordsworth and Clough has made us conscious of the presence of a great moral stability from their agency.

But the social influence of labour is, after all, its main power among men. The compulsory association of some men in great undertakings is only a type of the relations of labour throughout all the world, which unites the common contributions of mankind to the store of real riches. In the classic passage, so familiar, Carlyle, with perhaps too sorrowful a feeling, recognises the unselfish sacrifice which labour makes for others, thus fulfilling the highest social ideal. "Hardly entreated brother! For us was thy back so bent, for us were thy straight limbs and fingers so deformed; thou wert our conscript, on whom the lot fell, and fighting our battles wert so marred."

Common toil is a parable of deep meaning; it shadows forth for us the lofty destiny and complete unity of mankind, where each lives for the other, and all for God.

It is true, therefore, that the main power which labour exerts on the heart of man is to develop the social feeling; it is the strongest force against selfish individualism that the world has ever had. This isolation, which seems characteristic of ancient Greek life, the individual selfishness which marks much of their history, was largely due to the fact that they did not work together at any industrial task, but left it to slaves. In the Middle Ages, the guilds showed the need and the value of company, each helping the other by succour and hospitality; and in modern times, with not a little that is unwise pursuit of passing interest, rather than permanent, there is much generous self-sacrifice in the unions of our workmen in their various trades for collective action. For even though a man be a solitary workman, he works for others, and he is united to them by that labour and service. And if he work with a crowd, the lessons of sympathy and need of dependence on others that such a life teaches him, rob him of selfish tendencies to isolation. The kindness and thoughtfulness which such joint labour brings are among the best gifts that earth can bestow on man.

Jesus came to develop the social life of the race, to bring men into union one with another; and He recognised as one of the best means of doing so, the taking upon Himself the duty of a labouring man. For we owe to each other more than mere pecuniary gifts, especially if such gift be the result of inherited wealth. We must give part of ourselves, our strength, our life, to mankind; and only by doing so can we realise the true brotherhood of humanity. The workman spends his life for others as well as with them; he is the unknown benefactor of all who enjoy the fruits of his toil, and by his labours unites all mankind. Merely to bestow money is an idle and worthless gift, and often the source of more evil than good. Even though a man's title to inherited wealth were undisputed, and his right to the usury which comes from others' work undoubted, the gifts which he gives from such a source are, as far as he is concerned, worthless. The pleasure of giving is great, and its blessing to giver and receiver one of the best of the lights of life; but to give what one has not wrought for, is to give naught. It is the joy of labour beyond what is needed for personal wants, that one can bestow on others; and in such bestowal one gives not the mere gold, but a part of life itself—time and strength. The social force of labour is thus unmeasured; it is the great bond which unites the human race.

It is clear that the future is to give a different distribution of manual toil. It will be divided more equally among all the members of the community, by the mere force of causes which are already present, but which are acquiring more force. The true duty to each other will be more fully recognised, and the blessings of art and poetry and beauty will be more equally distributed, as well as the social enjoyment of common toil.

CHAPTER VII

THE THEOLOGY OF JESUS

THE centre of the teaching of Christ is the great truth that God is our Father.

Need we inquire if it was known before His coming? Even if it were reached by the nobler and purer hearts of Israel in Old Testament times, it is not their usual thought of God. They did not commonly represent God by such a relation; nor had it entered into the hearts of the Jews of the time of Christ as a real belief. How could they have held to the faith that God was their Father, when they accused Jesus of blasphemy when He claimed sonship for Himself? Their great birthright was hid from their sight till Jesus revealed its glory. There is no importance in the fact that Christ was not the first teacher of this doctrine; nor does it lessen His glory that in heathenism and Judaism there was a progress to the truth concerning God's Fatherhood; for Christ gave it a completeness and certainty which it had not known before His coming.

The Fatherhood of God was the sum of the revelation made by Christ. The Gospel of St. John differs in many ways from the other Gospels, but it shows no difference here. All the four evangelists represent Jesus as speaking of God as His Father, and as the universal Father of all men.

It is this which He impresses on His disciples as the thought of God which should be ever before their minds. For in the prayer He taught them, which embraces the whole of human life, He tells them to begin, *Our Father*. The Father He revealed to them was a Father who loved them and forgave them; who cared for their wants on earth and their dwelling in heaven; who blessed them with His Spirit, and sought the worship of all true hearts: but who withheld not His gifts from the unthankful and evil. "He maketh His sun to rise on the evil and the good, and sendeth rain on the just and the unjust." Like a Father, He loves all His children, and discerns in them some virtue or goodness which is hardly present to their own consciousness, and, always believing the best of their imperfect lives, has hope of them all. For they are His children, and even if they have long forgotten Him, if they have no claim on Him but their necessities, He still gives them His love and aid.

By direct teaching, and by parable, the great doctrine of the Divine Fatherhood was made plain to the hearts of the hearers of Jesus. The Sermon on the Mount is the sum of the truth regarding it, and the parable of the Prodigal Son shows all the heart of God to the trembling child of man, who had for ages been offering his sacrifice of blood to propitiate some dark power, whom his thought had pictured as supreme, in place of the Father of infinite love.[1] And if the inquiring soul of man asked yet further

[1] The conception of God which underlies sacrifice is that which is

knowledge of the divine goodness of the universal Father, he had but to consider the work and character of His Son. "Philip saith, Show us the Father, and it sufficeth us. Jesus saith unto him, Have I been so long time with you, and yet hast thou not known Me, Philip? He that hath seen Me hath seen the Father."

To understand the moral nature of God, we are told we must examine the life of Jesus. He revealed the divine Father, not only through His word, but through all that He did, through every relation He had with man. He presents His own life as the best knowledge man could have of the nature of God. His love and kindness, His sympathy with men in all the surroundings of their life, His forgiveness and tenderness, are so many revelations of the heavenly Father, of whom He was the express image. He appeals, indeed, to the common experience of mankind in support of His teaching, and exhibits the providence of God as having the breadth and universality of His love. He directs our attention to those facts of life which bear out the view He wishes to impress, which help to create the filial feeling on which the Christian rests.

Jesus shows clearly the purpose which the religion He gave to man was destined to serve, by this revelation

---

found in natural religion, and is fundamentally different from that revealed by Christ. This fact opens up trains of inquiry as to the relation which Christianity bears to the heathen religions and to Judaism, but shows that it cannot be called an ordinary development from them. Still less true is the older naturalistic thought, found in the English deists and their German contemporaries, that Christianity is simply a republication of the truths of natural religion.

of God. He unveils Him to our sight, but in no other light than as a Father; for Christ's mission to men was moral, not intellectual. He desires them to realise that they are all alike children of the one heavenly Father, and that their life finds its crown in acting as sons of the divine Father, moved by love like His, generous and universal. "Be ye perfect, as your Father in heaven is perfect."

The conception of God thus given by Jesus is wholly an ethical representation for an ethical purpose—the salvation of mankind. We must not think it is given us as a complete exhibition of the divine nature or attributes; though, indeed, to speak of such completeness of understanding of God is an impossibility, for no finite can comprehend the Infinite. Our Saviour Himself assures His hearers of this when He says: "No man hath seen God at any time." The nature of God must always remain an insoluble mystery to man. But does such a belief in the limitation of our powers necessarily repel us from the inquiry? Surely the philosophy, whether of Spencer or Hamilton or Mansel, bears no such meaning. Even if we are baffled, and our result is almost naught, may we not still aspire? Is it not something to know that the nature of God is beyond our knowledge?

We may, in the words of St. Paul, yet *feel after* God; for, though we cannot put our knowledge in words, He may yet manifest Himself to our souls. Justin Martyr asks: "Can a man know God, as we know arithmetic or astronomy?" Our knowledge may not be entirely coherent; we may not be able to arrange it into a perfect system, yet every point of knowledge gained is a fresh insight into truth.

Suppose now a conflict between the ethical revelation and the scientific attainment of man. These must essentially harmonise, but it is doubtful if our faculties will ever be able to reach the reconciliation, though they may ever tend to it. Meanwhile, however, we assume that a discrepancy occurs; which shall we follow?[1]

[1] We here come in sight of the theory of the double truth, which is expressed in the familiar words: "I believe as a Christian what I cannot believe as a philosopher." The Platonists have always inclined to this view with more or less adjustment. One of the best of the Humanists, Pomponazzi, clearly expounds this aspect of the apparent discrepancy between reason and faith. He holds that there is a speculative and practical reason; the one inquires into truth, the other regulates conduct. The danger is that here we have theology removed from the rank of a science and made a mere collection of unconnected precepts; but Pomponazzi was not really interested in favour of Christianity. The Platonic theory of a γεννᾶιον ψεῦδος, by which we can teach what will influence men without regard to its truth, was doubtless present to his mind; but it is a dangerous theory, and the needless thought of a spurious superiority. It was intellectual vanity as well as dishonesty which made Synesius, an earlier Platonist, say: "If I am made bishop, I must be allowed to philosophise in my own mind, while I talk mythology to the people." It was this imagined opposition which was the death of scholasticism, which did not survive the condemnation of the double truth by the Council of the Lateran in 1513. Descartes was sincere in his expression of belief when he said: "If God reveals anything about Himself or others that is beyond the natural powers of our mind, such as the mysteries of the Incarnation and Trinity, we are not entitled to refuse to believe in them, although we may not clearly understand them." We must never forget there is an inner circle of the soul, to which mere reasoning never penetrates, and which is, after all, the centre of our faith. It was Neander who said of Pascal that he was "a witness to that religious conviction which is founded in immediate perception, and is elevated above all reflection."

The answer in the experience of mankind is that we must trust and obey the ethical truth as Jesus gives it to us. We do not now consider what the authority of Jesus is, as we shall afterwards examine its source; but even here we may find the direction in which one form of that authority points, the practical soundness of His commands as regulating human conduct.

The position here taken up is the exact contrary of what Mr. Frederic Harrison gives as the Christian view. He asserts that " bishops, priests, and deacons, for the most part sweep theology away from the whole field of systematic thought and active life. Science, they say, explains the laws of nature and the laws of society; social motives are an adequate explanation of worldly activity." I doubt if Mr. Harrison states truly the position of those whom he opposes; but even if he be accurate, it is worth pointing out that the view we present looks towards the opposite direction.

The inquiries of man into the universe are by no means restrained by this attitude to scientific inquiry, whose difference with the ethical view of Jesus may be no more than a possible theory. Man may, with the reason given to him, examine into the relation of God to the universe, and find out what is revealed in the creation. He may search for the laws by which this frame of things is held together, or came into being, and form some idea of the Infinite Power behind them all. But is there an absolute need that we should try to reconcile the knowledge gained by scientific inquiry and that given by the teaching of Christ? Whether there is need or not, we cannot withhold our minds from the effort.

The link between the two forms of knowledge may not be given to us; these forms come from two separate sources, which we know are distinct in their appeal to our souls. They stand related to each other, since they both speak truth to us, but we may not discern any other relation between them. They are apprehended by different mental states, the one by faith, and the other by reason. We set ourselves a hard task when we try to find a harmony between our scientific knowledge and the fatherhood of God; but, we ask, is a complete synthesis necessary, even if possible?

There cannot be a doubt that the human mind craves for unity, and desires to see the same God that communes with the soul realising Himself in creation. We rejoice to find any confirmation of our religious faith in the teachings of science; and every new correspondence which we discover between the Father whom our hearts love, and the Almighty Power that rules the universe, gives us gladness. But what of the dark chasms which no light illumines? There are mysterious gaps in our knowledge which we have not yet bridged, such as are found in the slow evolution of nature as well as in its cataclysms.

We know we *cannot* arrive at all the truth; these gaps must, some of them, always exist; and we do not give up our faith because some scientific man has lighted on a question which he cannot answer. Human conduct is within our sphere; we have the power to survey it all, and any defects in our system of morals are corrected by the growing experience of ages. As a practical science it advances, but all its possibilities are before us in the ideal of goodness. We have therefore within us a moral and religious consciousness which we cannot fully bring into harmony with the world around us, but which enables us to unite ourselves to God and man in love and duty. We can show a complete view of the moral nature of man, which includes all the tendencies he has ever manifested, which takes count of his progress, which harmonises with the divine truths that have been given to him, as well as with the discoveries in morals which he has toilsomely reached; and this result of our scientific study has nothing in it except what strengthens our belief in the Fatherhood of God. We cannot lay down as an ascertained fact the position of man in relation to the wide universe which lies beyond our knowledge, except in the vast generalisations of astronomical theory; still less can we see the being of God as revealed in His works.

Jesus does not enter the field of science at all, which is altogether left for the mind of man to explore. He presents theology to us solely with a view to the regulation of our conduct, and all the speculations of man's reason may still go on undisturbed by any check from His command. As He interfered not with the social or family life of man, but sanctioned it by His gracious sympathy in rejoicing with them that did rejoice, and weeping with them that wept; as He overturned not the religious authority which ruled the temple worship, nor the secular that governed the national affairs, but gave tribute to both; as He encouraged all the manifold activities of man, by His sharing in the industry of a carpenter: so He left the mind of man free to pursue its speculations in physics, or metaphysics, or theology.

Not only does He not discourage the inquiries of human reason, or cast doubt on its truthfulness; He even seems to put value on the conclusions our speculative thought arrives at. "If it were not so," He said, speaking of the belief in a future life, "I would have told you." Does He not practically tell us that the instincts within us, the "moving about in worlds not realised," are a means whereby we come to know truth, and truth of the deepest moment. He really assures His followers that if one of these interior thoughts of the soul were false, He would have told them, nor let them cherish a delusion. The light of human reason, He tells us in almost as many words, glows with a divine radiance, and is a real guiding star, not a mere Will-o'-the-wisp deception. He encourages us, therefore, in our search for the synthesis of all knowledge; but however far onward we may go, we are not promised an arrival at the goal. To know God we must be divine. As an actual fact, we have seen that we find the synthesis in moral progress. Man always makes the ethical purpose the standard of his life. There is a sureness of foot on the highway of conduct which the soul does not find in any other walk of life. Hence it is that ordinary men seize on the centre truth of Christ's teaching in a way that the professed theologian is often a stranger to.

Through the history of the Church, amid all its dogmatic speculation, the humble Christian has always a practical belief in the Fatherhood of God. Even those doctrinal systems which more or less keep this truth in the background, such as Calvinism, do not lessen the hold of this great principle on the minds of the devout multitude. The modern theology, which makes the doctrine of the Fatherhood of God a central point from which all truth radiates, only puts into more or less scientific form what has always been the unexpressed though general conviction of Christendom.

The movement of doctrine among theologians follows the guiding of philosophical systems. Plato, Aristotle, Kant, Hegel, are the steersmen at different times to the ship of doctrine. But it is otherwise with the ordinary life of faith in the Church. The truth is conducted from soul to soul by the intercommunication of men, and as it passes, the non-essential elements fall into oblivion, the real and living heart alone abiding. It is, after all, a certain disposition of the heart, call it faith or love,[1] by which man receives and retains the living gospel, which is the same for all generations.

It is the ethical element which the heart of man absorbs in the religion of Christ, for that religion revealed truth in ethical forms and for ethical ends. How profound was the saying of Napoleon: "For my part, it is not the mystery of the Incarnation which I discover in religion, but the mystery of social order, which associates with heaven that idea of equality which prevents the rich from destroying the poor"!

But though the teaching of Jesus has this ethical form and purpose, we are not restrained from doctrinal inquiry or speculation. As St. Augustine says: "The Christian

[1] Julius Müller said that Glaube, *faith*, and Liebe, *love*, were etymologically the same.

claims as his Master's own possession every fragment of truth, wherever it may be found." The unity of truth must exist, though we may but imperfectly apprehend it; and our reason must go fearlessly on, for all the land of truth which lies before us is subject to the same divine law. Nothing but gain can come from the pursuit of knowledge in religion; we are certain to find seemingly parallel rays, which yet are coming from the one centre, if we could stretch our vision far enough into the infinite.

But Christ reveals to us, not only God as our Father, but also Himself as the Son of God; and He gives the assurance that he who hath seen Him hath seen the Father. As Jesus revealed God as the Father, and revealed Him only in that ethical aspect; so, in like manner, He teaches the divine Sonship. He enters into no metaphysical statements such as after ages have thought it needful to make, but, while asserting His own divinity, dwells on the moral attributes of His Sonship.

He renders perfect obedience as a Son, and thus becomes a model for all mankind. He has complete union with God as His Father, and He calls men to share that union, and in it to find peace and rest. "Come unto me all ye that labour and are heavy laden, and I will give you rest." "I have declared unto them Thy name, and will declare it; that the love wherewith Thou hast loved me may be in them, and I in them." Jesus did not teach all the truth about Himself or His Father. We cannot but ask why. Is it not plain that He confined His teaching to the great purpose of His life? He wished to restore man to a unity of brotherhood and love, and revealed what was necessary for that purpose. The doctrine of Christ about God has a *practical* end, and is limited by that practical end. What is told us about Father, Son, and Holy Ghost is given with a view of creating the filial and brotherly feeling in man, of completing the divine purpose of unity in him.

The life of Jesus shows the same limitations. He cured the sick, but did not stay the hand of disease and death in the Holy Land while He dwelt there, still less in the world at large. The laws of nature went on their regular course without interruption from Him. Nay, He often appeals to the order of all things, as pointing to some moral thought. His perfect submission to the dominion of law is seen when He speaks of the people on whom the tower of Siloam fell. Why were they cut off? The Jews thought it was a judgment on them: He simply saw an instance of universal natural law. How was that law brought into the normal relations of our human life? Why were lives useful and happy cut off suddenly? He offers no reply to such questions, which, indeed, may be asked of every death that ever happened. These may imply some unknown standpoint which human intelligence may not fully reach. It seems as if Jesus took the simple attitude, here as elsewhere, of trust in the inscrutable providence. Whatever happens, God is our Father. Do not ask to know the secret of His workings, but confide in His love. De Maistre expresses this with fine insight: " The just law is not that which is executed upon all, but that which is made for all. To find difficulties in such an order of things, one must love them. . . . Strange that we should find it easier to be just to man than to God!"[1] Who cannot see that the inner unity of God's providence cannot be unfolded to our imperfect sight? We are not ourselves divine, but mere creatures dependent on that providence. What way is there out of the darkness, but to say with Calvin that the absolute decrees of God cannot be known by us? Not that the Reformer thought that the decree was arbitrary, as we think it, but that it was outside our power to harmonize. The completely filial attitude of Jesus is seen in Gethsemane, when He prays as He taught us, *Thy will be done.*

Jesus refers to the limitations of His knowledge here and elsewhere when He says the Father only knows the appointed time; that the knowledge is not in the Son's possession. Much thought has been given to this subject of the limitations of the human life of Christ, and many theories, especially in recent times, have been formed upon it. We do not stay to discuss them, but simply would point out that Jesus ever keeps in view the filial relation He had to the divine Father. His purpose in speaking at all about God was to bring men to the knowledge of their true sonship; and no other thought of God is taken heed of in the life and words of Jesus Christ. All that would strengthen men's hearts to that great divine end is dwelt upon, but the many questions which our minds may ask are left unsolved, and the problem of immortality itself is referred solely to the Father's love. "In My Father's house are many mansions."

It is manifest that Jesus confined His presentation

[1] *Soirées de St. Petersbourg*, i. p. 25.

of the divine nature as it was in Himself to its moral manifestations. This may have been because it is only in these aspects that man can be like God, and only in these qualities could the divine appear in mortal flesh. All other divine attributes are impossible to humanity. But certain it is that if Christ was divine, He must be perfectly pure and holy, the absolute moral ideal. His goodness is not the mere effort after perfection that we make by a process of trial and error; as He says: "I have glorified Thee on the earth; I have finished the work which Thou gavest Me to do."

Men's strivings after goodness are mere temporary resting-places in the great progress to perfection, but His life was a complete view of that perfection laid bare to the sight of men. As the eye in seeing a wheel revolving cannot discern aught but a dim circle in which the separate parts are blended, but with the sudden gleam which a lightning flash gives can distinguish each spoke as if at rest; so the human gaze which can trace a slow development in man, and hope for its completion in far distant time, was able to learn by a divine illumination the divine end of humanity shown in Jesus Christ.

His knowledge, though divine, was conditioned by the form of human thought, which cannot express the divine ideas except through a long development in time. He could not know as man what man could not apprehend. But to God the long development is an immediate perception: its unfolding is a condition of our thought alone; for it is we alone who are the bond-servants of time and space.

In moral ideas the same development is seen, but they are not beyond the reach of mortal speech. The ethical presentation of the divine character of Jesus was within the apprehension of man, who saw enwrapped in Him the perfect union of the whole human race.[1] The theology of Jesus unfolded the great and final goal of the universal brotherhood of man in God.

The teaching of Jesus exhibited therefore the Fatherhood of God, and in His life He shows Himself the Son of Man, so that men might know the perfect love of God from His words and works, and also realise their true filial relation by His example. Christ had the one purpose steadfastly before Him, to unite men with one another and with God. It is with this thought in His mind that He unfolds the doctrine of the Holy Spirit. The divine Spirit is to make and keep alive in the hearts of men the teaching and life of Jesus, and thus establish and perpetuate their brotherly union. "He shall teach you all things, and bring all things to your remembrance, whatsoever I have said unto you." St. Paul tells us how this became an ever-increasing reality in the experience of mankind.

We have been told that our present age is the dispensation of the Spirit; and the signs of the times assure us of the fact. The increase of human sympathy and charity, the desire for peace and unity among nations, the progress in the knowledge of the work of God in universal nature, are all evidences of the ceaseless operations of the Spirit, who is sent to guide us into all truth. St. Paul will unfold for us more fully the working of the

[1] St. John xii. 32.

Spirit, but Christ completed His work of love by revealing, not only God as our Father, but also the Holy Spirit, who confirms us in our filial position, *and beareth witness with our spirit that we are the children of God.*

CHAPTER VIII

THE ETHICAL PRINCIPLE OF JESUS

THE ethical teaching of Jesus groups itself round the central thought of the Fatherhood of God and its consequent, the brotherhood of man. The Master does not give set commandments which fence in the daily life, but bestows an inward principle of love, which allows the whole being a perfect freedom. The follower of Christ must regard himself through all his life as a member of the human family, and all his actions must be conditioned by his regard to others. Jesus gave a summary of the commandments which embodies this idea—love to God leading to love to our neighbour.

The question has been asked, whether Christ added any new ethical principle to the life of man? Had His teaching any law of life to lay down which man had not known before? His own attitude seems to disclaim any novel doctrine, for He says He came to fulfil the law, not to destroy it. Human nature was not altered by the coming of Christ; the natural relations which the soul has to God are eternal in their character; and the laws of conduct must therefore have a certain form which is essentially permanent, though appearing only in an ever-developing idea. It is by degrees, therefore, that men can understand them and apply them; and every age shows an advance in practical morality. The human race leaves behind it its days of the weakness of childhood, and goes on to ever-renewing strength. Men have grown in their knowledge of duty; they better see how to act to each other so as to promote the general welfare. All their best thoughts are aided by the teaching and example of Christ, who showed in His life and death an absolute sacrifice. Those who have chosen to look have found forerunners of almost all His teachings in different moralists; but no such perfect life has ever been known.

The absolutely pure life of Christ gave a new ideal to mankind. In our weakness we shelter ourselves under the shadow of a great man's sins. We remember that our hero was of like passions, and often, without following his nobleness, we excuse our own baseness by his sometime fall. All the moral teaching in the world up to Christ's time had lacked the sanction of a stainless life. This He gave, and thus gave a baptism of power to mankind. The divine purity became incarnate in man, and opened up a new ideal of human life and character. The dispensation of Jesus may be said truly, therefore, to be a new ethical revelation, both in man's relation to the absolute good, and in his relation of love to his fellow-men. But that the rudiments of all that is true and good are in the soul of man, we dare not deny, and it is because Jesus saw them that He was able to lead us upward.

It may accordingly have been no new revelation when Jesus summed up His teaching in the words which follow; but He spoke with a voice of authority, and not as the scribes: "Thou shalt love the Lord thy God with all thy heart, and with all thy soul, and with all thy mind. This is the first and great commandment. And the second is like unto it, Thou shalt love thy neighbour as thyself. On these two commandments hang all the law and the prophets."

What is the nature of the love which we are to bear to God? It is that which children ought to have to a perfectly loving father; when we know that God is our Father, that knowledge will always beget that love in our souls. It implies, therefore, a complete trust in God; and since we trust Him, we yield ourselves to His will. We are convinced that that will is perfectly wise and kind, and we do not question its behests. The efforts of mystics to realise an absorption of the spirit into God are not acts of reason, but are the imperfect efforts of deep affection to express itself. Between mortals in this earthly life there are certain possibilities of unspoken love, the glance of the eye, the touch of the hand, the joy in the presence of the loved one, which lead the soul to crave some analogy in its relations with God. Without saying, with Kant, that we cannot feel a passive love to God, and can only show it in action, it yet remains true that the filial love of the soul must mainly find its utterance in love of the brethren, as St. John teaches: "He that loveth not his brother, whom he hath seen, how can he love God, whom he hath not seen?"

The words of Jesus, which command us to give the love of our heart and soul and mind to God, seem, however, to imply that the filial attitude of the soul to God is in itself a love of Him. But to make love no more than such a filial attitude is the very summit of selfishness, and assumes that God has no children but ourselves. The motive of love which Christ appeals to is the grateful acknowledgment of the gifts we receive from God, gifts which reach their crown in the forgiveness of sins. Those who tell us that we should love God with pure adoration, from a sense of this perfection, say what they cannot find easy to prove. For we cannot think of Him except in relation to ourselves; to think of Him as our Father, is to be moved by filial affection into which a certain amount of gratitude enters. It is true that in such love there must always be an element of self; but how can man escape from his own consciousness? Fénélon tells us that the special self-interest which we manifest in such feelings removes from them their highest glory. "Love," he says, "without any motive of self-interest, with a view to blessedness, is evidently more perfect than that which is mingled with such a motive." Such may be the case with reference to an anticipation of future rewards, the thought of which must awake the selfishness of man's nature, but it does not apply to that feeling of grateful thanksgiving for the present and the past. Men feel that Xavier's hymn speaks truthfully with reference to the love to God we have at our best moments—

> "Not that in heaven my home may be,
> Not lest I die eternally,—
> Not from the hopes of joys above me,
> But even as Thou Thyself didst love me,
> So love I and will ever love Thee." [1]

---

[1] Longfellow's translation. It is more probable that the hymn was St. Teresa's.

The references which Christ makes to the love which man bears to God are fewer than might be supposed from the intensity with which the mystics have urged this on mankind as the supreme ideal of religion. He knew the limitations of our nature, and directs His disciples to give brotherly love to Him and to each other, apparently because the love of God which the mystics delight to speak of, was well-nigh, if not altogether, unattainable. Beyond the words in which He sums up the commandments, He does not speak much to His disciples of the duty of love we owe to God, but rather directs their thoughts to the practical fruits of it in the brotherly life. Even to the Jews, He points out that if they really loved God as their Father, it would be more than a mere word with them: it would bring out of their hearts a real affection for Jesus, His Son, instead of a constant mistrust and hatred. The love of God is the essential condition of the new life, but Christ concerns Himself rather with its practical applications than with discussing its source and mental consciousness. In this He differs from His followers, who have too much occupied themselves with theories, and not enough applied their energies to a world whose sin and sorrow are ever calling for comfort and guidance.

The practical teaching of Christ is not hard to understand, yet it is not often that we meet with men who try to carry it out. It depends for its motive on a loving knowledge of the principle of brotherhood, which is not easily won in a world where the struggle for life is so fierce as it is with us. Its general form is that of the golden rule: *Whatsoever ye would that men should do to you, do ye even so to them.* This is said to be found in the utterances of earlier teachers of mankind, such as Confucius; but when it is a mere maxim, without the inspiring principle of love, it lacks power. To act in such wise is easy enough when one loves another, as in a family; one does not consciously apply the rule, which, though it lies hidden in the mind, is yet the secret spring of action. The flower of all generous action is its unconsciousness: morality is ruined when it becomes a thing of set enactments which we con over and try to obey. Yet such is the weakness of our heart, that the direct guidance of a definite command is a great help to us. In the teaching of Christ there are few such commandments, and those that seem plain enough are rarely observed.

The root of the practice of brotherhood is love. And over and over again Jesus enforces it on His hearers. " A new commandment I give unto you, That ye love one another." " Love your enemies." " By this shall all men know that ye are My disciples, if ye love one another." " This is My commandment, That ye love one another, as I have loved you." There is no essential difference between St. John and the Synoptic Gospels, but the form of the commandment is more restricted in the later writer. Church ideas seem to have come in to narrow his views and cloud his vision of truth; and he omits the wide and generous thoughts of the universal love which we find in the Sermon on the Mount.

That men's chief duty is social, is enforced throughout all the life of Jesus; a duty which stays not at the sacrifice of life itself. What light we have we must give to others; we must let our *light so shine before men that they may see our good works*. Virtue which is private and individual loses its real power, which is to promote the welfare of mankind. The parable of the Talents enforces the same truth. Every moral precept is referred to the same standard. Truthfulness, purity, mercy, are all considered with a view to the duty which members of the same family owe to each other. The whole ethical field is social; and individual life has no meaning apart from its fellowship with mankind. A thoughtful writer [1] has in recent times denied that Christianity teaches this. Deeply interested in social questions, he seems to see that Christianity fails to rise to the highest social ideal, while yet admitting that the central spirit of Christianity is the spirit of self-sacrifice, the effacement of personal ambition for the general welfare. What nobler form of social life could exist? *Greater love hath no man than this, that he lay down his life for his friends.* The same writer thinks there was a fatal taint of individualism in the followers of Christ, if not in Jesus Himself; and that the reason of this is, that the key to the character of Christ was lost. But that is a mere assumption. We have shown that Christ revealed, as never had been done before, the Fatherhood of God. He tells us that love for His Father, and obedience to that compelling love, moved Him to love men and to die for them. The same love He desired His disciples to share, even though they could only show it in a less degree. Of all the religions, and of all the forms of moral life, which the world has ever

[1] J. S. Mackenzie, in the *International Journal of Ethics*, April 1892, p. 331.

seen, the religion of Jesus is the least individual, and affords the largest and most generous social ideal.

To represent it as a life lived for the world beyond, is equally untrue. The life of Christ was eminently a full human life, taking count of material needs and enjoyments, as well as of spiritual desires. It is a caricature of Christianity which we see in the monkish or ecclesiastical ideal, which is neither a service of God nor man, but simply of self. The golden rule has an individualistic aspect, which is increased when we read into it the sum of the commandments, " Love thy neighbour as thyself." But the precepts enjoining non-resistance to evil, recommending lending where no repayment is possible, and giving love without hope of return, shed a more generous light on the practical application of it. We are not to make mere justice the standard of our life, for God does not do so with us, but to yield to others a love which is self-sacrificing even to giving life itself for others. The rule of duty seems to be a development higher than loving our neighbour as ourselves; we are to love him more. We must give up our happiness to secure his goodness, our ease to recover his health, our possessions at his demand. And what is left for us? The joy of being like God; and the power which our self-sacrificing love gives of purifying the world, and making all men united in the love and service of God. The gospel is the uncompromising teacher of altruism, specially because it has assurance of a great end in view.

Among Christian writers, Vinet is the most eloquent and philosophic advocate of individualism. His teaching represents a phase of life which is now past, and in

Christian thought his ideas are rarely present. The individualist theory of politics which is associated in our land with Mr. Mill has gone into the limbo of lost causes; and Vinet's religious ideas, which have the same parentage, are little else than matters of history. Vinet points out that it is the individual who possesses conscience and responsibility who will be brought to judgment, and who alone can have direct relation with God. But the theology of Vinet is defective. The future of humanity is not to be thought of as a group of beings separately existing, but as a restored world. *We are all members one of another*, and we lose our independent life for the sake of each other. The world was redeemed, and the world will be finally restored, as a unity. The individual is higher than society, says Vinet, which is the mere aggregation of men. But whence comes this maxim? If we live for mankind, is not the human race greater than any of the items which compose it? His theory would not destroy the Church so much as the family. It is the clearest expression of much of our modern selfish Protestantism, which deserves much of the invective which Positivists lavish on it.

We see the same type of mind in Channing, who also preached the gospel of individualism. He tells that "society is chiefly important as it ministers to, and calls forth, intellectual and moral energy and freedom. Our social nature and connections are means. Inward power is the end." Surely this is only partly true: if we have inward power, it is that we may promote the good of our fellow-men. We exist for the whole good of mankind, in so far as we can promote it. What did Christ say?

"Inasmuch as ye have done it unto one of the least of these My brethren, ye have done it unto Me." We serve God in serving man; indeed, it is our truest way of showing our love to Him. We may deceive ourselves about that abstract love which Fénélon urges on us,—love which is true enough as to its origin in the sense of the divine Fatherhood, but which vanishes into a mist if it does not breathe the outer air of human fellowship and duty. Dr. Channing regretted that religion had not done more to promote the enlarged intercourse of minds; but he need not have had any surprise, if religion is to be of so intensely individual a type. Individualism of any form is destined to perish as an influence over mankind, which is daily awaking to a richer knowledge of this social unity. When Madame Chantal said she was willing to be damned for God's glory if it so pleased Him, she could not really have trusted His fatherly love; and when Madame Guyon was hardly conscious of her own existence, to such a degree of holy quietude had she reached, she had forgotten that she was but one of a great family, many of whom had too hard a fight with life to have the possibility of such raptures, and whose necessities were calling ever for aid and sympathy.

There is indeed a disease of the contemplative soul which wraps itself in its individual life, and this malady appears in various forms of religious belief. We see it in the Amiels and Senancours[1] as well as the more

---

[1] Not that Senancour or Amiel were selfishly heedless of others, but they did not realise their duty as *social* beings. Senancour says the peace he desires is the peace which all good men long for—"peace in the peace of all men."

religious solitaries. Nature avenges herself for such disobedience to our best instincts; and the nobler the soul, the deeper the sorrow of a lonely and fruitless life. What Sainte-Beuve said of Obermann is true of all such careers. "He is the type of the dumb and abortive genius, of the full spring of sensibility wasted upon desert sands, of the hail-smitten harvest which never matures its gold." Man must not make the life of contemplation an end in itself: our years are too few to spend on ourselves. We must indeed take time to think over our actions, if we would not have them unwise; but we must not think for thinking's sake. The desire of culture which Goethe taught men is a part of our nature, but the culture should bear fruit. The longing for rest and peace, which is the poet's dream, will be satisfied if we earn it by work for others. The time we spend in thought and prayer is the time of refreshing, but we must use the strength we get from our quiet hours. Such is Jesus' teaching: "Work while it is day: the night cometh when no man can work."

The harvest Christ called His disciples to was not the harvest of their own souls, but of mankind. The whole scheme of Christian morals starts from this idea, and moves steadily onward to the goal of universal brotherhood.

It is true that the gospel gives us the freedom of children, but it is that we may serve others. *Whosoever will be great, let him be a servant.* The servant has often work from which his soul shrinks, but let him remember the divine Master, and his service will be freedom and joy. How untrue are the words of Renan, untrue in their application to St. Paul, of whom they were spoken, but equally false as regards all human life. " The man of action, though noble, and working for a noble end, is less near to God than he who has lived in the pure love of the true, the good, and the beautiful. The contact with reality always soils a little. The first places in the kingdom are reserved for those who adore the ideal alone. We must even, I think, place Paul below Francis of Assisi and the author of the *Imitation*, who both saw Jesus much nearer." This is the preference of an unhealthy nature, to whom all things were distorted.

Do not let us be deceived by such false thoughts, which come to us sometimes as temptations. It is by the active life that we show our love to God; the service of man is the service of our own souls. It is an essential principle of Christ's teaching, that mankind is one social body, for the welfare of which all are bound to labour. The individual is entirely lost in the duty to mankind, as Christ assures us that our private affections may become a temptation to us, and may gender selfishness in our heart by confining its sympathies to our own narrow sphere. *He that loveth father or mother more than Me, is not worthy of Me.* No more startling paradox has ever been uttered on the social relations of mankind than these words. They have their parallel in the Republic of Plato, where family life was to lose its isolation, and become a universal affection.

The ethical principle of Christ is entirely social, and has for its root the well-being of the whole human family. But to give it a standard, He asks His disciples to make their conduct to Him a rule for all men. If they would give everything to Jesus, then so are they to act to all men; if they feel a love to Him, so are they to love all men, even their enemies. Some see in this command of Jesus to give to others as to Himself, a representation of Him as the ideal man, the type of humanity. I doubt if such thoughts entered into the minds of His followers then, or if at any time they are easily conceivable. A philosophical conception such as the ideal man does not readily enter the sphere of active life, and the ethics of Jesus were for the common people, who *heard Him gladly*. For plain men the remembrance of Him, especially of His dying love, is a stimulus of surpassing sympathetic power. It is a standard of action which affords hardly any limit to the philanthropic feeling. *Love one another, as I have loved you.*

We here arrive at the Christian *conscience*. The conscience consists of a perception of duty, accompanied with an element of pleasure and pain. This emotional element in ordinary life in all likelihood arises from the opinion of our fellow-men. Their approval or disapproval is really the standard of our emotional attitude to conduct. An individual may defy such opinion, but it is because he has come to the conclusion that the judgment of other men is ill-founded. Jesus reprobates the conscience which is limited by the standard of the ordinary human life about the disciples. *Woe unto you, when all men shall speak well of you. Except your righteousness shall exceed the righteousness of the scribes and Pharisees, ye shall in no case enter into the kingdom of heaven. If ye love them which love you, what reward have ye? Do not even the publicans the same?* What then does He supply instead of this public opinion, made up of the *traditions of the elders* ? He asks them to remember Him, and do according to His commandment, ever dwelling in His love. The writer to the Hebrews speaks of *crucifying the Son of God afresh*, which expresses the extreme form of remorse of conscience ; but in all spheres of life this feeling becomes the standard. In the ideal judgment which men are subjected to in the parable which Christ gives of the Son of Man coming in glory, the righteous are accepted because they saw their Master hungered and gave Him meat ; thirsty, and gave Him drink ; a stranger, and took Him in ; naked, and clothed Him ; sick, and visited Him ; in prison, and came unto Him. They had not so served Christ, but He said : " Inasmuch as ye have done it unto one of the least of these of My brethren, ye have done it unto Me." What power has this conscience when awakened in a man ! It is the strongest moral force in the world, and may be seen in its typical example in the case of Zinzendorf, whose whole life was changed by seeing under an *Ecce Homo* : " This have I done for thee : what hast thou done for Me ? "

The ordinary conscience has few moments of approval : it only visits us when we have wandered from the path of right. To do our duty is apt to make us feel that at best we are but unprofitable servants. But the Christian conscience has a joy in service which ordinary life is hardly conscious of. Bitter is our regret when we come short of our duty, as indeed we always do ; but the gladness of seeming to serve, however poorly, so kind a Master, is one of the highest happinesses in life. The emotion of pleasure which generally accompanies an act of kindness is sometimes disappointed by ingratitude, and the man who finds his chief joy in benevolence from the happiness it gives others, has his feelings overcast by almost as dark a shadow as a bad conscience gives. Mere moral rectitude can hardly bear up against open indifference to the giver of some benefit; but it is otherwise with the Christian conscience. What was done, was done for His sake; and the reward of service is thus a constant quantity, whatever be the effect on the receiver of the kindness. That the disciple is one with Christ, is shown us in the parable of the Vine and the Branches; and St. Paul carries this feeling of unity to the inner sources of being.

The law of the Christian conscience is to do to all men as we should do to the best, to Jesus Himself. In actual practice it sometimes takes another form, to do as Jesus Himself did. The imitation of Christ has been the effort of His followers in all ages, and is counselled by the apostles. Too often has such effort been limited to the devout life, as in à Kempis's treatise; but the imitation is there most imperfect. The greater part of Christ's life was spent in active work in which intervals of retirement rarely appear. How the monastic ideal of the Roman Church could come to take such a life as its source, is one of the mysteries of the wayward reason of man.

The whole theory of life by rule, which monkery bred in men's minds, is contrary to the organic freedom of the soul. To serve men because it is a duty, to help them from fear of hell or hope of heaven, are all clumsy methods of existence. The Christian heart should have laid them all aside, for they are but the measured rightcousness of the scribes and Pharisees. Love to mankind not consciously doled out by drops from some phial daily filled, as in the monastic life, but a free movement of the organic principle within the heart, is the true impelling power. We do not feed a man because we are told to do so, but because he is hungry, and our fellow mortal. Accompanying this act there may be that tacit appeal to the remembrance of Christ which we have called conscience; but it may lie latent within us, and only appear on great occasions when there is a strife of opinion within our soul. The man who has truly reached the social ideal of Christianity, will feed another with as little conscious motive as he feeds himself. This is the complete arrival at the goal of Christian ethics. It is not necessarily an enthusiastic feeling; it is no necessarily exhilarating atmosphere; but is simply our common air. We must have regard to others in all we do; and we must actively seek their good. But may not there be a conflict in our life; may we not neglect ourselves while helping other men? There need be none, for we shall attain our highest ideal in the desire to give men the best we can do for them; as Christ illustrates by the parable of the Talents.

But we are not called to random benevolence, which takes no heed of consequences. Ordinary worldly people are fond of giving because it warms their heart. It may ruin the receiver of charity, it may pauperise a whole generation; but that is naught, if the giver has a passing glow of benevolence. This is what St. Paul condemns, and assures us that no gift is worth anything if love be not its root. St. Paul had in view the error of regarding giving as the sum of our charity. Are we to do no more than bestow our surplus on men? Are we to regard life simply as a hospital where we are all nurses? Surely it were wise to find out the reason why so many soldiers are down with the camp fever, and remove the deadly poison. We must blame the Roman Church with its noxious theories of good works counted up and paid for by the divine Treasury, and weighed out as in the balance of the Mohammedan judgment day, for the effeminate folly of copious and undiscerning charity. We are bound to give to men our wise thoughts as well as our gifts: to give without reflection is to deprive them of the benefit of our knowledge. This is against the teaching of the gospel, which ever teaches us that our inner life is to take account of other men; that even in our thoughts we must neither withhold from them any good nor do them any injustice. Such, indeed, is the true meaning of love, which is a feeling within us, more than a plan of action without. Real love for men will think over how best to serve them, and will not idly run into frantic showers of gold. When Carlyle and Dickens poured their scorn on "model prisons," the philanthropic world felt a thrill as if some revived heathenism were among us, and speaking through them. After all, it was only a call to men to see that their ways were wise. Good intentions, so called, are not everything; an indulgent parent is not the best. Our Lord gives His sanction to no such weak and thoughtless way of viewing life; nor do His apostles.

And here we come to the kernel of practical wisdom in our social conduct. Christianity lays down as *absolute* the law of altruism. We are bound to live for others, and in all things consider their highest advantage, which it tells us is their union in a race of brothers who love God and serve each other.

How is this to be attained? Christ gives no complete system of ethical detail; as in His theology, He leaves it open for the mind of man to philosophise. The great principles of human conduct are discoverable by reason, as the efforts of the ancient moralists show; and these should be our guidance. We must modify all our thoughts by the supreme authority of love, but otherwise they have free play. What is best for the community? Such must be our question. Everyone must sacrifice his personal preferences to the urgent needs of social welfare. If it be required that one should bestow all his goods to feed the poor, then it must be done; but if it be good that men should gather wealth that they may distribute it wisely, then let rich men increase their stores. Christ supplies the general principle which should fill our hearts—the feeling of love to all mankind; He sets before us the ideal at which we must aim, the brotherly communion of all men in all that is good and true and beautiful, in all that is happy and peaceful and hopeful—in love to man and love to God.

All ethical systems help to this end, since to the Christian they receive their sanction from Jesus. The wisest system is His best helper. Utilitarianism, intuitionalism, the ethics of the evolutionary and of the Hegelian schools, are all alike maps of the territory of human conduct, and will guide us well, provided we have the true compass—the love of man inspired by love to God and to His Son Jesus Christ. Our Saviour regards sin as the departure from this great principle. We are lost sheep, if we leave the love of God; and our selfish wanderings, as He teaches in the parable of the Prodigal Son, lead us further and further into the mire and darkness of a sinful life. It is love that brings us back; and dwelling in love we abide in purity, and are in deed and truth the sons of God.

CHAPTER IX

THE AUTHORITY OF JESUS

THE pious mind does not question the authority of Jesus Christ. It accepts Him as the divine Saviour, and lays aside every doubt of His absolute truth and the perpetual obligation of His commands. The inner intuition of love admits of no change in the constant trust which the soul gives. No reasonings could alter a conviction which has become part of the life of the Christian. The verification of experience which the devout man has had, is an assurance far above the conclusions of reason. "The heart has reasons which the reason has no knowledge of," said Pascal; and the voice of mankind has spoken assent to his words in many phases of life. This acceptance of Christ may come from a distinct considering of His claims, and concluding that He is divine, and therefore infallible; or from feeling that the heart gives a response to His teaching, and has received a divine illumination.

To the thoughtful observer the need of a divine sanction for the duties of life becomes a self-evident fact. We must find it in some phase of the divine revelation to man. "Religion," said Kant, "is the recognition of all our duties as divine commands." That form of ethical science which regards our life as a gradual growth towards a divine ideal, brings before us, with great clearness, the ever constant presence of God's working in the human soul. It sees that a God distant from men, as the Epicureans fabled their deities, is not readily received by the human heart at its best. To such a view may be traced the severance between morals and religion in the ancient world; though one cannot but think the divorce is sometimes exaggerated, when we see how the poets appeal to the gods as the final arbiters of all human conduct. To such a view, also, is to be attributed the divorce between outward piety and honesty of which our commercial world has shown too many instances. Men say God is far away: He is not with us; and He enters not into our life.

To know that there is a God who approves of goodness is not enough to satisfy the human heart. We need a divine sanction, but it must be in our very sight. It must come into our consciousness, and become a factor of all our moral judgments. Such an influence is sometimes seen in the thought of rewards and punishments. The knowledge that God "is a jealous God," still has its force in human hearts. The hope of heaven and the fear of hell still move mankind, though it is the latter that has the heaviest weight. No universalism has ever been able to shake the invincible sense of justice within the average man; and if his idea as to the method of divine retribution be crude, it is unwavering in its fidelity to the great principle that what a man sows that shall he reap.

But the Christian soul has found a better way than the stony path where we are driven by the scourge of the law as reluctant travellers to some land which we are told is pleasant, but of which all we know is that it is far off. This better way is that identification of the soul with Christ which is felt in true faith. When Luther said, "I am Christ," he did not go far beyond the words of St. Paul, who finds the "life of Jesus manifest in his mortal flesh." This faith does not come from knowing that Jesus was divine, from His proving Himself so by His word and works, by His life and death. It does not arise from our carefully weighing the evidence as if we were the judges in the case. Books are written to gather up all the facts which may help men to right thought on this doctrine about Jesus; and they have doubtless some value. But the fact is that the knowledge comes after the inner life is begun, and is not the highway thither. The writer of the Epistle known as that of the Second of St. Peter puts this very clearly. He puts faith first, then the practical proof of that faith—virtue, and knowledge follows. This agrees with the words of Jesus, who tells the Jews that obedience precedes knowledge[1] as to His authority, whether it is divine or human.

Many devout men can give a very meagre account of Christian dogma, and may make many departures from what the Church has laid down, while all the time having within them a true faith. True union with Christ does not result from accurate thinking, but from love to God and man, which is shown in the life. With most, the motive which fills the soul is the memory of Jesus, and especially of His death, which excites the emotion of grateful love to a passionate height. But the inner experience of the soul does not willingly lend itself to

[1] St. John vii. 17.

analysis, and no man knows himself well enough to tell us his secret heart. Still less can anyone penetrate into the consciousness of another; for even if he could have such sympathy as to understand it, he would translate it into his own soul-workings. Men are isolated from each other in the form of their union with God. They are united in the fruit which that union bears of love to Him and to their fellow-men.

The inner certainty is the only real certainty we have of God. We only can conceive Him to our hearts in His fatherly love as revealed in Jesus. Finding that trust in Jesus gives us that inexpressible confidence, that hidden impulse of life in our souls, we cannot withhold our being from the assurance that He is divine.

There is an analogy in our emotion of joy and solemnity in the presence or memory of the beauty of nature. There is nothing before our mind, even if we reflect, but a great scheme of cause and effect; yet our heart knows there is a higher thought enwrapped. Who has not felt, on a bright morning in spring, when the earth was revealing her life and fairness, a thrill of assurance that God was the universal life of all, that a glimpse was given of

> "That Light whose smile kindles the universe,
> That Beauty in which all things work and move"?

And the certainty to the inner life of the divine nature of Christ comes on us with a like mysterious movement as much beyond the understanding. "The light of soul consciousness," says Baader, "is born of the lightning."

When once the whole being has grasped the belief in Christ, all His teaching and life have a divine sanction.

Not that one takes the commands of the Master as separate precepts, and recalls them at need, for such mechanical obedience is foreign to true love. But the soul is so united to the life of Christ, and has such sympathy with Him, even to the fellowship of His sufferings, that the moral life flows as a natural stream from the heart of faith.

There are many ways of expressing the inner truth of faith, each of which is but an approach to the reality. The feeling of dependence we have on Jesus has been interpreted by many human facts, which are in part analogies, in part actual verities. But they all combine to strengthen the soul in that faith which is the centre of her true life of brotherhood, which leads to the perpetual joy of love and service. This feeling of inward response to Jesus may be aided by the natural dependence we have on great teachers, whatever their claims may be. Many who do not acknowledge Jesus as divine, who regard Him merely as a Jewish rabbi, yet carry out with unvarying diligence His commandments. When we see the devotion of certain thinkers to such a man as Comte, it is not difficult to understand how the wisest and best of men would bow before the will of Jesus, though they thought Him but a fellow mortal.

The influence of great minds on their followers is one of the most wonderful facts of life. It is an appointed way for the mass of mankind to know truth ; for they can only learn it after it has passed through another's mind. Most people need to be fed with knowledge ; there are few that can roam through the world, and, like hunters, find game ready to their guns. The natural loyalty of the human heart is a powerful lever for human progress; for it is the best men who come to lead, and the divine voice speaks through them.

Is it not true that all great movements have been led by a great man? Whence he arises, we ask not; if he is the mere creature of the influences of his time, he comes from God, who rules the course of time. And if he is the mere product of his age, he gathers into a focus the light of his age, so that all men turn to him. Not only during his own brief day does his light shine, but the generations after him are also blessed. It was some feeling of admiration for the truly lofty in man that brought the disciples first to Jesus' feet; and it was long before they knew how high they had climbed. But had it not been for that inborn loyalty of the human heart to the great and good, the first step would not have been taken. Carlyle must be quoted here, for no other has told us the truth about great men so nobly as he. " No nobler feeling than this of admiration for one higher than himself dwells in the breast of man. It is to this hour, and at all hours, the vivifying influence in man's life. Religions, I find, stand upon it; not paganism only, but far higher and truer religions—all religions hitherto known. Hero worship, heartfelt prostrate admiration, submission, burning, boundless, for a noblest God-like Form of Man,—is not that the germ of Christianity itself? . . . Is not all loyalty akin to religious faith? Faith is loyalty to some inspired teacher, some spiritual hero."

When Jesus Himself was asked as to the character of His earthly work, whether He were really the divine Son, what did He reply? We have His reply to St.

John the Baptist, who in prison inquired as to the mission of Jesus. In replying, Christ simply appealed to certain facts, without discussing any theology, such as the Jews seemed to find pleasure in. In effect He said: " Here am I doing all these good works, healing, comforting, preaching to the poor. If these things do not prove My divine message, then there is no proof worth having." We are directed again, as we have been already, in considering the theology of Jesus, to a purely ethical and not a doctrinal view, to observe the fruits of a loving heart shown in the life. What now do we need from God? Is it His power that He would teach us? Do we not see it in the majesty of the creation? It is His love that we seek, and Jesus proves that He comes from God by the kind, and helpful, and generous life He leads.

Nor, in connection with that great truth of brotherhood we are enforcing, should we forget that He laid stress on the gospel being preached to the poor. Is this an important part of Christ's mission, so important that it is an evidence of it? It surely cannot be that the poor for the first time had the blessings of religion opened to them; for in the Jewish temple their sacrifice was as acceptable as the rich man's more splendid gift, and in the heathen worship there was a like equality. Does it not mean that it is the beginning of that universal reign of love, when the poor shall no longer suffer for their poverty, for they shall dwell among friends and brothers? The divine mission to unite humanity was here announced in this gospel, " Goodwill to men." At other times in His life Jesus drew attention to His works of love, so proving His divine nature.

"The same works that I do bear witness of Me that the Father hath sent Me." "Though ye believe not Me, believe the works; that ye may know and believe that the Father is in Me, and I in Him." "Believe Me that I am in the Father, and the Father in Me; or else believe Me for the very works' sake."

These words did not lose their applicability because the generation passed that saw these works. Men in our time have yet more wonderful works to look on. They can see how the religion of Jesus has never lost its power; how, during all the centuries, it has been the beacon light of mankind; how it has purified, ennobled, and united men; and how it speaks of worlds yet to be entered, of love and peace, and eternal brotherhood.

Believe for the works' sake. The authority of Jesus has been proved in the experience of mankind. They have found Him their best guide and friend, and His religion the noblest ideal possible to the human soul, with a future of ever-increasing brightness before it.

The life of Jesus is found to be the secret of the true life of mankind. "In Him was life, and the life was the light of men." Any other life falls short of the ideal of humanity revealed by science. It is not a personal experience this, not an inner conviction which might be an individual illusion, but the conclusion formed by a study of the developing life of the human race. What is the goal they are marching towards? The answer of all our best ethical thinkers is, that we are realising by degrees the life of Jesus and the mission of Jesus in the hopes of mankind, which are daily receiving more and more fulfilment.

The utilitarian system has perhaps least alliance with the teaching of Jesus; yet its moral services, which have been of immense value to our modern world, have arisen from its widening the range of sympathy, and making men feel a desire to benefit others as largely as possible. It is but an imperfect version of the universal charity of Christ, and confirms His authority by approaching to His methods. "In so far as utilitarianism is more rigorous than Common Sense in exacting the sacrifice of the individual's happiness to that of mankind generally, it is strictly in accordance with the most characteristic teachings of Christianity."[1]

The views of Mr. Herbert Spencer, in the *Data of Ethics*, are essentially Christian in their ideal; and since they are said to be reached by purely scientific reasoning, we find an evidence that in man there are native instincts which point to the divine purposes which Christ revealed. "In the future," Mr. Spencer says, "a regard for others will eventually become so large a source of pleasure, as to compete with in its amount, and indeed overgrow, the pleasure which is derived from direct egoistic gratification. . . . Eventually, then, along with the approximately complete adaptation of man to the social state, along with the evolution of a society complete in its adjustments . . . there will also come a state in which egoism and altruism are so conciliated that the one merges in the other."[2]

Kant's theory of morals can only be rightly under-

[1] Sidgwick's *Methods of Ethics*, 2nd edition, p. 464. See also Green's *Prolegomena*, p. 361.
[2] *Data of Ethics*, 3rd edition, Appendix, p. 300.

stood in connection with his religious views. In the *Critique of Practical Reason* it has an individualistic character; but if we read into it the views and hopes expressed in his *Philosophy of Religion* and his *Idea of a Universal History*, we cannot but hear the echoes or overtones of the divine Word. In its very form it implies an ideal man in an ideal fellowship of men; and in its practical issues a recent writer rightly described it as showing the moral " end as self-sacrifice." [1] To say that every ethical system which seeks the highest good is a confirmation of the authority of Christ, is no new thing, for we find it plainly taught in the writings of Campanella in the sixteenth century. He maintained that there was a general law throughout mankind which brought them by the exercise of their reason to the true life, and that law was alone found in Christ's teaching, which therefore had the supreme authority of truth.

Still more striking is the agreement between Positivism and Christianity as to the end of life; but the system of the Positivists is in its nature eclectic, and cannot be regarded as logically coherent. The religion and morality of Comte and his followers are taken from all sources, and the reconciling power is found in offering them all up on the altar of humanity. Lofty thoughts are expressed and great purposes are sought by the advocates of Positivism; and though its intellectual basis is by no means clear, its moral ends are generous. That such a system should be based on purely secular grounds is in itself a testimony to the divine Author of Christianity.

Even the gloomy philosophy of Schopenhauer is not

[1] Mr. J. H. Muirhead, *Elements of Ethics*.

without a divine ray. He maintains that to cling to one's own will as against existence outside of us is individualism, which is in itself the principle of evil; but if we blend our own will by sympathy with all men and all things, we are living a truly good life. The supreme good is only to be found when we give up entirely our own selfish desires, and yield ourselves entirely as a sacrifice to the general welfare of all men. In this we shall find peace and freedom. Strange it is to find ethics so pure coming from a philosophy so perverse in its theories; but if Schopenhauer's reflections are the fruit of study of this world, they point to its destiny in obeying the commands of Christ.

But the moral teacher who in our day has been most honoured, and worthily so, is Mr. T. H. Green. His ethics are based on what we may call a natural foundation, and yet his conclusions are entirely Christian. "The realisation and fulfilment" of the human spirit "can only take place in and through society." "There may be reason to hold that there are capacities of the human spirit not realisable in persons under the conditions of any society we know, or can positively conceive, or that may be capable of existing on the earth. . . . We may justify the supposition that the personal life, which historically or on earth is lived under conditions which thwart its development, is continued in a society with which we have no means of communication through the senses, but which shares in and carries further every measure of perfection attained by man under the conditions of life that we know." [1]

[1] *Prolegomena to Ethics*, 2nd edition, pp. 199, 195.

Men who have no thought of moral or theological theories have found that their life is only truly lived if lived according to Christ; and, believing as they do that God gave the life of their bodies, they cannot but believe that it is God also who has given this life to their souls.[1] Thinkers who have examined the nature and tendencies of the soul have come very near the divine truth of Jesus, near enough to strengthen our faith in His supreme authority. As far as we can grasp His clue to human life we are sure He leads us right, and we trust Him for the rest. "For even moral honesty itself is part of the law of God and an adumbration of the divine life. So that, when regeneration has more thoroughly illuminated his understanding, I doubt not but that he will fall into that pious admiration and speech of the ancient patriarch: 'Verily God was in this place, and I knew it not.'"[2]

We must not think that Christ refuses the homage of deeds which are done in His spirit, though not in His name. The gifts of the Magi are not spurned, though they return again to their far land. Did He not say Himself: "Whosoever shall do the will of My Father which is in heaven, the same is My brother and sister and mother." The philosophers may unconsciously do this will, but though they know not the relation in which they stand to God by their acts, the divine wisdom does not disregard the kinship of love. Strange it is, indeed, that simple faith can reach at a step the height

---

[1] See Mr. Matthew Arnold's *Literature and Dogma*, chap. x. § 3, for a naturalistic statement of this.

[2] Henry More, *Divine Dialogues*.

which the wisest thought toils long after, if ever it attains at all. But the heart of man, when it turns to goodness, is irresistibly drawn to the ways and works of Christ, and by following His example shows its belief "for the works' sake." Belief indeed it is, lying hidden under all kinds of dead mummies of rational thought, but the unconscious and perhaps unwilling faith is not to be scorned by man if God is ready to receive it. Fichte said that if Christ were now to return to earth, it would concern Him but little though His name and person were forgotten, if He only found men enthusiastic in His cause and labouring for it. What he means is clear enough: to do the works of Christ is to admit His authority, whatever strange turn our thoughts may take about Him. It is not by our mind and speech only, in this world of ours, that we can acknowledge Christ to be supreme, for love binds us in its golden cords, and though we know it not, as we are yielding to our affectionate desires for the welfare of mankind, it brings us to the feet of Jesus. No man, however little creed he may profess, can labour earnestly for his fellow-men without revealing in his enthusiasm glimpses of a deeper faith than he acknowledges. The very steadfastness of his unselfish purpose implies such a belief in human brotherhood and the overruling love of God, as unites him in unconscious submission to the Saviour of mankind.

CHAPTER X

BROTHERHOOD IN THE EPISTLES

THAT there were oppositions in the early Church between the apostles in their teaching, is told us in the Acts. How far these went is a matter of opinion. Men may judge from the documents and from the subsequent history of the Church how much truth there is in the Tübingen theories. But the apostles were agreed in one thing, that it was their duty to love one another, and keep the unity of the brotherhood.

It is true that ecclesiastical ideas soon entered into their hearts, and their sympathies seem to have limited themselves too much to the brotherhood of the faithful, and overlooked the wider thought of general humanity. But in their writings as well as in their acts they could not help showing that the divine Spirit was leading them into opener heavens than they knew. Their earnestness to give all men the blessing of the gospel was in itself a testimony to human brotherhood, and we can see how the truth they taught, with but imperfect apprehension of its fuller meanings, has been read with a keener insight than their own by the developing life of humanity.

It is in the First Epistle of St. Peter that we find the

expression, "Love the brotherhood"; and it does not stand alone as an injunction to charity and unity. For the whole Epistle is inspired by such thoughts of love and humility. "See that ye love one another with a pure heart fervently." The Christian unity is exemplified by the figure of a building in which the individual believers are stones; and the whole idea of the Epistle is that love and unity come from the indwelling Spirit, and are the fruits of faith. There are some resemblances between this First Epistle and the Gospel of St. Mark, but there is even a closer connection with St. Paul's Epistle to the Ephesians. Both lay stress on the graces of faith, hope, and love as springing from the unity of the Church. There is in this Epistle a recognition of duty to the Gentiles, and a specific command to " honour all men," which is in itself a proof of the influence of Christ on a mind which has always been regarded as essentially Jewish.

The other apostle who may be placed in the same class is St. James, who shows many links which bind him to St. Peter. But in this teacher of the morality of Christianity how kind and brotherly a spirit is shown. He tells those to whom he writes that the whole spirit of religion is active love. His sympathy with the poor, with the sorrowful, with "the fatherless and widows in their affliction," is a treasury of comfort and exhortation for men; and he follows closely in the footsteps of his Master. His exaltation of good works is one of the most precious things in all the Epistles, and reminds us of the words of Jesus: "Not every one that saith unto Me, Lord, Lord, shall enter into the kingdom of heaven; but he that doeth the will of My Father which is in heaven." Indeed, not a few resemblances have been found between the teaching of the Sermon on the Mount and the words of St. James; and it is clear that they both express the divine law as it was given by Christ—" the royal law, Thou shalt love thy neighbour as thyself."

This doctrine receives its supreme exposition in the writings of St. John, who is indeed the Apostle of Love. He doubts the possibility of any love to God which does not show itself in love to the brotherhood; and in this he echoes his Master's words. It is an oft-told story of the conclusion of his life, that when no longer able to manifest his love in action, he leaves it to men as his dying exhortation: " Little children, love one another."

But St. John brings before us the ideal Christian society. No believer is a mere unit of mankind: he is a member of a great family. The Church is the exhibition of a perfect harmony, which is symbolized in the Apocalypse in the concord of music. It is in St. John's Apocalypse that we see that brotherly union is an end in itself; that to rest in the love of the brethren and of God in a united humanity is the perfect destiny of man. Our earthly lives teach us this: we do not toil for labour's sake, but to bless others by the fruits of our work; we do not deny ourselves for the mere sake of ascetic discipline, but that others may benefit; we seek a higher end than the mere training of self, or the occupation of the hour. In all this, are we not unconsciously pointing, by our family love, and our helpful charity, and our work for others, to that great harmony of perfect brotherhood which is in itself the end of existence? Are love, friendship, and the communion of souls on earth not ends in themselves? Are they not a sufficient reason for their own being? And do we not know that, while our earthly labours perish, and their memory is forgotten, our love is our immortal part? So St. John brings before us the Church not as a mere instrument for spreading the gospel, but as the actual embodiment of that gospel. The Church, according to him, is the end of mankind, and shows the perfect restitution into eternal harmony of the whole life of mankind in God.

The same sublime thoughts inspire St. Paul, who has been the great teacher of the Christian Church. He develops the doctrine of Christian unity with great fulness, and views it from various standpoints, and at last leads up to a final prospect of the perfect realisation of a united humanity.

He teaches that the Church is an *organic* unity, not a mere voluntary association. This unity is obtained, not by dead monotony, but by diverse members performing duties which tend to a perfect harmony. On the divine side, the bond of the union is the Spirit; while, on the human, it is love, which is the essence and form of the communion of man. The Church is, with St. Paul, the city of the saints and the household of God. He sums up the features which constitute the unity of the Church in the Epistle to the Ephesians. Christians have one Head—" one Lord"; they are united in their faith, their baptism, their hope of eternal life; they are one in love, and they express their unity in an outward form, " one body." The position from which St. Paul starts is that of the freedom of all men in Christ. The old distinction which the Jews prided themselves on, which marked them out from other peoples, was at best but a shadow of the future. It may be that their national unity was a good thing; but it was but a type of a wider and more generous union. "For as many of you as have been baptized into Christ have put on Christ. There is neither Jew nor Greek, there is neither bond nor free, there is neither male nor female: for ye are all one in Christ Jesus."

How St. Paul rejoices in the breaking down of the "middle wall of partition," which made the world no longer a gathering of "strangers and foreigners," but of fellow-citizens! And yet we know he clung to his Jewish nationality, and loved his own people dearly. Was it not the sorrow of his heart that they received him so coldly? He used his birthright as he used his individual life, not to wrap himself in it as a defensive cloak, but as a means whereby he might serve all mankind.

It is with this view that he asserts the individual freedom of the follower of Christ from any limitations which the world may have made as to our fellowship with men. The soul of man, in its inner life, knows nothing of the narrow boundaries which hedge in its outward existence; and when it realises its union to Christ, it refuses to be held in any human trammels.

St. Paul it is, of all the New Testament writers, who reaches highest in the conception of a universal humanity. This he does by looking at Christ as the ideal man, to whom all men are related, and therefore claim our love.

For we are not freed from the limitations of earth in order that we may assert our independence of our brethren: " For, brethren, ye have been called unto liberty; only use not liberty for an occasion to the flesh, but by love be slaves to one another."

St. Paul himself acted on this maxim, for his whole life was one long self-sacrifice. No man came so near his Master in his love for men as the Apostle of the Gentiles. Gladly did he spend and was spent for mankind; and took " pleasure in infirmities, in reproaches, in necessities, in persecutions, in distresses," if his work of love still went on. He was willing that he should be accursed from Christ for his brethren, his kinsmen according to the flesh. To such height did his patriotic feeling of true religious brotherhood attain. Far off comes the famous saying of Danton, who had his strange baptism of fraternity or death, and cared not if his name were blighted, if only France were free. Few men can calmly go forward to such awful conclusions to our little life, with its passion for eternity, which takes all forms, from the pantheon of history, in which Danton hoped to dwell, to that presence of God which the apostle longed to win. But a true belief in the unity and brotherhood of man will enable men so to yield themselves for others. It was because St. Paul followed his Master in identifying himself with humanity, that he was capable of such self-sacrifice as almost passes our belief.

His writings abound with exhortations to love and peace and unity, and to labour for each other; for it was the God of love and peace who was the universal Father. The Fatherhood, indeed, he saw more clearly in Christ;

and our union with the Son assured us of the possession of God as our Father, "of whom are all things, and we in Him." But our kinship to Christ enforces on us the truth that "none of us liveth unto himself." When we sin against the brethren, he tells us, we sin against Christ.

It is characteristic of St. Paul, that it is he who has preserved to us that saying of Jesus which is not given in the Gospels: "It is more blessed to give than to receive."[1] It is from St. Paul also that we have the sublime hymn on love, in his First Epistle to the Corinthians. Here he opens to us the principle of his doctrine of man, that love is the goal and perfection of our nature. He does not look on love as a means to an end, but as the purpose of our being. All the efforts of reason are but the striving after that harmony which finds its consummation in love. Knowledge in all its manifestations is but the groping of a child after that perfection which is realised in the union of love. So St. John in the Apocalypse represents the future state of man as one of musical harmony. Mankind are to exist for the sake of their harmony one with another; love is to be its own end; and the perfect concord which is symbolised in the harpers harping with their harps, and the new song, are shown to us as the law of our new and eternal being. A shadow of this great truth is seen in the *Banquet* of Plato, which Shelley rightly calls the most beautiful and perfect of all the works of Plato; and the poet himself has taught us to see the "beauty in which all things work and move," as an expression of a real

[1] In his address to the elders of Ephesus at Miletus, Acts xx. 25.

harmony which tells us what the end of the creation is, as well as opens to our gaze the law which guides it.

It is this thought of the unity of all things which inspires St. Paul's speculations on the final union of all men. Mr. Arnold tells us that the two main ethical thoughts which govern St. Paul are these: "the one, the earnest insistence with which he recommended 'bowels of mercies,' as he calls them, meekness, humbleness of mind, gentleness, unwearying forbearance, crowned all of them with that charity 'which is the bond of perfectness'; the other, the force with which he dwells on the *solidarity* of man—the joint interest, that is, which binds humanity together, the duty of respecting every one's part in it, and doing justice to his efforts to fulfil that part."[1] Mr. Arnold is a somewhat cold interpreter of St. Paul, and cannot translate the apostle's fiery enthusiasm into his own measured words, but he has hold of the substantial truth. These are really central ideas of St. Paul, who relates them both, however, to Christ, and finds in Him their unity. It is because He died for men that we are to love them, since He showed us the brotherhood of all men; it is because He so unites all men that we hold to their solidarity, not only as a principle, but as a practical guide.

St. Paul carries this idea of the solidarity of mankind to yet higher issues, and brings before our bewildered gaze the prospect of a general restoration.

The language of the apostle is very strong, and has excited much thought from the earliest times till now. He tells us that it is the divine purpose "that in the

[1] *St. Paul and Protestantism*, p. 32.

dispensation of the fulness of times He might gather together in one all things in Christ, both which are in heaven and which are on earth." Christ is the Head of the human race, who are so inspired with His life, that " as in Adam all die, even so in Christ shall all be made alive."

We have here a conception brought before us of the unity of mankind as the final goal of their being. With this idea St. Paul struggled, and in vain attempted to give a complete thought of it which should be ethically intelligible to us. To his mind, a final separation between mankind could not seem a resting-place for the thought and hope of the devout believer in the union of the human race with Christ its Head. As he passionately repudiated the division between Jew and Gentile, and rejoiced at the destruction of the "wall of partition," so did his thought try to compass a final union of all mankind. He was convinced at least of this, that such a union was in the divine purpose of love, however man might thwart it.

The vision which St. Paul had of the universal harmony of all things is not completely intelligible to us, but we can see how it elevates and strengthens his ideal of human unity, and gives him courage and hope for the future. To discuss the theories of universal restoration which have been based on it from the days of Origen till now, which fascinated the minds of Bengel and Schleiermacher, is not within our purpose, which withholds itself from any consideration of the future life—

"I do not ask to see
The distant scene, one step enough for me."

It is better to regard the statements of St. Paul as revealing the profound truth of the solidarity of mankind,—a truth which, in all its aspects, we may fail to grasp, but which is the root-principle of human life.

There is, indeed, an earthly fulfilment to which they look forward. We have a vision of a united humanity, as a family of love and peace, to which all the thoughts and works of mankind will be brought to consolidate. The Apocalypse turns its gaze on the same *earthly* Paradise, for the great voice from heaven says: "Behold the tabernacle of God is with men, and He will dwell with them, and they shall be His people." It is not our earthly Jerusalem that rises to heaven, we must remember, but "the holy city, the new Jerusalem," which comes down from God.

The same lofty thought inspires the writer to the Hebrews, whose Epistle is full of the spirit of sonship and of brotherly love. He has a deep sense of the unity through all time of mankind, and sees that the future alone can complete the present. The heroes of faith were not perfect till their brethren of ages after them had received the "better thing" provided for them. What the full meaning of that deep saying is, who can unfold? But does it not speak to us of a gradual raising up of all men to the level of the highest?[1] If the patriarchs were not perfect till they attained the knowledge and purity of the later ages, is the same thing not true of all undeveloped men? The final salvation of the soul does not consist in individual

[1] It is this thought which led Origen and Clement and their successors to the belief in universalism.

exaltation so much, as in a communion of the whole of redeemed mankind. This is the lofty purpose of Christ, as we are taught in the Epistles; and to that purpose the whole forces of man's life are ever contributing. "What a thought for each man! I am a member of mankind, universal mankind, of which Christ is the Head, and God is the indwelling Spirit! When all are perfect, I shall be perfect. I am permitted to contribute to the whole divine empire of humanity, but much more will the whole empire contribute to me, infuse strength into me, and everlastingly renew and refresh my heart, my mind, and all my powers."[1]

[1] Pulsford, *The Supremacy of Man*, p. 263.

CHAPTER XI

INDIVIDUALISM IN THE LIFE OF THE CHURCH

WE have seen that the theology of Christianity under the teaching of Jesus and His apostles began from an idea of the human race viewed as a unity. This meant more than the fact that men are linked together in their life, so that they work for each other, and with each other, and exert a mutual influence. It meant more than the common relationships and interdependence of our social existence. It takes heed of the fact that our personality is controlled by heredity and surroundings, by our character born with us, and made for us by the world we live in. Individual life is a plant conditioned by its environment to such an extent that it loses much of its individual character. The belief in an actual unity and solidarity of the race is an essential foundation of the early Christian theology. Apparently we are taught that men are one, not only by their mental and physical structure, by the sum of their being, but are one also by their origin, in that they are children of Adam. Some theologians regard the Adamic descent as a mere figure of the actual unity of the race, and pointing to no reality outside of that unity. Whatever it signify, it is clear that sin and salvation, as taught to the first learners of Christianity, imply a historical and collective unity of mankind. The idea is familiar enough to modern thought as being used by Comte for the purposes of his religion. Some thinkers are of opinion that this idea is carried so far in the Scriptures as to imply that no personal guilt attaches to man in respect of his inborn character or that acquired by surroundings, although it may bring his share of the sorrows of the human race, as they happen to fall heavily or lightly on him. And similarly, they read in St. Paul's teaching a doctrine that the salvation of any one man is incomplete till the whole race is raised to the destined height of purity.

Whether these views have full warrant or not, it is plain that the Christian is taught to regard himself not as an individual, but as a member of a family, whose interests on earth, and whose destiny hereafter, are so bound up with his own that it is impossible to sever himself from them, and that in all his life he must have regard to this unity. The sacraments of Baptism and the Eucharist tended to strengthen this communion; such is their basis, and such should have been their result. And yet the truth that "we are members one of another," soon began to be obscured, and Christianity became individualistic in its tendency.

The causes of this change are worth inquiring into. What influence did the Church come under which weakened its sense of its true unity? The need of independent action, which would often arise in the midst of a hostile world, may have helped to make the Christian self-reliant. Solitary, and in danger of his life, he must have had strong courage and individual convictions. To profess his faith must have cut him off from family ties, and little opportunity may have been given him of making a new kinship with those of like creed with himself. Times of persecution may, indeed, bind the persecuted more closely together, where they have the power to meet each other, but it oftener scatters them, and turns them forth as lonely wanderers from the fellowship of men. The surroundings of the primitive Christian must have had a strong moulding power over the form of his practical religion.

In like manner, the times of trouble which the Jews had to pass through before the coming of Jesus gave birth to the Essenes. They renounced fellowship with their own people, because the nation was too corrupt to be reformed, as Elijah had in days before gone into the desert alone. The idea of nationality was entirely forgotten, when the nation presented no longer the form of a united people, but a war of opposing forces, political and religious. The only hope they could have was to save their own souls amidst the ruin around them. It is a natural impulse which finds expression in all times of human history. It concerns us not by what outside religious forces Essenism was moulded; the idea of seclusion and individualism was created by the circumstances in which its founders were placed, and which gave them at once a following.

Such of the early Christians as were Jews were exposed to the same influences as were round the Essenes; and their character was apt to take the same form. The practice of asceticism here found its origin;

and events favoured its development, till it culminated in the excesses of the solitary and monastic life.

The apostolic Fathers are still in the current of the New Testament teaching, and their general view of Christianity is largely social, rather than individual; but the Church soon turned aside from the old path, and conformed to the Gnostic and Judaic theories of individual life. The theological diversity thus occasioned was no rupture of the principle of union; for though the *odium theologicum* does strain hard the outward relationships of men, it rarely touches the inner unity, which belongs to all true seekers after truth. If men are free to think, they must sometimes differ as to the conclusions they come to; but though that difference may sever them to the eye, their antagonism may be merely the process by which truth may find a reconciliation. Hence we look rather at practical than at doctrinal divergence.

The first break in the social unity of the Church came from distinction between religion of the higher culture and that of the simpler faith, which was begun by Clement of Alexandria. The teaching of Plato is here brought into Christianity, and the moral effect is not good. What was fit enough for Plato's system was out of keeping with the franker teaching of Jesus, whom "the common people heard gladly." The strong intellectual tendency of the Alexandrian Platonists had elements of disservice to the Christian life. The Montanists were foes to that intellectualism, yet they made the same distinctions between the spiritually-minded Christians and those who were merely carnal (or psychic) in their souls. The effect of these lines of demarcation soon made itself felt in the life of the Church. Men were not content with the fellowship in goodness which they had with their brothers of the same faith; they longed for some special gift for themselves. The Montanist prophet, like the Irvingite copyist of modern times, felt that he was exalted above the level of ordinary Christian brotherhood; and his orthodox brother, who looked askance on his spiritual utterances, longed for a corresponding elevation. This he found in the practice of asceticism and celibacy. He confined himself in these by his view of the contrast between matter and spirit, which made life consist in the Buddhist ideal of extinguishing the sense-element in our existence. In all this the individualising tendency which was seen in Greek philosophy in the teaching of the Stoics, and which had its part in Roman civilisation, from the heart of which the profane crowd were withdrawn, was manifested. It is a natural growth of man's intellectual life, and shows itself in the fastidiousness of modern culture, which shrinks from contact with the unwashed mob. But it is a tendency which early Christianity was at war with; for it not only sins against true human brotherhood, but renders impossible the advancement of the ignorant, and the progress of man. In this the old Toryism of this and other lands, which had its highest point in the *ancien régime* of France, was a sin, not only against political freedom, but also against the love of Christ Himself. It was hostile to the heart of the Christian faith.

The ancient individualism had its own merits: it was

a renunciation of evil and of self; from which, indeed, if evil were conquered, self emerged with greater power than ever. The new superior culture which would enjoy the fruits of the toil of others without thinking of them, which would dwell in luxury while others are in penury, seems to have no merit whatever; and doubtless some strong tide of human and divine vengeance will rise to sweep it away, as happened a century since in France.

Despite the influence of Novatianism, which kept before it the ideal of a Christian brotherhood, and the compromising efforts of Cyprian, who placed before mankind the idea of a united Church, the individualistic tendency went on its triumphant way. An ideal of higher perfection was laid down, which found embodiment in monasticism and the life which endeavoured more or less to reach the monastic excellence. This view of life can hardly be said yet to be extinct, and an ascetic spirit pervades much of modern religiosity. It is extraordinary to find writers identifying it with Calvinism, which is represented as a gloomy shadow over human life, hostile to art and to social freedom. As a fact, Calvinism was one of the means by which men were freed from the pursuit of the monastic ideal, although it was not able wholly to purge itself from the ascetic admixture.

There is a sense, as we shall see, in which the Christian faith accepts the self-denial which is found in asceticism; but in its Church form the practice is rather pagan than Christian. It is not even Jewish; for the people of Israel rejoiced in life with its social duties, and its patriotic enthusiasm, and trusted that Jehovah would cause His face to shine on them. To the Jews, life was a period of sunshine, with a darkness overshadowing its close; to the monk, a long slavery with much suffering, which at last earned paradise. The ascetic ideal fostered individualism by its division of the Christian people into the religious and secular,—an error which has borne the bitterest fruits. It has removed the best influences of religion from the concerns of ordinary life, and has retarded the growth of moral enlightenment. To separate men from each other under different laws of life, is seriously to endanger the moral sanction of both codes of law. But to separate men in that which, they are assured, is of primary importance, is to strike a heavy blow at the unity and solidarity of man. Every man becomes a law unto himself; and as the religious life becomes more distinctly religious, the secular has less and less of piety. The whole conception of religious superiority is foreign to the humble spirit of Christianity.[1] The sects which close their doors to any but the initiated are destitute of the first principles of the teaching of Jesus, which tells us that our love and service and fellowship are to be given to the evil and the

[1] The striking words of Jovinian, who strove against this separating tendency, are worth quoting: "There is but one divine element of life, which all believers share in common; but one fellowship with Christ, which proceeds from faith in Him; but one new birth. All who possess this in common with each other have the same calling, the same dignity, the same heavenly blessings; the diversity of outward circumstances creating no difference in this respect." Both St. Jerome and St. Augustine regard Jovinian as a heretic; but such views as these could stand any test that the Church might make of their orthodoxy.

good; that the distinctions we make as men are not regarded by the universal Father, who makes His sun to rise on the evil and the good, and sendeth rain on the just and the unjust. It may be that there are men better than others, nay, it must be so; but the way is open to all. Still more, we must recognise that in all men there is the germ of goodness, and the possibility of the highest goodness. Our Saviour never forgot this, and His insight was able to discern it in those who were outcast from men by reason of their sins. If we are inclined to forget this, and our modern science seems to tend to make us doubt it, we can turn to the inspiring poems of Victor Hugo, who never forgets that every child of man, however low he has sunk, possesses a redeeming trait, a reflection of the universal love in which our life is bathed, as in the serene all-surrounding air. Plutarch expresses this truth with clearness, and his words are worth quoting: "God, when He takes in hand a human soul, sees the inchoate virtue that is invisible to every human eye, and the ignorance or weakness that to human eyes has taken the aspect of vice,—sees even in that which looks to human eyes a mere evidence of a mind inclined to evil, the signs of a latent vigour in things excellent."[1]

The division of religious callings, which leaves it open to individual choice as to their measure of piety, has its root in a mistrust of ordinary life. The daily occupations and social relations of mankind are suspected of evil; and it almost looks as if the

[1] Plutarch: "Animi ne an Corporis Affectiones sint pejores" (trans. Wedgwood).

ascetics thought the world was of the devil's making and not of God's, as the Gnostics attributed it to the Demiurge.

The idea that labour of the body was less worthy than meditation of the soul—that the body, in fact, by its appetites and desires was a hindrance to true communion with God—was a strange one for those who were followers of Jesus, who spent the greater part of His life in the work of carpentry. Not content with breaking up the Christian Church into two classes of more and less religious, so as to injure all sense of unity, the ascetics shattered the unity of man's nature, and looked with suspicion at the ordinary healthy impulses of the human frame. Food and sleep were but temptations, and life itself but a waiting for death. This wretched pessimism was the result of individualistic desires for a life other than has been given us, for a higher sphere than other men have to dwell in. It is an impossibility to sever the mind from the body; for to such an extent has this truth been admitted in our time, that the one is regarded but as a function of the other. The idealists say that our consciousness (through a kind of determination at the first moment of our existence) shapes not only our nature, but even our bodily form and features; and the materialists tell us that thought is a mere physical product of the brain. Whatever our philosophy teach us, our experience makes it very plain that we cannot separate the soul from the body in any view of life. Our life here depends on certain material conditions, and thought so wears out the brain that it requires food to repair the waste. To win the best results of life we must submit to its laws. "Your Father knoweth that ye have need of these things."

It is hard to say how much strong thinking and active virtue have been lost to the world through the lack of material sustenance which some good men have compelled themselves to endure. It is still harder to say how much of the purity of the mystic has been due to his fasting and solitude; some of his visions may have come from a brain tortured by unnatural treatment. But it is certain that for most men a certain physical ease in life is necessary to get the best work both from body and soul. Here and there an individual may be otherwise made, as there are giants and dwarfs in this world; but the rule of life is as Jesus expressed it, that we "have need of these things." It is the folly of individualism to strive after being more than human, when Christ Himself accepted all the conditions of our material life. A man may deny himself for the sake of others, as the wayfarer shares his crust with the poorer man he meets, though there is not enough for one scanty meal for either; and in doing so, will do what is good and generous. But to refuse God's gifts without reason, to regard the supply of every want as a temptation, to weaken the bodily strength so as to maim the usefulness, to be an ascetic for the sake of self, is to doubt the wisdom of God who has made us, soul and body, and His love who has bestowed upon us the means of satisfying the needs of both.

Practically, the solitary ascetic withdrew all his service from man. What contribution he was able to give to the general sum of human usefulness or happiness he withheld. His whole concern was in securing his own salvation, " in hopes to merit heaven by making earth a hell." The true life is the life of society with our fellows, whom we can serve and sympathise with; and this is the Christian ideal. To put our talent in a napkin and bury it away in a monastic cell, is to defraud men of what is due to them. To withdraw ourselves from the world while there is work to do therein, and we are able to help in it, with a view to saving our souls, is to reach the very acme of selfishness.[1] The individualistic tendency of Christian life continued throughout all the Middle Ages. It manifested itself in a mysticism of various forms, which, though making the individual soul as nothing before God, yet isolated it from true communion with men. The result of this was that men with mystical tendencies carried their individualism so far as to scorn ordinary morality; and the excesses of John of Leyden in Münster are a not unnatural conclusion to theorising so remote from true human life. It is the opinion of a solitary himself, the Abbé Roux in the *Pensées d'un Solitaire*, that men who rely wholly on intuitive experiences are bound to act now and then like fools. The history of religion supplies abundant proof of the statement; and it is one of the happiest results of the Reformation that we have

[1] St. Chrysostom's words may be quoted : "Though you fast, though your bed be the earth and your food ashes, though you mourn continually without doing good to others, you will make no progress. Though you practise the monastic perfection in its highest form, all the while recking not though others are going to destruction, you cannot keep a clear conscience in God's sight. Neither voluntary poverty, nor martyrdom, nor anything we do, will be to our credit, if we have not reached the supreme virtue of love."— *Hom. 25 in Ep. I. to Corinth*

left behind us the individual excesses in asceticism and seclusion from life which Christianity in its mediæval form shared with the religion of the Aztecs of Mexico and the Brahmans of India. The stagnation of morals and progress in Europe till the revival of letters was a result of this unhappy view of human life and of the Christian Church. For many centuries the ethical literature of the Church is very meagre; but it is not the absence of her literature we lament, it is the lack of the moulding influence of a true Christian life through the artificial sundering of religion and common duty.

The individualistic theory is not yet gone from among us. It no longer calls a man from his social relations, and separates him from family life; but it often gives a selfish bent to his thoughts. The popular preacher calls on him to save his soul; and, moved by desire of reward or fear of punishment, he bends his energy to the task. Assured of his salvation, he too often shuts himself in from sympathy with his fellow-men, and dwells with his own soul. It is a wonder to the observer of mankind how the religious person can see with such indifference the miseries of the poor and the sufferings of the weak. How they can have in any way entered into the following of Him who gave His life for men, is hard to be understood. And yet the religious class, who, by reason of their more worthy and steadfast character, are often prosperous, enjoy their comforts in selfish isolation, or share them only with their kindred. The fault lies in their view of Christianity and the Church, which is essentially a fellowship that calls on all to seek the good of others. The social union of mankind begins with the family; but with many of us, our social interests are exhausted in our own household. "Every Englishman is an island," said Novalis, and the only extension of boundary which he permits himself is his children and other kindred. Family life, which is meant to be the preparation for the brotherhood of man, often locks the door of wider sympathies, and becomes but another form of individualism. Herein we must hear the word of Jesus: "If any man come to Me, and hate not his father and mother, and wife and children, and brothers and sisters, yea, and his own life also, he cannot be My disciple."

In this Jesus simply means that family affection must not exclude from our hearts the wider and deeper sympathy which is due to all men.[1] The Christian must rise above the mere natural instincts of the heart, which are not even special to the human race. Yet there is no commoner form of individualism than this family affection, to the exclusion of all the world beside. Asceticism had in it the germ of all the theories of the Church which aimed at separation from the world. It was the parent of schisms and dissent; for its fundamental idea was that the Christian should be an island dweller in the sea of human life. The Novatianist idea of the Church as the exclusive congregation of saints may perhaps be the ideal of the fellowship of men, but

---

[1] As St. Augustine says: "Extend your love, then, and limit not to your wives and children. Such love is found even in beasts and sparrows. You know the sparrows and swallows, how they love their mates, how together they hatch their eggs and nourish their young together, by a sort of sweet and natural kindness, and with no thought of return,"—*Hom. in Matt.* 90.

its arbitrary interpretation of saintship, its love of erecting barriers around the Christian fellowship, deprive it of much human use and charity, and not a little insight into truth. Separatists of the centuries since Novatian have largely given up the ruling thoughts of their early forerunners, and it is only an uncharitable thought which will find in our modern dissent any likeness of the early narrowness, which is not also discoverable in the Churches who have kept in the primitive traditions. Still it is a chapter by no means fragrant with love and unity which tells us of the divisions in the Church of Christ.

Some early Separatists maintained, in opposition to St. Cyprian, that every association of Christians which met in the name of Christ was a Church. The movement which began so early, of separation from the general body of the Church without any sufficient reason, bore abundant fruits afterwards, some good, some evil. The progress into wider thoughts of the unity of the Church may have been aided by it; but it also prevented that collective Christian force, which union would have brought, from exercising its full weight in the world. St. Cyprian's answer to the Separatists was irrefutable. They quoted the promise of Jesus to be with two or three who met in His name. The bishop replied that the condition of Christ's presence was a union of hearts in love; "and how is it possible for one to agree with another who does not agree with the body of the Church? How can two or three be assembled together in the name of Christ, who are separated from Christ and His gospel?"

The alteration in the meaning and administration of

the Eucharist was also a development of individualism. At first a common meal, which was to develop the brotherly love of the partakers, it became an individual reception of some special blessing; and the love-feast which went along with it soon ceased to be a part of the Church service. Of this something will be said later on; and we only add another instance of the growth of individualism, which will also receive fuller treatment.

The foundation idea of the primitive fellowship of the Church implied a community of gifts to be used for the edification of the Church. There was no separation between clergy and laity, for the priestly calling and character were common to both. But very soon this idea of the universal priesthood was lost sight of, and a separate class claimed for their order a sacramental power which, so far as it existed at all, was the joint right of the whole Church. This, along with the ascetic and monastic ideas, was the greatest blow that the brotherhood of Christians received, and prevented the due development of Christianity in the brotherhood of man.

CHAPTER XII

THE FAMILY: ITS PAST AND FUTURE

IN the Book of Genesis we read that God gave to man two gifts at once, the family and the Church. The affection which unites man to man, was born along with that which unites man to God. These gifts are so noble and divine, that men have viewed them as ends in themselves, as ideals which were perfect and eternal. That death does not sever us from those we love, has been the faith of mankind, kept up in heathen races by their funeral rites, which involved the willing or unwilling doom of wives and servants of him who had died, in order that in the world to come he might not be alone and unattended; and in Christian peoples the same idea has been strengthened by the practice of prayers for the dead; so that it is an article of almost universal acceptance that families are again united in the world to come.[1] The teachings of the poets have lent their aid to the beautiful and consoling thought that there are inner realities in our souls sacred from the touch of death; and the instincts of the human race have compelled men to believe that the purest feelings of the soul cannot

[1] It is needless to refer to the theories of Swedenborg on this subject, although they are stated with his usual dogmatism.

share our mortality. In all our hopes there must be some truth, for our instincts were not given to mislead us. But are we right in thinking that the love and kinship of family is more than a mere education for something better? Is it not but a first step in an ascending scale of union with mankind, out of which we pass, and upwards?

The first step must, however, be taken if we are to reach the brotherhood of man as a universal fact. That brotherhood must spring from the natural kinship which exists among men. The very words we use express physical facts; for when we speak of brothers we mean children of the same parents. It matters not whether the family grow by paternal or maternal filiation, whether the children are reckoned of one family because they are of one mother or of one father. It is enough that they group themselves by natural kinship, which gives common duties and interests.

The family at first, however, was rather a means of separation than of union. The description of the Cyclops which Homer gives in the *Odyssey* [1]—"They had neither assemblies to deliberate or give sentence, but each ruled his wives and children, and took no heed of his neighbour" —is quoted by Plato,[2] with the remark that the same state of things existed in some parts of Greece and among barbarians. Aristotle also refers to it [3] as illustrating the following words: "That society which Nature has established for daily support is the domestic; but the society of many families is called a village, and a village is most naturally composed of the descendants of one family."

[1] *Od.* x. 112.   [2] *De Legg.* iii.   [3] *Polit.* i. 2.

The relation of families to each other was often one of jealousy, which, as occasion rose, might turn into hostility; but the internal unity was a certain fact. So much so, that, as Sir H. Maine says, " the unit of an ancient society was the family, of a modern society the individual."[1]

Some doubt has been cast on the theory that the family is the original condition of mankind. It has been maintained that some other mode of life must have existed, as many savage people seem to be without family union, living in a tribe where marriage ties, according to our common understanding of them, do not exist. There seem to be traces of some such custom of life in the early history of both Aryan and Semitic peoples. Those races in past days were divided into tribes, each of which was marked by a badge of some natural object, such as a plant or animal. This was held sacred, and the tradition was that the whole tribe descended from it in some mythical past. The evidence for this, in reference to early man, is found in such historical notices as survive of animal worship, descent through the mother, and marriage out of the tribe. The observation of travellers supplies proof of like habits among various savage peoples.

Did this state of life exist among primitive men? Has the world passed through this condition on the way to a higher and better order?

It seems clear that the family is the oldest human institution. In the early patriarchal life the father was the head of the family, being priest and king in his household. It does not need that we suppose that

[1] *Ancient Law*, p. 126.

man started from a life of innocence to establish this as highly probable. There is, even to the inquirer who will not make any postulate except that man started from animalism, not a little proof that the family life is the original. In all the peoples who dwell on the great continents, there is a universal worship of the male ancestors: surely this points to a unity of family, when they worshipped a common head. Darwin, in his studies of mankind from the point of view of his theory, came to the conclusion that mankind originally dwelt in family kinship. He says: " The most probable view is that primæval man aboriginally lived in small communities, each with as many wives as he could support or obtain. In primæval times, men would probably have lived as polygamists, or temporarily as monogamists. They would not, at that period, have lost one of the strongest of all instincts, the love of their young offspring."

An original family life seems to be a certainty from all we can learn: how did man come to fall from it to dwell in hordes? The answer to this is found in certain facts of human life, which are dark blots on man's history.

If men dwelt in hordes, the physical explanation is that there was not such an equality of sexes as would give a wife to every man. This equality is the natural condition of our life, and if it had passed away, there must have been a reason for it. The custom of female infanticide may account for the fewness of women, and would disturb the level of the sexes: it is certain that it is still practised, as a woman is less useful in savage life than a man. When we see that the life in hordes is rather an island custom than a continental, being found in countries which were peopled late in time, we are on the track of another important fact. Such groups of colonisers would naturally start with few women, and this unusual disproportion between the sexes would lead to the tribal union, with its unspeakable accompaniments. This form of life would last long after any need for it could be imagined; and the insecurity of settlers in a new country might help to retain it. Certain it seems, therefore, that some special circumstances had tended to degrade man to this bestial herding.

May we not find in the studies of the anthropologists some confirmation of the teaching of the Sacred Scriptures as to primitive man? And is it not noteworthy to find there the ancient record of aboriginal family life among the Semites, who, we learn from Professor Robertson Smith's inquiries, seem to have possessed in early days the lower form of horde life?

Everywhere, as we trace the footsteps of early mankind, we find faint marks of a fall from a better life. When men lost their first estate, how hard it was for them to regain it! But the divine purpose in human life was not obscurely shown. By slow effort men arose to the nobler family union, which was the ideal of humanity: the divine Spirit ever unfolding more fully the progressive life of the race.

The family is the highest stage possible of our earthly condition, and we cannot doubt that it is a permanent and divine institution.

But recent theorists have assailed its perpetuity, and have persuaded themselves that a better state of things might come to pass, and that, in the interests of universal brotherhood, family life should be abolished. A French writer,[1] who seems to glory in the shame of reducing man by his theories to his lowest and most brutal origin, speaks as follows: "We are justified in believing, contrary to the opinion of Mr. Herbert Spencer, that in certain societies at least, the part which the family now holds in everyday life will gradually tend to diminish. We cannot predict how this great transformation will be effected in our social organism. But before such a condition can be realised, altruism must altogether gain the upper hand over egoism, and the moral standard must be very considerably raised." Plato thought his ideal Republic would be the better of such a development; but he knew human nature was too strong for him to realise it, and, as he says, "if we might not see it on earth, in heaven there is probably a model of this our city, where he who wishes to behold it may see it."[2] The Nihilists of Russia, with their terrible "gospel" of individualism, are opposed to marriage and the family unity. They look to the time when the chains which are called "science, civilisation, property, marriage, morality, and justice, will snap asunder like threads." The only law of a human being, according to their view, should be his own happiness, and they are therefore bitterly opposed to any socialism, or communism, or co-operation in anything but destruction.

But without going to the extremes of these Russian anarchists, the institution of the family is threatened

[1] Letourneau, *Sociology*, trans. by Trollope, p. 379.
[2] Plato, *Republic*, ix. 592.

by forces nearer home. The frequency and facility of divorce in the United States have often been noted, and we are threatened in the United Kingdom with an approach to such a state of things. It is evident that the unity and sanctity of the family depend on the permanence of the marriage bond. Without taking any extreme view, such as the Roman Church holds in theory, that a divorce is altogether unlawful, we may well be alarmed at the state of opinion and law in the United States on this subject. Such causes as intoxication, or failure to support through idleness, or habitual indulgence of ungovernable temper, are regarded as sufficient. In Wisconsin and Kentucky, married persons may separate, by agreement, for a certain period as a preliminary to divorce at the end of that time. In Washington Territory a divorce may be given to people who seem unable to live together. It is found that divorce is least common among the wealthy classes, on account, as is said, of difficulties as to property arrangements, and that it abounds in the middle classes, which are usually considered the stronghold of religion and order. It seems as if the trend of legislation in America was towards making the marriage contract one which was easily entered into and easily dissolved, by this means shattering the unity and the very existence of the family. The figures which are given us tell of a remarkable state of things. In the State of Vermont, the ratio of divorces to marriages increased from one in twenty-three in 1860 to one in fourteen in 1878; but since then there has been a decrease. In Rhode Island the proportion is one in thirteen, which is not so large as that in Connecticut, where we find one divorce for every ten marriages.[1] This is an unnatural and dangerous state of things, which must affect the future of the country. It is said to be a development of the individualistic movement, and as such Humboldt and John Stuart Mill defend a general freedom of divorce, with hardly any restriction. But the world wishes now to move out of selfish regard for mere individual desires, and their arguments will have less weight than when they were written.

The danger which menaces us is that an ignorant socialistic movement may wish to annul the sanctity of marriage, as the Russian Nihilists do; but this may be checked by showing that all true social brotherhood is imperilled by the relaxation of the marriage bond. That there are unhappy marriages no one can doubt; but the remedy does not lie in freedom of divorce,—such liberty can only increase the number of unsuitable unions, for people are less careful about entering on any course from which they can readily escape. If marriage is rendered indissoluble except for gross offences against the marriage bond, it will not be so lightly considered. A due sense of the importance of care before taking a step which is practically irrevocable will do more to prevent unhappy unions than any facility for divorce. The habits of our society are less inclined to foster this than they might be. The sole thought that enters into the minds of the parents is generally the pecuniary conditions of the case; and if wealth or freedom from money troubles is likely to result, they pay little atten-

[1] Gladden, *Century Magazine*, 1882.

tion to anything else. On the part of the persons about to marry, it often happens that there is even less reflection. A hasty acquaintance, in which altogether but few hours have been spent, is often a preliminary to a life union, which is unhappy almost from the very nature of the case. The marriages of the working classes are, perhaps, generally happiest in this country, though in America a different state of things seems to prevail. The habits of forbearance which poorer people are compelled to learn enable them to endure much inconvenience, and the fact that both husband and wife equally share the toil of life gives the partnership more lasting elements. The main cause of unhappiness among the operative classes is the habit of intoxication, for which some legislative control other than divorce is imperatively necessary in the present state of society. It is clear that what is necessary to give marriage a certainty of adding to the happiness of life is not the opportunity of divorce should it turn out badly, but a due regard by people about to marry to the character of their proposed companion for life. And even though exceptional cases of hardship occur now and then, as they must, which no wise divorce law can reach, the sufferers must bear their wrongs for the good of the community. It may be a hard thing to say, but the happiness of some few individuals cannot be allowed to peril the general welfare of the whole people. If those who are in this bad plight remember this fact, it may serve to mitigate their sense of injustice.

The family life, with its union and affection, with its training in self-sacrifice and its labour for others, is the essential preliminary of the brotherhood of man. All hope of attaining such a glorious future is ended if this first condition be not fulfilled. The human heart can only be trained in the school of the home. If the sacred and divine institution of the family be impaired, the injury to the general cause of human brotherhood is irreparable. We should soon return to a selfish isolation, and barbarism of jealous hostility, which would render all progress in the social affections impossible. A system like Plato's, instead of leading to heaven, would point the way to hell. What safeguards have we that men will not revert to the primitive condition, when every man was at war with his neighbour? The conditions of modern life are harder, and competition fiercer; and the struggle for existence would but develop a deeper enmity. The one hope which mankind have as a foundation on which to build their temple of love and brotherhood, is the family: without that divine institution we can do nothing.

Having laid down as an absolute and permanent condition of brotherly feeling on earth, that the family must be kept untouched in its divine simplicity, we now proceed to ask if the purpose of the family is such as to render its existence perpetual in any higher state of life to which the future may bring us. Its ideal usefulness is even here not attained by a mutual affection among its members: it must not be a mere alliance for defence or advantage. Too often does our sympathy confine itself to the limits of our household; and our family affection often injures our sense of justice. A man is a hard master, an unscrupulous trader, in order that his means may increase so as to benefit his children. He cares nothing for himself; he denies himself pleasure and rest to work for them: but his view of duty does not extend beyond them. In so acting, he is abusing God's best gift to us; taking the pure gold of love, and turning it into the base alloy of selfish pride. The family union was not given to strengthen the power of selfishness over the soul of man, but to slowly extinguish it for the nobler feeling of human sympathy and human fellowship.

The purpose which the family serves, therefore, is to train in the habits of thought and action necessary for the promotion of universal brotherhood. That it does so is evident from our daily experience. Who does not at once recognise the motherly instinct which makes a mother kind to all children? or which makes men kind to a schoolboy when they think of their own? It is worth noting here that our public-school system has some dangers in developing selfishness by removing the boys from the sweeter influences of family life. A day-school education is to be preferred. Professor Sewell[1] said some years since what is still true: "The English Church has thought more of individuals than of families. It has created and dispersed abroad a power inadequate even to cope with children, certainly not adequate to control parents. And too often, especially of late, it has broken up the family relationship, by transplanting the children into large schools, and superseding the parental authority. It is the mistake rather of her poverty than of her will; but unless speedily and decidedly corrected,

[1] *On the Dialogues of Plato*, p. 270.

it will have led to serious mischief." The pauper children, when allowed to herd together in the workhouse, grow up amidst harsh discipline and imperfect training to be the foundation of a dangerous proletariat; but now, since they have been boarded out in private families, they will be trained in family affection, so as to know and to exercise the brotherhood of citizenship.[1] The modern idea, which recognises individuals rather than families, is only a makeshift for a time. But we must not have our family life isolated as in the patriarchal days; we must be closely interlocked with the community, and have interests and sympathy with all men. It is only thus that we can arrive at true human brotherhood.

Modern civilisation is manifesting great influence over the family union. The dispersion of families in pursuit of labour and commerce tends to weaken the family tie at too early an age, and the facilities of travel and communication are hardly enough to counteract the effects of the severance. There may, however, be the growth of a wider human sympathy as a result from the dispersion of mankind; and there may be also a closer form of association born of the creation of great centres of population. The questions which thus arise are somewhat complicated, and, like the astronomical problems of several bodies mutually influencing others in space, can only be approximately solved.

The influence of poor-law legislation, and its kindred

---

[1] A similar measure, with the best results, has been carried out in regard to Scottish "hospitals" for the education of children; although in a few cases some foolish people have prevented this very much needed change of method.

enactments with reference to education, are serious factors in our modern life. The family ties in the pauper classes are becoming dangerously lax, by the provisions which absolve men from family duties; and if the influence spreads upward, the coherence of the nation will be injured. We are doing our best, by the compulsory provision of poor relief, to which paupers may lay legal claim, to create a proletariat whose weakness is the only security against their power to bring the national life to chaos. For the family is not only the foundation of earthly happiness, but also of national stability as well as of human brotherhood.

Family life, however, has moved away from the patriarchal idea of the authority of the head, to centre itself rather in the sympathy and affectionate duty which parents owe to children. There is an increase in parental affection, at the same time that the filial respect seems weaker to the outward observer. A father or mother is willing to make any sacrifice or give any indulgence to their children. The loss of parental authority is easily explained by the gradual growth of the State, which tends to remove all sanctions from parental control except purely moral forces. The isolation of the family is lost, and the parent merges himself in the fabric of society. He no longer looks on his children as his property, but feels that he owes to society the duty of educating and caring for them, and in the task he develops new affections which were unknown to the older parental relationship. Motherhood always possessed this deep feeling of sacrificing love; but it has been the mission of Christianity to deepen this in the hearts of fathers, so as to prepare the way for the universal unselfishness of human brotherhood.

For the family, by its close union and mutual affection, was but a preparation of heart for something wider. The isolation in which the patriarchal family dwelt, and which marks, in a measure, family life in the present day, was a necessary part of its existence. It could not have held together unless by a strong bond, openly recognised; to loosen that bond was to open the way for promiscuous hordes. But its spiritual influence was none the less real, although not openly known ; the Spirit of God moved the heart of man to prepare the way for the great future, when every family would be but a wave on the great ocean of universal love.

The true object of religion is not the development of the individual life, but the social perfection. Individual truth and goodness and beauty are only beautiful and good and true when given for the service of man; and so family life is the great unconscious preparation for the one family in heaven and earth.

Accordingly, we are compelled to ask what is the ultimate destiny of family life. If the brotherhood of man should ever be attained, will it be necessary, in so glorious a communion of body and soul, to keep the family as a spiritual limitation in that ideal and celestial commonwealth?[1] Here we are wholly in the realm of the

[1] As a physical fact, the family is a permanent condition of earthly life ; but its inner spiritual meanings need not be limited by its physical characteristics. It is solely to these soul-relationships of love and union that our attention is directed. It may here be observed that the full meaning of human brotherhood is, in all likelihood (to speak from a merely philosophical standpoint), not

ideal, and we are departing a little from the earthly path to which we have limited ourselves; but it may be necessary to look upwards for a time to understand the fulness of the principle of human brotherhood as taught by Christ.

Plato, who knew that in the corrupt state of family life at Athens he had little hope of realising his ideal, assures us he does not wish to do without the affection which is the bond of family union. His hope was that it would be none the less strong because spread over a wider area. The whole State would, he hoped, be one of brothers, fathers, and sons, who should use these names endearingly.[1] He thought by these means to slay all selfishness, and to cultivate pure and generous hearts; and although he knew it was impracticable, he yet set it before the world as an ideal State.

In the teaching of Jesus there is at least one saying on this subject which needs considering; and possibly two. When the Sadducees came to Him with their question about the woman who had married seven husbands in succession, He replied: "In the resurrection they neither marry nor are given in marriage, but are as the angels of God in heaven." This sentence has not been easy to understand, and has awakened many thoughts. Kingsley, for one, seems to have been much exercised about it. He writes: "I know that if immortality is to include in my case identity of person, I shall feel to my wife for ever as I do now. That exhausted by the conditions of our mortal life. See the words of T. H. Green on p. 125, and of Lotze on p. 254. But, as we have said, we do not propose to consider this aspect of the subject in this treatise.

[1] *Republic*, v. 463, 472.

feeling may be developed in ways which I do not expect: it may have provided for it forms of expression very different from any which are among the holiest sacraments of life: of that I take no care. The union I believe to be as eternal as my own soul." Again: " In heaven they neither marry nor are given in marriage: but is marriage not the mere approximation to a unity which shall be perfect in heaven ? . . . All expressions of love here are but dim shadows of a union which shall be perfect, if we will but work here so as to work out our own salvation."[1] Here he has a glimpse of the great truth that family life is not an end in itself, but a means of preparing us for a deeper and eternal brotherhood. It is in the Church, says St. Ambrose, " that the names by which we express relationship receive their full meaning,—the reverence of sons, the piety of parents, the kinship of brothers."[2] The family is but the shadow of something better; the preparation for something we do not realise, but can look forward to. We can see how it fits us for a fuller earthly brother- hood : let us use our home affections so as to leave our hearts opener to a world-brotherhood, into which all lesser fellowships shall flow as rivers to the sea.

There is another saying attributed to Jesus which we find in the Second Epistle of St. Clement.[3] The Lord being asked by a certain man when His kingdom would come, replied: " When the two shall be one, and the external as the internal, and the male with the female, neither male nor female." This is said to be from a

[1] *C. Kingsley's Life*, by his wife, ii. 103, 104.
[2] St. Ambrose, *De Officiis*, i. 33.   [3] II. Epistle xii. 2.

work called the "Gospel according to the Egyptians," which is now lost, but was formerly used by the Encratites and other heretics. The authenticity of the saying is at least doubtful, though, as Lightfoot suggests, it may have been based on some saying of Christ's similar in meaning to St. Paul's words in the Epistle to the Galatians:[1] "There is neither male nor female." The meaning is evidently similar, though its mystical character, so different from the usual manner of our Lord in His speech as reported in the Gospels, renders it open to many interpretations. We can only conclude that we have here a vision of the ideal purpose of conjugal love and family affection in preparing the heart for a fuller and more generous draught of universal love and sympathy and brotherhood. Such a view does not make us value it less because it is incomplete in its purpose; but it teaches us to cherish it the more, as it is the means of so great and glorious a destiny. Every thought of love that fills the breast attunes it to receive more and more of the music which is the harmony of all things; and if we yield ourselves to the melody of the familiar song of home affection, we shall train our ears for deeper and more majestic harmonies that await us, and which one day we may attain.

[1] Gal. iii. 28.

CHAPTER XIII

THE SACRAMENTS

THE Christian religion in its most solemn rites declares its great purpose. As if to guard against any possible forgetfulness of the unity and brotherhood of man being the appointed goal of all human life and effort, Christ instituted the sacraments as perpetual witnesses to His divine end in giving life to the Church. Religion, said Novalis, is a social thing; without a Church it cannot exist. The union of the disciples to one another and to Christ, said the Master Himself, is an essential condition of true life. "As the branch cannot bear fruit of itself except it abide in the vine, no more can ye except ye abide in Me."

To give this union an outward form, the sacraments were appointed. By baptism we are admitted into the Church, and become ourselves living witnesses of that brotherhood which the Church exists to declare and advance.

That the Church is a universal brotherhood, is clear from the fact that we baptize infants. What right or title can one infant have to baptism more than another? There is no hint in the teaching of Jesus that any child is preferred before another. "Suffer the children to come unto Me, and forbid them not." "It is not the will of your Father which is in heaven that one of these little ones should perish."

It is not by baptism that we become sons of God; we are already His children. But we declare that we recognise our true position towards Him as our Father, who loves us, and has forgiven us. It is from this knowledge of our sonship to the divine Father that we come to realise our brotherly relation to man.

Although baptism is thus the entrance gate to the Church, it is essentially an individual act with an individual meaning. It is true that it is the way in which the Christian brotherhood receives into its fold those who are born into the human family; but is it not rather a declaration that all men are the sons of God, and therefore already in that family of which He is the Father? It is in baptism that the child is declared an heir to the great treasures of love and unity which God has appointed as the future possession of mankind.

That baptism is an act of universal meaning is clear from the doctrine held by the orthodox Church in all times, that the baptism of heretics is valid. The Councils of Laodicea and Constantinople and other Councils affirmed its entire validity, when administered in the name of the Trinity, however heterodox the person baptizing might be; and St. Augustine, St. Jerome, and many others of the early Christian writers, express the same opinion. If baptism is admission to the Christian community in any narrow sense, how could men admit to a community of which they were not themselves members?

Here we have a glimpse of one of these great universal truths which the Church preserved, while hardly knowing the full worth of her treasure. The recognition of heretic and schismatic baptism had for its inner meaning a recognition of the universal love of the divine Father, of the universal redemption of Christ, of the universal sonship of men. It was removed by a wide horizon from purely ecclesiastical acts such as ordination. The Church kept for herself this power, and refused to recognise schismatic orders, and insisted on reordaining those who had such orders. But baptism was not the peculiar possession of the orthodox; it was like the sunlight, the universal privilege of mankind. Hence it was that the baptism of the Baptist was regarded as an admission to the fellowship of the Church, for we read that Apollos was received into the Church apparently on the ground of this baptism.

This sacrament has therefore, in its essential principle, a foreshadowing of the great final unity of mankind. It is always spoken of in Scripture as an element of union, and one of the keys of God's world of peace and harmony to which He will one day bring mankind. The sacrament of baptism is, perhaps, not valued as it should be; but, notwithstanding man's ignorance of its power and beauty, it bears them, though they know it not, on a wide current of brotherly union into real and abiding love.

In the Holy Communion we have another form of the same brotherly influence brought before us. By uniting in the Eucharist we recognise our relationship to men, in that they are to share in our material possessions as well as in love and fellowship. And we acknowledge that union is to be consummated by realising the universal brotherhood of Christ Himself to all mankind.

In earlier times, it is apparent that sharing in the material elements of this life of ours took a more prominent place than it does now. For the agape was joined with the Eucharist, and the needy were aided by the gifts which were brought for the sacrament and for the feast.[1] At this weekly union the early Christians had an opportunity of laying aside the worldly seeking after selfish interests ; and the blessing of the bread and wine made them remember that all gifts come from the universal Father. The Church has never quite forgotten the communion in material things which the sacrament typifies, for there is no communion ever held without an almsgiving. In the old days the bread and wine for the communion were taken out of the offerings of the people, and then the rest consumed at the agape or given to the poor.[2]

This is an important view of the sacrament which must not be overlooked.

> "The Holy Supper is kept indeed,
> In whatso we share with another's need :
> Not what we give, but what we share,
> For the gift without the giver is bare ;
> Who gives himself with his alms feeds three—
> Himself, his hungering neighbour, and Me."

The Roman Church has much weakened the force of the two great sacraments which Christ appointed by adding others. By this means the true ideas of the

---
[1] Tertullian, *Apol.* c. 39.
[2] 1 Cor. ix. 21. Justin Martyr, *Apol.* ii. 98.

sacraments have been lost, and other notions added contrary to the divine teaching as well as to the human usefulness of the rites. Some have thought that there are too few sacraments;[1] but if they express the sum of existence, how can they be added to? The one brings before us the individual life, which is asserted in baptism to consist in the sonship which we have to the divine Father. When that individual life has been fully realised by us, when we are old enough to have it as an actual possession, we come to the second sacrament, and yield it to the brotherhood. Not for ourselves was our life given, but for others. "No man liveth unto himself."

The so-called other sacraments have little relation to these ideas, with, perhaps, the single exception of marriage, which might have been retained, as in a sense a sacrament of humanity; but its logical position would have been difficult in that case to define.

A communion in material things is nothing, as St. Paul tells us, without charity. The sacrament, therefore, had for its essence the true brotherly love. A feast of joy is a feast of friendship, for it implies a sharing of our joy with others, and the communion had this for its chief ethical idea.

The early Christians accordingly were anxious that no thought of strife should enter into their hearts while together at this feast. Tertullian, in the well-known chapter of his *Apology*, tells the Christians who had any dispute to be reconciled, and not make a mockery of

[1] Goethe thought so (*Wahrheit und Dichtung*, B. 7), and some Lutherans (*e.g.* Vilmar) and Anglicans wish to add to their number.

their communion of love by inward variance while professing outward union.

It is clear how far off the Roman Church (and perhaps every Church more or less) has wandered from the early intent of this sacrament, by making it a matter of individual reception rather than brotherly communion. The Christian sects who sit down together seem to come nearer the original idea in outward form, whatever their inward thought may be.

Brotherhood brings gladness to the heart, and the feast of communion was a feast of thanksgiving. They remembered with gladness the divine Father whose children they were, and whose bounties they were receiving, and bathed themselves in the brotherhood of man, which they thought of, not only as embracing the living, but also the dead, from whom their life, both physical and moral, came; and this great brotherhood they specially traced to its divine source in Christ Himself.

When Emerson says, "What was once a mere circumstance, that the best and the worst men in the parish, the poor and the rich, the learned and the ignorant, young and old, should meet one day as fellows in one house, in sign of an equal right in the soul, has come to a paramount motive for going thither," he really touches the heart of Christianity, though he knows it not. At no time was the common brotherhood of man a mere circumstance; at all times it was the essential aim of Christianity: and if advancing progress has brought its true meaning more into prominence, such is the natural result of the process of education through which the human race is going. Through the sieve of the years only the finer wheat falls, and the coarser is cast away, for it is useless. The appetite craves better food than the old husks, and the true aim of religion is cleared of its unserviceable accretions.

The social and brotherly element is the foundation purpose of the communion. If we remember that it closed a series of teachings given by Jesus as to the importance of brotherly love and perfect union, it will be plain to us that it was a mere symbolic summing up of all that He had said. He prayed that His own might be one, even as He and His Father were one; that they might be made perfect in one. And He had exhorted them over and over again that they should love one another, as He had loved them.

He appeals to that motive which we have called the Christian conscience — the remembrance of His love. And the sacrament specially brings this before us, for it is to be taken in remembrance of Him. His desire for unity, His death for men, are all to be in our hearts as we unite together in this holy rite.

The meaning of the sacrament one would think it impossible to obscure; but how have men darkened it! By elaborate ritual, by mysterious doctrine, by strange talk about fasting and the like, they have clouded its primary purpose from the vision of men.

Still, when we consider the ethical evolution of the Christian doctrine with reference to the sacraments, we see how the dogma served to keep the idea before the mind of the Church. In baptism, the theory of baptismal regeneration was a strong presentation of the fact that the child was a child of God, and had the blessing of a Father's love. The washing with water brings vividly to view the truth that God has pardoned our sins, and that to come before Him with sacrifices of atonement, as in the days of ignorance, was to doubt the work of Christ. In some form or other, accordingly, the Church still clings to a doctrine of baptismal grace.

In the communion the real fellowship of men with each other through Christ was enforced by the teaching as to His real presence with them. They felt that it was from Him that the true unity proceeded, and without Him the soul would lose its sense of the ideal completeness of that unity, and the future perfection to which it must attain. Under various forms the Church exhibited this truth; and at the Reformation the German and Swiss and English Reformers felt that it must be preserved. It is sometimes said that Zwingli did not hold this doctrine; but his writings testify to the contrary.[1] To lose this truth was to lose the great blessing of the sacrament; so the Church has held. On the other hand, the teaching of some branches of the Church, which regards the Eucharist as an efficacious sacrificial act,[2] was

[1] See his confession sent to King Francis I., quoted by Schaff.
[2] The simpler form of this doctrine, which represents it as a commemoration of the sacrifice of Christ, is an effort to realise that united worship and atmosphere of brotherly life which the individual reception, and still more the priestly reception, as in later times, put into the background. St. Chrysostom and St. Augustine teach this view, the latter with remarkable beauty. The whole city of God, the communion of saints, is the offering presented to God by our High Priest; and so the Church, commemorating the offering of Christ, presents itself as a sacrifice to God. So did St. Augustine, who, of all theologians, brings best before us the thought of the Eucharist as a communion, endeavour to strengthen our hold on the great reality of united mankind.

an addition to the Christian faith, which did not appear for some centuries, and departed from the meaning of the sacrament. It would not endure the spirit of inquiry which the Reformation brought, and accordingly was swept out of true Christian thought for ever after. Nothing illustrates more clearly the process of time in developing the ethical purpose of Christianity, than the history of Christian doctrine as to the sacraments. The true purpose becomes clearer with increasing light; all dogma that obscured that purpose falls away; and even the very form of celebration rises from individualism, as in the Roman, to collective worship, as in the Reformed Churches. Perhaps the ordinary Protestant view, that faith is necessary to the benefit of the sacrament, is a little narrowly interpreted by most people. Such a belief as brings men to the communion may not always be faith, as we understand it; but there must be some good come to the soul from the act of brotherly union. Imperfect, indeed, may be the conception of it, but there must be some unconscious groping after the truth, which cannot but lead to fuller enlightenment. It is a limited range of vision which shuts out men from the feast of communion with united humanity, because they do not fully realise the idea it enfolds. Who can shut them out from the great fact itself to which the history of man is ever advancing?

The Lutherans give the due prominence to the sacraments which their meaning requires. In the Churches which see little force in the sacraments, and which attach importance to pulpit instruction, there is a strong individualistic tendency, which in our age tends to weaken their testimony to the great fact of human brotherhood. They think too much of personal religion, and too little of the wider human fellowship which Christianity implies. Hence it is that as Churches they stand aloof from the modern altruistic movements; and their place is largely taken by those Churches which attach importance to the sacraments. A view of the Church which makes it a mere association for personal culture in religion, is false to the divine end it has before it. The Unitarians, perhaps, hold the extreme form of this opinion; but many Protestant Churches, such as the Congregationalists and Presbyterians, also tend in the same direction.

The sacraments are the external representation of the great fact of human unity. Faith in that fact may exist and grow to completeness without the outward form; as we see in the Quakers, whose intense effort to realise the spiritual unity in some cases is rewarded by a vision of that unity. But life cannot be carried on through thought alone; it must figure itself in action. Love which has no symbols of affection may live in the sublimer hearts of mankind; but ordinary mortals cling to its expression in tender caresses, without which, they fear, it would die. Union which is only felt in the heart, without being strengthened by some sign that men can see, some seal that impresses it on the soul, is apt to lose reality.

As I have said, the more recent Lutheran theologians seem to have before them the true thought as to the brotherly idea of the sacrament, and its importance in the life of the Church. It is really the best ordinary means of bringing men to realise their brotherhood, and keeping them in it. The teaching of Delitzsch and Kliefoth,[1] especially the latter, is of great value in enforcing this practical truth.

The Anglican theories, though in many ways valuable, have less coherence, as they are not a natural development, and have an individualist character which makes the sacrament little but a kind of commentary or appendix to preaching. The Church of England seems partly to have forgotten the truth, which Schleiermacher, who was in one sense the prophet of individualism, taught with such clearness, that Christianity is a *social* religion. Hence some English theologians, and also Bishop Martensen, seem to have departed from the essential doctrine of the sacraments, which declares that in them the whole body of the Church acts, and not a priestly order. We find that Justin Martyr, in his *Apology*, regards the congregation as a whole as the acting priests in the Eucharist, and not any special officers of the congregation. The same view is confirmed by Tertullian and St. Augustine; and no other opinion can be made to correspond with the true idea of the sacrament as the symbol and seal of brotherhood. All must move their souls by the same feeling of love, and must unite in giving as well as receiving the sacrament.

It is a crude theological arrangement which we find in the Augsburg Confession and the Westminster Confession, which classifies the sacraments as means of grace. Why, the whole of our life, with all its changes and chances, is a

[1] See an admirable summary in Lichtenberger's *Theology of the Nineteenth Century*, Clark's edition.

means of grace. To view the sacraments as one of the means of grace, along with other spiritual exercises, is to remove them from the central position. Secular writers, like Goethe, have recognised more fully their true place than many theologians. The sacrament of the Communion is the visible expression of the sum and end of the Christian faith, and occupies a distinctive position, therefore, in the Christian life, which is not satisfied by ranging it alongside preaching as one of the means of grace. It is this blindness which has made our Christianity so individual, which has exposed it to the taunts, not undeserved, of being a selfish effort to "make the best of both worlds" for our personality, and of turning the sublime altruism which Jesus taught us by His life and death into a glorified egoism. The sacraments have in their outward presentation a grand testimony to the truth that the salvation of God is for the whole of humanity as a regenerated brotherhood. Are all the great promises of the general blessing of mankind, which Christ and His apostles gave us, to be reduced to one narrow thought of an individual safety? What becomes of the sayings of Jesus Himself, such as that which St. John tells us of, that He would draw all men unto Him? What did St. Paul mean when he said, "the free gift came upon all men," "that God might have mercy upon all," that "in Christ all might be made alive"? This is not the place to discuss the subtleties of the "restitution" theory of many devout hearts from Origen to Bengel and Schleiermacher, for it passes into that region of speculation which we must carefully guard from influencing our practical religion;

and besides, as Rothe has convincingly pointed out, injures the whole ethical side of Christianity, by dealing a deadly blow at the free receiving of it by the souls of men. But a more generous form of saving faith is found in the New Testament than that which occupies itself as John Bunyan's Pilgrim did, with a solitary effort to "flee from the wrath to come." That faith is permanently held before the vision of mankind in the great sacrament of love and brotherhood.

CHAPTER XIV

ENTRANCE INTO THE LIFE OF BROTHERHOOD, AND PROGRESS THEREIN

THE heart which trusts the words of Jesus must believe that its sins are forgiven. There can be no other beginning in the life of a son than to believe in the Father's love. It is perhaps hard to realise that God could forgive sins so great as they sometimes appear to our consciousness. But to doubt the love of God is to doubt His Fatherhood. We may count it impossible for human beings to "believe and tremble"; for if our hearts are filled with terror at the knowledge that there is a God above us, we are really sceptics as to His being, which is love. It is not our faith which makes us sons, for we are sons however far we wander from God; but our faith helps us to see that we are children of the Father of love. This knowledge sometimes comes on us like a flash, though we may have been long toiling after it. It comes at last, as all God's best gifts fall on us, like the joy of the dawn, without our effort, or even our prayer. How true was the old doctrine of God's grace as it appeared to St. Augustine and his followers since; and how close it follows the analogy of all our divine Father's dealings with men. We are borne out of the mist of self, with its shadow of sacrifices offered in fear, into the ampler ether of the adoption of sons.

The state of mind that goes before the recognition of this truth is often a heavy burden to the soul. We feel our entire isolation, and our hearts are dark. Never were the thoughts of the darkness of such an hour better given voice to than by Richter, who, if he speaks more in the language of our modern scientific days than of the earlier ages, yet expresses the universal feeling of mankind: " As he saw the grinding press of worlds . . . he raised his eyes to the void Immensity, and said . . . How is each so solitary in the wide grave of the All! I am alone with myself! O Father, O Father, where is Thy infinite bosom, that I might rest on it! Ah! if each soul is its own father and creator, why cannot it be its own destroyer too?"

When such thoughts cast their shadow over us, and no light appears, we cry, as we loathe our lonely selfhood, which chills us as if we were bound to a corpse: "*O wretched man that I am, who will deliver me from this body of death?*"

But this sense of sin, this morbid distrust of the divine Fatherhood, is a disease of the soul. It is a malaria born of the marshy land of selfish life. The Reformers, when they proclaimed the great truth of justification by faith, taught us that we must not spend our days in self-contemplation, and raking up the sins of the past. All is forgiven, and now let us *forget those things which are behind, and reach forth to those things which are before.* When the seeker after God offered sacrifice to Him, he was ignorant of His fatherly love.

Men in past times dreaded God as an unknown power, whose anger might be death to His creature; and with no higher thought than fear of the might of God, and desire to appease Him, they deluged their altars with blood.

The Aryan view of the divine Being, which sprung from their scientific inquiry as to the origin of things, and naturally impressed the devout thinker with a sense of mysterious power; and the Semitic, which regarded Him chiefly as the Holy One, equally gave birth to this awful view of the divine character. In the Vedas we can read the awestruck heart in the words of the prayer: "Let me not yet, Varuna, enter into the house of clay: have mercy, Almighty, have mercy! If I go trembling like a cloud driven before the wind, have mercy, Almighty, have mercy!" The gradual growth of the knowledge that God was the divine Father turned the hearts of the Jews from their old thoughts, which regarded Him as an angry Being who desired sacrifices. The words of Samuel give a glimpse of the idea of filial duty as a better attitude than that of the wish to propitiate a dread Power. "To obey is better than sacrifice; and to hearken, than the fat of rams." And David, in the depth of his remorse for sin, has a ray of hope even from his imperfect apprehension of the true nature of God's fatherly love. "The sacrifices of God are a broken spirit; a broken and a contrite heart Thou wilt not despise." While, still later, we see how Micah arrived at the gate of light after the long darkness of the human soul. "Shall I come before the Lord with burnt-offerings? Shall I give my firstborn for my transgression, the fruit of my body for the sin of my soul? He hath showed thee, O man, what is good: and what doth the Lord require of thee, but to do justly, and to love mercy, and to walk humbly with thy God?" And after the Captivity still more did the Jews realise the true nature of God, and man's relations to Him. We read in the Second Isaiah that there were no sacrifices offered;[1] and in the Song of the Three Children, that "there was at that time neither burnt-offering, nor sacrifice, nor oblation, nor incense, nor place to sacrifice."[2]

The thought of men upon this change has turned on the contrast between ceremonial and spiritual worship; but the advance in religious life did not really take that form. Dean Stanley is especially ready to mark the distinction between priest and prophet, and apparently the progress from the one to the other; but in this his position is not historically justified. It was not because the worship was less ceremonial, for their circumstances in a foreign land might account for that; but because it disclosed a new thought of God as the Father who rejoiced to receive His children, and from whose love no sin of theirs could cut them off. It is not till we come to the Second Isaiah, to Malachi, and to the Psalms written after the Exile, that we find recognition of God as our Father.[3] This entered into Jewish thought, though they grasped it but feebly, and prepared the way for the sublime statement of the truth in the teaching and life of Jesus.

The first step in the new life is to realise that we are

[1] Isa. xliii. 23.   [2] Vers. 14, 15.
[3] Isa. lxiii. 16, lxiv. 8; Mal. ii. 10; Ps. lxxxix., ciii.

the children of God, and therefore bound by essential ties of duty and affection toward all his family. What a caricature of true religion is the popular view, that our efforts are to be given to save *our own* soul. The conscious desire for personal salvation often keeps men long out of the knowledge of God's love, and their own sonship. We have but to realise that God is a Father, and we at once are certain that no sins of ours can keep His love from us. Once the heart knows God's divine Fatherhood, we come to the belief that all children have, that the parental affection cannot be lost by wrong-doing. To trust this infinite love makes us tender, forgiving to others, and eager to serve them.

The history of all those who have come to know God as their Father follows the same general course. St. Paul teaches that *the love of God is shed abroad in our hearts by the Holy Ghost*; and St. John assures us that *we love Him because He first loved us*. St. Cyprian[1] tells us that "no bound or measure can be assigned in the reception of divine gifts, as is the case with earthly benefits." St. Hilary of Poitiers says: "Since the Son of God became man, men may become the sons of God. A man who with gladness receives this doctrine, renews his spirit by faith, and conceives a hope full of immortality. Having once learned to believe, he rejects the captious difficulties, and no longer judges after the maxims of the world."[2] St. Augustine came to see, through the study of some of the Platonists, that everything that came from God was good, and that universal nature was justly called on to bless God for His goodness. "Too late did I love

[1] *Epistle to Donatus*   [2] *De Trinitate.*

Thee, Thou primeval Beauty. Thou didst call aloud and overcome my deafness; Thou didst shine and dispel my darkness." "I am a little child, but my Father always lives."[1] St. Bernard says: "One man confesses to God because He is mighty; another, because He is kind to him who confesses; a third, because God is good, and for naught else. The first is a slave, and fears for himself; the second is mercenary, and seeks only his own advantage; the third is a son, and acts dutifully to a Father."[2]

The road to the new life is not through examining one's own heart, but by seeking after God as Jesus reveals Him. Truly does He say that He is the way. The discovery of the divine Fatherhood is the entrance to a new state of being. As Luther says: " To such a Father, who overwhelms me with His inestimable loving-kindness, must I not liberally, cheerfully, and with my whole heart, do everything which I shall know to be pleasing in His sight?"[3]

It is to be remembered that St. John, who of the evangelists gives us most light on the beginning of the true life, speaks of the new birth, as we have done, chiefly, if not solely, with reference to the future. It is a new impulse which leads a man onward to life. We have simply entered on the way, but all the journey is before us. It is not without good reason that Wordsworth, in his "Ode on the Intimation of Immortality from Recollections of early Childhood," regards the child as conscious of certain truths which fade away with man-

---

[1] *Confessions*, x. [2] Epistle 11.
[3] Luther, "Of the Freedom of a Christian Man."

hood. It is only by effort that we regain that sense of sonship which is natural to us as children. The knowledge that God is our Father is indeed latent in our souls, and may rarely take any form except the love of our earthly father, who stands as the type of the divine and perfect Fatherhood; but the spiritual attitude of the child's nature is a necessity of the human soul. As Jesus said: "*Except ye be converted, and become as little children, ye shall not enter the kingdom of heaven.*"

To become a member of the human brotherhood, or rather to realise our membership since we already belong to it, as St. Bernard says, "God's gifts in creation and redemption are the common heritage of all men," we must first know that we have a common Father, and have our heart filled with love to Him. When this entrance into the life of brotherhood is made, we are prepared to go forward, our heart ever expanding toward the fulness of love to all men which God has, and which we are to strive after. The sacrament of baptism has been given as the outward type of this new life. The rite is symbolical of the forgiveness of sins which is already given to the world, and only needs to be received by the devout heart. It does not make men God's children, but simply declares that they are. Hence it is a form which the Church should never dispense with, lest mankind lose the truth which it is appointed to teach.

Nothing can be more true to the root-idea of the Christian faith, to the real position of men to God, than to baptize children. It brings them into surroundings where they will grow into a deeper knowledge of the love and brotherhood which are the highest manifestations of man's inner and outer life. But it must not be forgotten and laid aside as a mere memory of childhood: it must be kept before the mind as an acknowledgment of the birthright of men as sons of God. St. Augustine lamented that he had not been baptized when a child: he would have known God sooner than he did, if his parents had brought him to his heavenly Father.

Perhaps it is the surest foundation for a permanent life of brotherhood, that one should be early taught to know one's true relation to men and God. There is no essential difference between the sudden enlightenment of the soul which St. Paul experienced, and the gradual growth of a pure spirit from childhood, for both are entrances into the filial feeling. But when the nature is gently trained into true sympathy, its actions are sweeter and more uniformly fraternal. The gusts of selfishness that rush over the hearts of men, who have had a great change come on them like a lightning flash, sometimes extinguish the lamp of love which has begun to shine within them. Plato desired his young people to have truth infused into them by association, till they had their being attuned to its harmony. And so too would St. Augustine desire for all that they be early brought into the "citadel of faith," that they may be strengthened before they have to fight, and taught goodness before they learn evil. If we have "a golden gift from God" within us in our filial love as children, let us not lightly esteem it. Above all, let us not begin to doubt our sonship, and torture our souls as too many young people do, with the doubt whether they are "converted." The teaching of Aristotle, that we must search for truth through doubts, is common enough in religion; but it is seldom the way to peace. Do not make children sceptics in their youth; remember the Saviour's teaching: "Whoso shall offend one of these little ones that believe in Me, it were better for him that a millstone were hanged about his neck, and that he were drowned in the depth of the sea."

Our children have a part in the organic life of the family and of the community which shapes their soul towards the true faith. The spiritual life of the parents is communicated to the child in a thousand other ways than direct instruction. The mysterious links which bind soul to soul are not fully known to us; but we can see the results of their action, and so strong a force one must not pass by.[1]

The life of Christ is in this, as in all other respects, an example; and happy are they who increase in wisdom with their stature, and in favour with God and man. The narrowness which we deplore in St. Augustine, and the fierceness of Loyola, are reversions to that selfish heedlessness of others out of which they awoke to the love of God and men, and some such weakness accompanies all such violent experiences. A popular religion which

[1] "So glued is our mental habit to the impression that religious character is wholly the result of choice in the individual, or, if generated by a divine ictus, preceded by absolute necessity by convictions and struggles, that we cannot comprehend that a child should be prepared for God by causes prior to his own will" (Bushnell, *Argument for Discourses on Christian Nurture*, p. 39). "A godly education is God's first and ordinary appointed means for the begetting of actual faith" (Baxter, *Christian Directory*). "Family education and order are some of the chief means of grace" (Jonathan Edwards).

demands such from all men, cannot but result in an increase of selfish forms of religious thought, and is a real danger to the progress of true, and generous, and self-sacrificing brotherhood.

Once that the soul has grasped the truth of its sonship, its path is ever onward. We recognise that other men are also sons, however they may be, like ourselves, unworthy of the divine and Fatherly love. By loving and serving them, we enter into a purer thought of our kinship to them, and become more worthy children of our divine Father. Forgiving, and loving, and working for men, whoever they be, we are like our Father, who maketh *His sun to rise on the evil and the good, and sendeth rain on the just and on the unjust*, and we slowly approach the divine ideal: " Be ye perfect, as your Father in heaven is perfect."

The way of holiness is by work; but that work is perverted from its purpose if it be done with conscious purpose of purity. It must be done from love of mankind. St. Paul says: "Work out your own salvation." Develop in your soul a growing principle of loving altruism, not for the sake of having a loving soul, but to benefit mankind and promote the human brotherhood. You must not work for your own sake, but for others.

This is the essence of sanctification.[1] It must not be pursued in a selfish spirit, for the reward of purity, for it cannot be so reached. Every good action will only add more to the selfish corruption of the heart. Herein is the fatal error of justification by works. To

---

[1] The word ἁγιασμός means a consecration to *service*.

serve God or men for personal reward or benefit, is to take all the value from the service; for the real object is to serve self all the while. Here is the evil of asceticism. For what do we deny ourselves? That we may serve others? Such a thought is far from the heart of the ascetic: he dreams only of himself, and some distant reward. Whether the work be in Christian lands or in Thibet or India, the motive is the same, individualism; and unworthy a man, born to serve men. Nay, each successive act begets a self-satisfaction which is the foe of real goodness. The rapture of the pictures of the solitary saints expresses the congratulations of self, not the joy of service or of God. When Thorwaldsen was advanced in life, he doubted his skill was gone; for, as he said, "Here is my statue of Christ: it is the first of my works that I have ever felt satisfied with. Till now my idea has always been far beyond what I could execute. But it is no longer so. I shall never have a great idea again." The calm which breathes from the features of these saintly pictures is a sign that the onward movement of the soul has ceased. It is a quiet pool of self, not a stream flowing on to God through the service of man.

The only way to holiness is to serve others: to slay self day by day, as St. Paul told us to do.

Every kind act that we do is a purifying of our soul. We have rid ourselves by it of some little part of our burden of self. Nor think that the burden of self is a mere figure which carries no deep meaning with it; for if the end of our being is a union with man and God, all that keeps from that union must be like a weight on our soul, and make our forward steps heavy. What is the beginning of the new life in our practical conduct? We know it is love in our hearts; but we are also assured by Christ and His apostles,[1] that the sign of it in our lives is the ceasing to live to self and to seek our own joys and interests; and to strive to live for others. It is the beginning, the middle, and the end of the true life. Through it we make constant progress; but our progress has no higher purpose than to continue in the unselfish life. Many are the sides from which this progress may be viewed. It is doubt of God which keeps us outside His great purpose of union among men. We cherish our little life as if it were our all, not knowing how rich it becomes when we live for others. Faith in God and man leads us out of our isolation, and we yield ourselves to the great stream of destiny, trusting that God will bring us to richer fields of being than we dream of now.

Man is an imperfect creature: he is only the possibility of something higher and nobler, to which he ever tends, if in the true line of the divine purpose. All sin comes from the will turning aside from that purpose. The soul in its darkness loses sight of the divine end, and seeks some near object which seems to "show good." To know and work to the divine future of brotherhood defends the soul against those temptations of the way, and every kind act gives a

[1] St. Luke xiv. 26; St. John xii. 25; Rom. xiv. 7, 8; Gal. ii. 20; Phil. ii. 3, etc.

glimpse of the celestial city of universal love. How brightly illumined the heart becomes with the radiance of its own unselfish desires. Evil is a privation of good, and has no real existence in itself. The whole universe is an expression of the will of God, and more and more tends to realise that will. Evil is a stay of the process, in which man tries a path of his own to his own loss.[1] Or it may be that he merely refuses to go on, while the river of divine destiny flows past him. As Fichte said, the sinfulness of man proceeds from "an inherent inertia or indolence of human nature."

With what energy St. Paul entreats us to work out our own salvation: it is high time, he says, to awake out of sleep. As Goethe says in the second part of *Faust*—

"Whoe'er aspires unweariedly
Is not beyond redeeming."

It is effort which cleanses our soul: as work cleanses and strengthens the outer man, and the healthful perspiration removes the impurities of our body; so to strive for others gives an ever-renewing sanctification. We are in the divine Spirit when so we work, and so long as we yield ourselves to His influence we shall not slack our energies.

Some thinkers[2] have told us that our very independent existence, implying as it does a departure

---

[1] The student of philosophy will recognise in the above statements the thought of St. Augustine in his anti-Manichæan works, and Leibnitz in his *Theodicée*.

[2] In its extreme form this theory is found in Blasche's *Evil in Harmony with Natural Law*.

from unity, is a condition from which we should strive to rise out of. To be born is in itself a fall, and our life is to be given to restore ourselves to that unity we thus have lost. The original sin is to have an individual life at all, and we must, day by day, have it purged by our endeavours. This we are assured is the thought of Buddhism, and it is essentially a shadow of the truth. To enter on the new birth is to know that we have our Father's will to realise in the unity of men through love; and to that purpose we must offer the sacrifice of self.

CHAPTER XV

THE CHRISTIAN PERSONALITY

WHEN Socrates said that no man is willingly wicked, he uttered a truth which goes to the root of human personality.[1] Man as an individual knows that he exists, and supposes that he has free will. His consciousness of existence and his free will make up his personality. But if his free will should turn out to be a mere supposition, what becomes of his personality?

We hear the voice of physical science telling us loudly, that as the world is a great chain of cause and effect, we are but links in the chain, and our thoughts, our desires, and our acts are as inevitable as the sunrise or the dew. Is it not true of many men that their lives are little better than this unthinking automatism?

> "Most men eddy about
> Here and there, eat and drink,
> Chatter and love and hate,
> Gather and squander, are raised
> Aloft, are hurled in the dust,
> Striving blindly, achieving
> Nothing; and then they die—

---

[1] Plato, in the *Gorgias*, puts this into the mouth of Socrates, whose opinion we know it was from Aristotle and Xenophon: his own matured view takes a different form.

> Perish, and no one asks
> Who or what they have been,
> More than he asks what waves,
> In the moonlit solitudes mild
> Of the midmost ocean, have swelled,
> Foamed for a moment, and gone."

"The average man," said Schopenhauer, "is engrossed in the vortex and turmoil of existence, to which he is bound hand and foot." It is hard, indeed, to realise that we are aught but the plaything of forces about us, and it is only after slow steps and long years that man reaches his personal consciousness.

When we turn to St. Paul, we find that he seems to agree with Socrates, for he says the evil he does is not done by himself, but sin that dwelleth in him. There is within us, he would seem to say, a blind force which leads whither we would not willingly go, like the Homeric Atè which Helen says caused her to be unfaithful.

Apparently we have here a recognition that man sinks part of his personality when he sins; that he is not really himself, but a mere manifestation of unintelligible powers. If we hold in any way, as many wise men have held, the bondage of the human will, we must assent to this view. For if man is bound, by what is he bound? Not surely by himself, for then would he make himself free. Then it must be by some external force, such as his inherited tendencies, or his life-surroundings. Or you may seek still further back, and image, as Julius Müller and many other thinkers have followed the Platonists in representing, some dark shadow of a life before the present which hangs like a pall over us.

It is a simpler way, however, to take the facts as we find them without any speculation. When a man comes to know God, he hates sin. He learns that God is his Father, and he would not grieve Him willingly. Sometimes the old unreflecting nature comes back, and his soul is in misery. Will he never outgrow the time when he was a mere child of the world, and subject to its commanding tide?

A man is not a real person until he knows God as his Father. Before that consciousness comes to him, he has only within him the possibility of being a person. He is a child, speaking as a child, understanding as a child, thinking as a child; but when the consciousness of God visits his soul, he becomes a man. A full and complete personality belongs only to the man renewed by the knowledge of God. It is with him as with the heir to a throne who knows not his royal birth: till the day it is told him, he is but a plain citizen, although all the time he was in reality a prince. Our being slumbers in its ignorance, and we only awake when we realise that we are sons of God: we become free, as Jesus tells us, by the truth.

Our awaking does not make us the sons of God, for we were born in His image; but as far as our birthright was concerned, we might as well not possess it while we are ignorant of it.

Personality, in a man, consists in knowing the relation his ego bears to the God in whom he lives. While we are children, the sense of individuality is only slowly acquired: it is long before we know that we are in any way self-conscious. Still, we are individuals, and separate existences, though we are not able to represent the fact to ourselves; and we are likewise related to God, though the God-consciousness is dormant within us.

The only glimpses of the moral ideal which men have are through the consciousness of their sonship to God. Imperfectly, indeed, they may possess it, but it always bears the fruit of good living to the honour and praise of His name. In no man is this consciousness always present, for we fit our hearts day by day for the dwelling of the divine Spirit. The good men of heathen times, as St. Paul tells us, were similarly guided, though perhaps their personality was more intermittent and their fruits less regularly harvested.

It is commonly said that Christianity first taught men the value of the individual life. The world learned that infinity was wrapped up in a single soul from the intense passion for personal salvation which Christians showed. But it might be more truly said that it was the Christian religion that gave the power of personality to man.

The savage can hardly be called a free agent; he is so much the creature of his surroundings. He is so mobile, so easily affected, that he cannot be said to bring motives into the province of reason at all. The civilised child is a being possessing far more government of the will than the ordinary savage, who seems to yield to outside influences like a tree or the wild animals. From what paroxysms of sorrow the savage passes in a moment to joy as wild! A few beads, a child's trumpet, some scarlet cloth, will affect him to rapturous tears. Nor has he to any extent the power of voluntary association: he acts with uncontrolled impulse, which seems communicated from mind to mind, in a mob, whose passion subsides like the wind, as rapidly as it rose. Our lower classes in great cities have many features that resemble these traits of savage life, for their personality is to some extent in like manner undeveloped; and they are

> "A pipe for Fortune's finger,
> To sound what stop she please."

The full consciousness of personality comes to the savage and the uneducated from his knowing that he is the child of God, that he has an individual soul which is dear to his Father. It is an essential preliminary of the life of brotherhood that the sense of the personality should be aroused. The Christian must feel that he is not a slave, a mere "living tool" of the world and man, but a son, with power of individual action to love, and help, and work for others. As Jesus said to His disciples: "Henceforth I call you not servants."

We awake to the consciousness of self, but not to dwell in proud independence. Freedom is the essential condition of all duty, which does not rise to moral height if the doer is not free to perform it. But the freedom we possess simply to resign it: free from all, we, like the apostles, make ourselves servant to all. As Christ told us: "Whosoever will be chief, let him be a servant." As in *Measure for Measure* we read that the Provost said to the Duke: "I am your free dependent." We are dependent on each other, but none the less free. The essence of love is, that the heart cannot be compelled into it; and it is in love to God that the soul awakes to its consciousness of real existence.

The common possession of this God-consciousness by those who meet each other, leads to an instant sympathy: "Whoever doeth the will of My Father which is in heaven, the same is My brother, and sister, and mother." The walls in which we fortify our personality are broken down, and we are admitted into the common life of the brotherhood of man.

It has been said that this sympathy leads to an assimilation. Husband and wife who live long together become like each other in thought and feature; and men trace a remarkable resemblance between those who live in communities, such as Moravians, Shakers, and monks. Furthermore, the union in industries which is so common in our time, coupled, doubtless, with the struggle for existence, which tends to make people shun any distinguishing peculiarity if they wish to pass their life in tranquillity, as the ermine turns white in the winter snows, brings about a monotony of character and feature in our large cities and in our modern life. These things point to the gradual growth of a family resemblance among men, specially in the thoughts of the soul.

Since filial love is the main feeling of the Christian, it is possessed by all, and has the same kind of influence in every life, though it differs in degree. It must therefore tend to make all the brothers of the great family of man resemble each other. Here we are brought in sight of a closer unity than has hitherto marked the human race. We arrive at personality, simply to surrender our independence by constant service of each other.

Accordingly, though this personality of ours is a gain of our new life, we need not think that it exhausts the fulness of that life. The naturalistic ethics is inclined to find in personality the complete consummation of our moral life. Mr. T. H. Green asks: "If society is the condition of all development of our personality, and if the necessities of social life, as alone we can know or conceive it, put limits to our personal development, can we suppose it to be in persons that the spirit operative in men finds its full expression and realisation?"[1]

Let us look at the question before we hear Mr. Green's answer. It is in the service of men, whom the child of God knows as his brethren, that he finds the purification of his soul from self; and it is by that service he unites himself to men. The bond of union is love given and received, and that love unites him to God. In this sacrifice of self he comes to his true personality; and what need is there for any limitation to the sacrifice, if, by the complete yielding of the individual soul, the great purpose of the perfect unity of man is assured? "No man liveth unto himself."

Mr. Green says: "The spiritual progress of mankind is an unmeaning phrase, unless it means a progress of personal character and to personal character. It is simply unintelligible, unless understood to be in the direction of more perfect forms of personal life."[2] We must accept this as evident, under the present condition of humanity. As we live now, and as we are likely to live on the earth, there does not seem any other form of the ideal of mankind within our thought. All men are steadily to advance by the spreading of the virtues of the good among those who are less good. Men are to share their

[1] *Prolegomena to Ethics*, p. 192.   [2] *Ibid.* p. 195.

moral riches with their fellows, as they now see it their duty more and more to share their actual possessions with the needy. The divine ideal of mankind becomes realised by the spread of the consciousness of brotherhood among men, leading both from and to that of the Fatherhood of God.

But is this all? Is the soul of man satisfied; and are the hopes and promises of revelation exhausted with this? It is a glorious consummation, a city of God, from whose gateway we are yet far; but God has yet greater riches in store for mankind, as the writer we have quoted himself hopes.

When St. John said, "Beloved, now are we the sons of God: and it doth not yet appear what we shall be: but we know that, when He shall appear, we shall be like Him; for we shall see Him as He is," he looked forward to a closer union of mankind in God than we can conceive. When St. Paul said, "It is no longer I that live, but Christ that liveth in me," he had a foretaste of a more perfect love and communion than often dawns upon our selfish hearts. He does not cling frantically to the poor possession of personal individuality we have here, but seems to see himself merged in a glorious and unspeakable unity. This sublime thought is beyond our feeble grasp; but there are moments when reflections of its radiance illumine our earthly life, to prepare us for the great and unknown future.

CHAPTER XVI

BROTHERHOOD IN THE EARLY CHURCH

THE law of brotherhood, which was the idea of the Church, had little to check its operations in primitive times. The Church had a free course to develop itself, independent of any outside influence, for its numbers were small and its disciples obscure. But the early Christians were, by the nature of their surroundings, driven to form a society which, like that of the Jews in modern times, was a kind of close corporation. The persecutions which they had to face, and which were practically universal throughout the world they dwelt in, for it was all under the Roman dominion, supplied them with motive sufficient for retiring from the public view and forming a fellowship apart. No other practical solution was possible to them at the time; but whether their method agreed with the teaching of Jesus, is doubtful. Christ prayed for His disciples, not that they should be taken out of the world, but that they might be kept from the evil.[1] And their seclusion bore unkindly fruit; for the narrow idea of the Church, which was fostered by the circumstances of the primitive Christians, at last

[1] Tertullian contrasts Christians with the solitaries of India, for, he says, the Christians mix with the world.

developed into the excesses of monasticism. But the monastic life could not be carried out in its completeness among creatures who were human and not angelic; and there was a parallel movement which more closely represented the idea of the Church and its operations as seen in the Scriptures. The Church was content to ask from most men but a nominal adherence to its creed, trusting to the educative influence of the great principles on which it was founded to develop a higher type of life.

The apostles held a wider view of the Church. The vision which St. Peter saw when called to go to Cornelius, enlarged his heart as well as his intelligence. The idea of the Church which he seems to have had before this vision was that of a Jewish society, linked together by mutual love and remembrance of Jesus. He does not even seem to have been conscious of claims of outside people on his services, far less his love and brotherhood. The fact is that the doctrine of universal brotherhood was the crucial question at the outset of Christianity. If it was to be an exclusive fellowship of Jews, its great purpose would be unfulfilled. Cornelius was in reality already a member of the Church, though he had not received any seal of such membership. And, indeed, the question arises as to the essential character of such a seal; but we must not digress to consider it. Similarly, too, when St. Paul met the disciples of St. John the Baptist, who were ignorant of anything but what they had received from him, he did not hesitate to commune with them as of the true fellowship. It is hard to see where a line can be drawn between those men of imperfect knowledge and the purest of the heathen of the times of the apostles. The early apologists were in the right path when they traced the resemblances between the best thought and life of the philosophic paganism and the Christian faith. It was due to such efforts, however imperfect their conception of the true nature of the connection was, that ecclesiastical Christianity took up its universal position. The apostle speaks in his Epistle to the Ephesians of the whole family in heaven and earth. Whom did he think of when he wrote these words? Is there any reason to suppose that he had no wider vision than of the professing Church? Did the apostle, who had so just a view of the ethical position of the natural man who was "a law unto himself," who gave so tolerant a description of the "times of ignorance," hedge in *the family* by any barriers of ecclesiasticism? He who came, not to baptize, but to preach the gospel, was unlikely to take a restricted view of the fellowship of men.

For, after all, the family of men must mean the whole of humanity, to whom Christ united Himself, and of whom He was the Head. It was doubtless this exclusiveness of the early Church which kept it hid from the observation of the poets, historians, and philosophers who lived at the time, and whose writings have been preserved to us. There remain but few notices of the first days of Christianity from the heathen writers who saw its early growth. The persecutions which it endured are the chief occasion for mentioning it; otherwise its very existence would have been unrecorded by the great moral historian of antiquity — Tacitus. The only passage in which Marcus Aurelius refers to the Christians is where he stigmatises them as willing to die from mere obstinacy, evidently regarding them as a kind of insensate barbarians.[1] Epictetus knows as little about them, and seems to have only in view the more fanatical members of the Church, who, he says, are free from fear of death "through habit."[2] The younger Pliny is one of the most attractive characters of ancient times; his letters show him an earnest seeker after wisdom, and a kind-hearted and tolerant man;[3] yet his examination of Christianity could only bring him to the conclusion that it was an "extraordinary and extravagant superstition," as he styles it in his famous letter to Trajan.[4] In the writings of Plutarch there is no reference, favourable or unfavourable, to Christianity; while Lucian merely speaks of Christians with a kind of pity, as simple people whom knaves imposed on;[5] and Celsus, whom Origen confuted, seems to have regarded it as a secret society.

This silence or slighting statement about Christianity is an evidence of the seclusion in which the faithful lived. The fact that all kinds of dark deeds were laid to their charge as taking place in their secret assemblies, is only one sign of the retirement in which they passed their lives. Probably no other method was possible for them: the temper of the times was violent against them; but one seems to see a wider door which might have opened for the mission of the early faith, if its claims had been duly considered by the nobler and better spirits of the time.

---

[1] xi. 3.   [2] iv. 7.
[3] See his description of Euphrates (i. 10), and his view of the equal treatment of freedmen.
[4] x. 98.   [5] *De Morte Peregrini*.

The beginnings of this spirit of exclusiveness are seen in the Gospel of St. John, which has a more ecclesiastical character than the Synoptists. When we remember when it was written, we cannot wonder at this feature. The Church had lost its original simple unity, and the disciples were scattered far and wide. Thrown in on themselves, on their inner life, and such little fellowship as they had with kindred believers, they dwelt on those phases of Christ's teaching which fostered this individual faith.

In the Synoptists, the love which men are to show is not confined to the brethren, as in St. John, for the idea of a limited brotherhood had not appeared. The kernel of the teaching of Jesus in the Sermon on the Mount is that divine obligation of forgiveness and love to all men, whatever they are in character, even though they are enemies to God and man. God Himself shows this forgiving love, and we must *be perfect, as our Father in heaven is perfect*. St. John does not give us this teaching; but shows us Jesus enjoining over and over again the love of *the brethren*. He loves to recollect that Jesus spoke about laying down His life for His *friends*. This narrowing of the scope of the universal Love is born of the age when the Gospel appeared.

We find St. John representing Jesus as at first having an inner circle of friends, to whom He told His great mission before He spread it abroad to the whole people. In the other Gospels, the message of Jesus is at once proclaimed openly. He suddenly flashes on the horizon of Capernaum, where He was unknown. In all this we may see the jealousy of the disciple, who could not bear to see His Master's love lightly considered. Should He squander a treasure on those who loved Him not? Since our possession is so infinitely precious, let us guard it carefully. Such must have been the thought of the disciples in these early and dangerous times, and St. John gave voice to it.

Take also the central thought of St. John's Gospel and place it beside that of the Synoptists. They speak of the kingdom of heaven as the object of the mission of Jesus to men, and see in it a mighty influence which shall regenerate all mankind, because it includes all the activities of humanity within its scope. To this St. John makes few references: his idea of the coming of Jesus is the eternal life which is given to the individual believer. To St. John the salvation is an individual blessing: to the Synoptists, a general restoration of all men. Such teaching as that of St. John's Gospel must have been a welcome influence in an age whose thought it so fully embodied, and it confirmed the early Christians in their isolation.

Doubtless we have glorious beams of the universal Love shining in the page of St. John, where we read that Christ takes away the sin of the world. And is there another view of the purpose of God shown when the blessing is only given to *those who believe*, in the conversation with Nicodemus?[1] Where else do we see so clearly the Light of the world revealed to men, that Light which lighteth every man which cometh into the world? Or where do we breathe more fully the free

[1] What is the meaning of belief? Much depends on the answer to such a question.

air of the universal Spirit than in the words to the woman of Samaria: "God is a Spirit, and they that worship Him must worship Him in spirit and in truth." The difference does not lie in any narrowing of the divine thoughts, but in their application to men: while the other evangelists think of a union of humanity, St. John dwells on the union with God.

He is the father of all the mystics, who have always been the disbelievers in a wide, social religion. Their intense affection shrinks from the rude touch of the outer world, and the light which should be seen of men is hidden away in some lonely cell. St. John's early religious impressions were coloured by this mystic or ascetic element. He was a pupil of the Baptist, who seems to have a relation to the Essenes, and he was in later life a diligent student of Philo. Personally, he seems to have had a larger view of truth than many of his followers took, for he loves to record the sayings of Jesus on the need of work, which they ignored. But the selective tendency of men to choose in divine teaching what is most in accord with their outer life let these things pass unheeded, and fixed its grasp on the individualism of the Gospel. Unnoticed were the great cosmical ideas in which St. John, like St. Paul, delighted to absorb his thought, for the depth of these was bewildering to the Christian mind. But personal affection, close union to the Master, a love and communion which were eternal,—these they could feel; and these made the sum of their religion. The brotherhood of man became restricted to the brotherhood of the faithful; and the little flock were more and more inclined to keep themselves apart from the world, forgetting the prayer of Jesus : " I pray not that Thou shouldest take them out of the world, but that Thou shouldest keep them from the evil."

The candid student of Church history will bring no reproach on the early Christians for their isolation from the world. How could they do otherwise amid hostile forces so great? Their war was not alone with heathenism outside in forms of State intolerance, but with foes among themselves, which threatened the very existence of their religion, not to speak of its purity. Entrusted as they had been with a sacred deposit for mankind, they felt that they must hand down, unstained and undiminished, to future generations, the heritage of knowledge. Watch must be kept on the speech, nay, on the hearts of each one, lest they should lose a drop of the water of life. A few pilgrims on a perilous journey, their only hope for future generations was that they should keep together, and thus by joint effort preserve the faith from corruption. Such was their thought, and such their action ; and we cannot say it was not wise.

It was a necessary part in the development of the Church that she should become a reality before she tried to leaven the world ; and, though our impatient hearts would have had the Church leave her seclusion, to come forth too soon, and try to blend with the world, would have sapped her life and wrecked her future. She must abide awhile in her solitude ere she dwelt in the busy life of men.

In the providential guiding of the Church, this period

of her history was her sojourn in the wilderness, when, like Moses, she prepared herself for the great task of leading the world into freedom and brotherhood.

But the internal life of the Christians at this time was led in accordance with the principles of Christ, though the separation from the world was not in accord with His teaching. The very circumstances that kept them separate from the world bound them closer together. The community of goods which the disciples at Jerusalem established practically continued for many years, though it was rather a voluntary giving than a complete resignation of individual possession. Justin Martyr and Tertullian both declare that the Christians had all things in common, and in the Teaching of the Twelve Apostles we read: "Thou shalt not turn away from him that is in want, but shalt share all things with thy brother, nor claim them for thine own; for if you together share in the things that perish not, how much more in those that perish!" But though this existed as a motive to charity, it does not seem to have been an invariable or compulsory arrangement. The very case of Ananias and Sapphira, whom St. Peter asked, "Whiles it remained, was it not thine own; and after it was sold, was it not in thine own power?" proves that it was no religious obligation in any outward form, though the spirit was essential to true brotherhood. The claims of family life and circumstances were acknowledged, and the duty of the Church did not interfere with these. Accordingly, Clement of Alexandria considered "community of goods as contrary to the order of things appointed by God." By and by it came to be a tenet of heretics, such as the

Apostolici or Encratites, of whom St. Augustine[1] says: "They will not receive into their communion any who possessed private property. They considered those who did not follow the same practice as themselves to have no hope of salvation."

The evils which might have attended the custom may have led to its decline; but it is quite as likely that the change was caused by the diminution of the brotherly spirit. The first enthusiasm of discipleship passed away, and the Christians lost hold of the fundamental principle of their morals. The rise of Neo-Platonism, with its intense individualism, with its indifference to all social and civic duties, was the most powerful factor in the change. Still we find the purer minds looking back to the spring-time of the Church, and longing for its return. St. Chrysostom[2] saw how an actual presentation of the gospel of brotherhood, such as it showed, would win the attention of the surrounding heathen. The social anomalies of the time struck the early Church with greater force than they have done in any time since till our own age. The unequal division of the world's goods seemed to them due to some neglect of the true laws of life. Their political economy based itself on morals, and they thought the obligation to charity should prevent accumulation. St. Ambrose says that "all things are made by nature for common use; and if any is excluded from the enjoyment of the fruits of the earth, it is an unnatural state of things."[3] St. Augustine, with many professions that he only counsels and does not compel

---

[1] Aug. *De Hæres.* c. 40.   [2] Chrysostom, *Homil. in Act*
[3] *De Off. Minist.* i. 29.

advises men to give freely of their means. Speaking of rich and poor, he addresses the rich man: "God set you both one and the same journey, this present life; you have found that you are fellow-travellers in it, you are walking one way; he is carrying nothing with him, thou art carrying with thee more than thou dost need. Give him of that thou hast: so shalt thou at once feed him, and lessen thine own burden." [1]

St. Augustine gives here the true philosophy of life, as well as the reason of brotherly feelings and actions. The same journey lies before us; the same needs we feel: why should we not cheerfully recognise the fact? The early apologists lay their principal stress on the outward moral progress and brotherly union of Christians. The dogmas which in later ages took a chief place, are kept in the background, and the atonement and its mysteries are little spoken of. Justin Martyr points out how men have been brought to Christianity by observing the lives of Christians; and Tertullian says that the contrast between the selfish isolation of heathenism and the love of Christians, seemed extraordinary to the heathen. The kiss of peace, which was a part of their eucharistic worship, and which was one of the welcomes given to the baptized, was an index of the state of heart which prevailed. The community liberally provided for widows, orphans, and the poor; and had care of those in prison or slavery. And one Church helped another: it was sufficient that any should be in need, to have a claim on the charity of the faithful. Although hospitality and kindness were chiefly given to

[1] *Hom. in Mat.* 61.

those who professed themselves Christians, the claims of the outside world were not forgotten. During the plague at Carthage, when the pagans left their dead unburied, the Christians perceived the call of duty and removed the bodies. St. Cyprian reminded them of the sublime teaching of Jesus. " If we do good only to our own, we do no more than the publicans and heathen. But if we are the children of God, who makes His sun to rise, and sends His rain on the just and unjust, who scatters His blessings, not merely on His own, but even on those whose hearts are far from Him, we must show it by our actions, striving to be perfect, as our Father in heaven is perfect."

Many instances of generous self-denial are handed down to us from these times; of which as noble as any is that one man would go into slavery to redeem another, or to give food to those in want. But the whole spirit of the early Church was one of community and brotherhood. The principle supplied the motive power, and its applications were easy. As we have seen, there was no absolute call for a community of goods, which in the nature of things would be hard to maintain, so much do men's tastes and habits differ; but every man held his possessions in trust. It was an essential condition of true religion to free the soul from covetous pride of possession. Luxury and splendour were not necessarily forbidden, but no one must starve alongside of it all. And if they interfere with the true feeling of Christian fellowship, they must be given up. Clement of Alexandria points out that where the love of money is in the heart, it is that which must be rooted out, rather than the mere possession given up. The great law of brotherhood was paramount over all other considerations, and thus led to a true socialism.

The Christians were apt to be limited in their views, and to help only those who professed to be faithful. Lucian tells us they were often deceived by people who sought them merely for their gifts; and The Teaching of the Twelve Apostles gives a caution against the encouragement of such people. But it would be little heeded; for there is, to this day, no readier passport to the purse of the professing Christian than a talk of religion from the lips of the beggar, with its natural result in the increase of hypocrisy. This results from a narrowing of the sympathies: indigence is of no creed; the poor are always with us; and surely to relieve the hunger of an irreligious man is as natural an act as to help a professing Christian, if we are to act on the principle of the Sermon on the Mount? The career of Christianity was checked in its outward flow by this exclusive spirit. It may have been necessary, as we saw, for the Church to dwell in seclusion that she might purify her heart in the desert, and keep herself free from foreign elements. We see, indeed, how soon these alien influences entered into her life, destroying her idea of the absolute unity of the Church, without gaining that of the brotherhood of man.

Christianity lost sight of the identification of Christ with the human race, and held to some other view of His incarnation. Christ, when He came to earth, took our natural body and was kin to all mankind. The Church was not then formed, and this relation to men cannot be limited to His union with the Church. The Apostle Paul looked forward to an absolute unity, not of the Church alone, but of the whole human race. To him the progress of the Church was not the development of an ecclesiastical fellowship, but of a universal humanity, from which none were excluded. The unity of the faith was but a means to a great end, "till we come unto a perfect man." The universal redemption of mankind is one of the chief truths in the gospel; and the Church too soon lost its hold on this great principle of life. The universal Fatherhood of God and the universal brotherhood of man are of the essence of the teaching of Jesus. These truths were not fully received by the Church in any age, so as to be put in practice, and we are only marching forward to them now; but the essential elements of these principles were already in operation in the early Church, "cribbed, cabined, and confined," but still alive.

To the great practical principles of brotherhood the early Church was true. We have seen with what love they lived together, and what charity they bestowed. Nor did they think, as too many do, that such liberality excused a heart of selfishness, or a life given to unscrupulous gain. For usury was condemned by them as contrary to that law of Christ which said: "Give to him that asketh of thee; and from him that would borrow of thee turn not away." "And if ye lend to them of whom ye hope to receive, what thanks have ye? for sinners also do the same." The early Fathers followed in the steps of Christ, condemning all interest, in which they were followed by the English and German Reformers.

"It is a sin," said St. Augustine, "to take back more than the debt which is due."[1] "Interest is an unjust possession, which should be restored: even the law and the judges decree its restitution."[2] Similar passages may be found in Tertullian, St. Cyprian, St. Ambrose, St. Jerome, St. Chrysostom, and other Fathers. The thought which fills them all is that usury is a return to the law of an eye for an eye, which Jesus condemned; and contrary to that principle of Christianity which regards the possessions of each as held for the advantage of all. It is as an index to this feeling that it has weight, proving, as it does, that men could make their religion an everyday fact, not a mere occasional theory. Our modern economists have seen need to think of the question of interest, not on mere religious grounds, as Mr. Ruskin looks at it, but with regard to the social welfare, as Mr. F. W. Newman points out. The fearful oppression of the poor which it causes,[3] which St. Augustine described as massacring the poor man with its exactions, makes some kind of check on certain kinds of usurers advisable for the common good. The same regard for the general good of the commonwealth which early Christianity had from motives of love, has become necessary from motives of prudence.

We shall often find the traces of the evolution of the community towards the social ideal of Christianity, to which the world is steadily progressing. In this men may see one of the strongest proofs of its truly divine

---

[1] *Contra Faustum*, 19. 25.   [2] Epist. 54.
[3] The expulsion of the Jews from Russia was a revolutionary way of adjusting a great social wrong.

character, as unfolding to us that secret of the destiny of man which we strive to enter into through the long and upward path of philosophy. The almost hopeless dulness of soul which some men have, makes them think that whatever the letter of Scripture does not forbid is not contrary to God's law. On this ground interest has been defended, and, what is hardly to be believed, the institution of slavery. Dr. Hodge took up this incredible position; and his misunderstanding of this question of slavery is enough to disqualify him from being heard in any way as an expounder of Christianity. There are surely certain principles of life by which we relate ourselves to our fellow-men, without seeking absolute precepts; but can we find any common ground on which to meet such irreligious speculation? On these general principles of Christian morals we must settle the question of interest, of slavery, and all practical conduct. The early Church had no doubt on the matter of slavery. The extraordinary obliquity of commentators is seen in their treatment of St. Paul's entreaty to Philemon to treat Onesimus as a brother. This they regard as not implying emancipation. What marvellous bondage to legal forms! How can a man be a slave, if he is a brother? The very idea of slavery implies an unnatural relation utterly inconsistent with brotherhood, which extinguishes that idea for ever. St. Paul simply enjoined Philemon to take the "slave" and keep him in his house, showing to him all the brotherly love due to a fellow-man. If those who try to make the sources of Christianity clear to their readers thought more of the spirit and less of the letter, the Church would not lag behind its true purpose as it does. Time was when it led the van of every such liberal and loving deed. It was so in the early Christian days; when man strove to put in action the true life of equal brotherhood, which is taught by Christ. A false note is struck often enough by such preachers as St. Ambrose and St. Chrysostom, which was born of their distrust of the material life. They see the sweet uses even of such adversity as Roman slavery was; and for their false ethics of life the world was long compelled to suffer this wrong; and after it had freed itself, driven again into ways of error from their example and their dull method of unfolding the true Christian life.

Meanwhile, while the popular preachers trimmed their sails, the humbler folks did their Christian duty. They redeemed captives taken in war, and debtors who became enslaved; they even went themselves to take the place of the unfortunate who had been brought into slavery; and by countless charities mitigated a great evil which they could not abolish in so great an empire, where they were themselves outcasts.

It was then as it always has been, the true heart of man beat in the simpler life of plain men. The refinements of theology and philosophy stifle common feeling as they often obscure common sense; and while the Hodges and Chrysostoms apologise for crimes against humanity, the soul of the universal man turns from their nauseous sophistries and looks to God Himself for guidance.

It is to the general feeling of humanity that we must make our last appeal. The early Christians, we know by the testimony of their enemies, were a generous, self-sacrificing set of men; and Heaven will never permit priests to tamper with the divine inspirations of love which the Spirit puts into the heart of the sons of God. The love and brotherhood of the early Christians were indeed imperfect; their sympathies were narrow; but their entire faith in the Fatherhood of God and the Christian brotherhood are worthy the imitation of all ages.

CHAPTER XVII

BROTHERHOOD IN THE MIDDLE AGES, WITH A VIEW OF
THE RELATION OF CHRISTIANITY TO CHILDHOOD

In the Mediæval Church we see the interpretation which the lives of men and the current of history put on the great ideas committed to them by the earlier ages. The ideas may have been unfolded in new forms, but they remained substantially the same in their inner being.

The unity of the Church became a more impressive fact as it extended its borders. To St. Augustine the world owes the grand thought of the universal Church. Against the Donatists,[1] who would make themselves the standard by which God's love was to be measured, he vindicated the freedom of Christian brotherhood, as Gregory of Nyssa overthrew the theory of Eunomius, which reserved the privileges of the Church for those who were experts in theology.[2] Well would it have been for men if St. Augustine's precept to keep love as our central motive had never been forgotten; but men have rather preferred to dwell on his interpretation of the words in the parable: "Compel them to come in."[3] There are ways of compulsion which are divine, and a

---
[1] See his treatise, *De unitate Ecclesiæ*.
[2] Gregory Nyssen, *Orat. adv. Eunomium*.   [3] Epist. 93.

love which the hardest heart cannot resist; but the Catholic Church has not always kept to these gentle persuasives. The bloody deeds of the Inquisition are a chapter in the history of mankind which does not speak of brotherhood. By them the unity of the Church was wrecked, some men think, never to be restored. It cannot be that this madness of intolerance is a product of the Catholic idea of the Church, any more than the awful deeds of the Reign of Terror are to be put to the account of the principles of Liberty, Equality, and Fraternity.

The Catholic idea of the Church is an attempt to realise the fellowship of mankind; and to make any barriers which are not in the essence of the nature of the Church, is to weaken its representation of united humanity. To shut out the ignorant, to exclude the sinner, from the education which the Church gives, is to throw away our hope of reforming the world. Though the gates of the Church are wide, the truths it teaches are unaltered, and the life which it inspires does not lose its vitality. What is sometimes called its compromise with heathenism was but the increase of its charity; for when the Church welcomed the barbarians to its fold, there came in a power which in after days renewed its life. To bring men into the outward Church was to strengthen their communion with Christ which was already begun, and so establish their fellowship with men. As St. Chrysostom says of prayer, that its blessing consists in the unity of feeling, the harmony of thought, and the bond of love which it realises; so St. Augustine says the true matter of the sacrament of the Eucharist is the fellowship of the body and its members, which fellowship constitutes the Church. According to the Catholic view, no one could be in the outward union without sharing some of the life which was the source and sustaining power of that outward union. This idea of the Church as a visible society was the salvation of the Middle Ages. Had that thought of the Church, which Neander so often dwells upon, been the ruling view of thinking men,—the thought of the Church as an invisible society of good men who are united in a spiritual communion,—the great moral power of Christianity would have been confined to the few who drank its deeper waters. Mr. Lecky[1] says that Christianity has rather leavened individuals than society; and so saying, he hardly speaks with accuracy; but if men had not had a strong hold of the Church as an outward body of men who, notwithstanding their different stages of attainment in virtue and knowledge, felt themselves members of one family, Mr. Lecky's conclusion would only have been too just. By the influence of the sublime unity of the Church, which was too lofty to take note of the lesser differences of mankind, the progress of mankind was assured in the virtues which led to true brotherhood. It is only in more recent times, when a mania of creed-making has invaded the Roman Church, that she has lost sight of the older principle of true catholicity, and surrendered the generous freedom of the Church in earlier days for a narrow and jealous exclusiveness. But the picture drawn by one of her sons in our own time is true with regard to the past. "The Catholicism of the Middle Ages, although recognising the

[1] *History of European Morals*, ii. 147.

supreme value of the individual soul, and addressing itself primarily to the individual conscience, yet by no means left men in introspective subjectivity, a chaos of disconnected atoms, but, drawing them together by the strongest principle of cohesion the world has ever known, a belief in a divine fraternity worked, according to the evangelical similitude, as leaven upon the mass of humanity. The Catholic Church was the Christian family, a *gens sancta*, and its members were *domestici Dei*. The great thought by which Christendom was permeated and knit together, was the thought of God, the beginning and final end of each soul; but apprehended in the household of faith, in which each soul had its fellowship of sacred things. This, then, was the organisation of human society in the Middle Ages, — an organisation based on the Fatherhood of God and the brotherhood of Christians as the great objective facts of life." [1]

The great fact of the Church's existence was a lofty testimony to human brotherhood. All lands were united in her communion; and the words of St. Paul, that there was neither Jew or Greek within her fold, were realised. The missionary activity of the Church, which flourished till the fourteenth century, was itself a perpetual witness to the doctrine of the equal birth of all men as sons of God. And in a feudal age, which still bore traces of the scars which slavery had left on human society, the fact that the career lay open to talent in the Church, served to give men a practical reminder of the essential brotherhood of men, in spite of original differences of rank or

[1] "The Goal of Modern Thought," *Nineteenth Century*, May 1882, by W. S. Lilly.

circumstances. So strong, indeed, is the force of the living presence of the Church as a demonstration of human unity, that it receives less attention from philosophers and theologians during the Middle Ages than it did during the first centuries of the Christian era. What need was there to prove one of the most evident facts of daily existence?

Philosophy and theology, accordingly, took a strong individualist tendency, which had its invariable accompaniment of pantheistic thought. Man cannot be satisfied with himself; and if he cuts himself off from true relation with his fellow-man, he seems naturally to think his individuality but an illusion, which he desires to escape from into the one Reality which absorbs him. The speculations of Scotus Erigena are but another side of the views of such mystics as Hugo of St. Victor and Bernard of Clairvaux. In both, man is isolated from his hereditary past, his surrounding present, and his collective future, and is viewed as a single phenomena. We have travelled far from the thought of St. Paul when we come up with speculations like these. Their influence was, however, but small; for the great fabric of the Church threw its vast shadow over them, and preached by its very existence the unity and continuity of man. Nor is the thought of mystical religion one which is easily grasped by the general mind of man. Men see their relation so much more clearly to their fellows than they do to their God, that a religion which is based on isolation from mankind cannot be accepted by any large number, even were it possible that the circumstances of life should permit it. Ordinary mortals find their true existence lie in their fellowship with other men; and if religion endeavours to train them to another way of life, it must begin by making something else of them than human beings. In this struggle with the conditions on which our life is founded, such forms of religion cannot prevail. The common instincts of mankind must at last overturn asceticism and mysticism.

The Catholic Church departed from its divine idea, and gave itself a fatal wound by its growing use of excommunication. It was a right at all times doubtful, and dangerous to true thoughts of charity and brotherhood; and men were unwilling to have recourse to it in the earlier ages. And when it did come into use, it was as a mere weapon of war, and had no real love for the honour and purity of the Church as its basis. Excommunications were issued at the desire of princes, and the Church lowered her lofty banner of peace and goodwill to promote some petty quarrel. Occasionally, indeed, she laid a whole kingdom under an interdict, and levelled her thunders against monarchs. In all this it was the Papacy which spoke for the Church, a right to which it had no claim; and began that career of ecclesiastical narrowness which made the Church as governed by the Pope the foe of true human unity and peace.

One of the most remarkable works of any age was the product of the conflict between papal individualism and the universality of the Church. In the *De Monarchia* of Dante we find those ideas of universal humanity which our century has rejoiced in as almost a new discovery. Mankind is a united, collective being with a common end in their activity. The unity of mankind, which God has given them, should be maintained by an outward unity of government. The centre of the thought of mankind constituted a universal natural religion, which again found expression in an empire of justice, whose seat should be Rome. With Dante, the Papacy would have to give way to a larger conception of the Church, its unity, and its mission. Condemned by the Papacy, the work of Dante fell into oblivion, and remained rather a landmark of thought than a stimulus to action.

The errors of the Papacy were not, however, able to counteract the influence of the Church, whose divine life made her a strong force on the side of the brotherhood of man. All through the Middle Ages there was a recollection of the best thoughts of the Latin philosophers and of Aristotle. This universal element acted as a breath of freer air amid the clouds of narrow ecclesiasticism. The Church did not disown her obligations to the ancient teachers of morality. Abelard regarded the Greek moralists as nearer to Christian truth than the Jewish law. Christianity, in his view, only enabled men to win as a common possession what, in the days before it, had belonged to a few specially gifted men. And Aquinas raised Aristotle to an equal position of authority with the Sacred Scriptures; while the brilliant and beautiful speculations of Nicolaus of Cusa summed up the best thought of the comprehensive charity of the Middle Ages at their close.

Throughout all the Middle Ages we can see a steadfast effort to realise the views of St. Paul with respect to the universal freedom of mankind. There is a gradual diminution of slavery, and the freeing of slaves and prisoners was a frequent religious act, often recorded in charters, and connected with holy festivals. In almost all the countries of Europe, through the influence of the Church, slavery was extinct by the fourteenth century. It left, however, its legacy of unequal conditions, and the great body of the people were in little better plight than the slaves of the older world. It was not until the spreading of a purer view of Christianity, such as Wiclif taught, that the villeins of the feudal system acquired their freedom. The progress of the true religion of Christ has ever been the means of the advancement of human freedom and brotherhood; and it was the Reformation which swept away the last traces of the feudal tyrannies. Russia was outside the current of the European movement, and it has been reserved for the nineteenth century to see the abolition of serfdom; but it is foreign to our present purpose to consider its case, or the extraordinary slavery of the United States of America, which lived so long in a land of free Christian people. But we must not ourselves dwell in a fool's paradise in this matter of slavery. To Carlyle's view, the working classes were nought but slaves, whose only freedom was their power to starve and die; and most thoughtful men will find much to confirm his sad words. Mr. Zincke compared the Egyptian fellah with the English peasant, and found their lot much alike,—hard toil, poor fare, and a life lacking enjoyment and hope. In name, serfdom may be abolished, but the thing still abides with us, and many of the mitigating influences of the feudal system are absent from our modern society. Christianity has yet a hard task before it, ere it bring about a reign of brotherly feeling in the lives of men.

The Middle Ages showed many different tendencies with regard to the position of women. They were benefited by the sacramental character which was given to marriage by the Church; but they were injured by the assumption of ascetic superiority in the celibate condition. The mere fact of the clergy holding aloof from the married condition was in itself a stigma on the equality of women. It was a form of the same feeling which condemned second marriages, and put the man or woman who contracted them under certain disabilities.[1] In the best days of classical times a depth of personal regard sometimes kept sacred the memory of the wife who had been loved and lost, but the Middle Ages gave few instances of a like passion.

The peculiar devotion paid to women by the later chivalry had its origin in the Arabian love songs, and it is doubtful whether the artificial homage paid was compensation enough for the looseness of manners which accompanied it. It was an unnatural state of things at best to treat women even in theory as angels, and had its root in the base Mohammedan habit which made them but the playthings of men. But the troubadour was a mere excrescence in chivalry, whose heart we can read in the mediæval romances. In these, women occupy a leading place, and though their position is different in the sterner Nibelung legends from that which we find in the Chansons de Geste, we see in

---

[1] For example, a person who had married two wives in succession, or one widow, was excluded from "benefit of clergy."

them all that practical equality in mind and in action which implies that the doctrine of the subjection of women was a thing of the past, and their true place in life had been won by the influences of Christianity. Of the rightful position of women, the worship of the Virgin Mary was both an evidence and a guarantee for permanence. It was one of the most humanising influences of the Middle Ages; and since it is a necessary part of the true unity of man that woman should have her due place, that worship cannot be overlooked as one of the causes that tended to promote human brotherhood.

Whether it embodied the feminine ideal of Christianity, which we are often told is the essence of its moral excellence, is at least doubtful. The worship of Mary had its fullest developments in the most warlike period of mediæval times. To the cry of the Mohammedan devotee, which gave the name of the Prophet as the word of battle, the Christian soldier opposed the invocation of Our Lady. Nor, indeed, did Christianity promote peace, as its early preachers hoped. The early Fathers lived at a time when war was outside the lines of their life, and discouraged the followers of Christ from taking the sword. Their successors in the Middle Ages saw no reason why the God of battles should not accompany the Christian armies as He had aided the Jews; and the gospel of peace was forgotten. The world is no better in this respect since these days; but as long as it is possible to find the Church defending war by recollecting the old times of Judaic narrowness, the reign of brotherhood is yet far off. We can only say that if Christianity has not removed war, nor apparently sought to do so, it has lessened its horrors, and taught men clemency to conquered foes, and a brotherly kindness to prisoners taken in battle.

It is in the movement of charity that we see the onward march of true Christianity. The institution of hospitals, and the kindly care which noble women gave the sick in them, were a following in the footsteps of Jesus. The legends of the saints abound with instances of self-sacrifice for the poor and the suffering; and it matters not whether they were true or not, for they show the ideal of the times which produced them, and in which they were current. The familiar tales of St. Elizabeth of Hungary, of St. Martin of Tours, and of the Cid taking the leper on his own horse to sup with him at the inn, prove how deeply the parable of the Good Samaritan had sunk into the heart of man. It is these tales which are the real lustre of the Middle Ages, and it seems as if their radiance had a clearer light than the less personal charity of our own times can yield.

It is no long step that we take from the worship of the Virgin to that of the child Jesus; from the reverence for womanhood, which begat so many kindly virtues, to the care of children, who appeal to all the tender thoughts of the heart. To deny oneself for offspring is the first form in which altruism manifests itself; but savage life shows a frequent indifference to the young. Infanticide is an almost invariable accompaniment of the lower stages of human barbarism, whether in Arctic lands or South Sea Islands. Where children are spared, and where the parents do take care of them, that care does not last long. It is an instinct which soon perishes, and a new interest easily overpowers it. Slowly, indeed, does man advance to a recognition of the weak and helpless as truly his brothers, with a claim on his love; and how easy it is for him to revert to his barbarous indifference to them. A state of luxury almost always manifests a dark border of savage selfishness. We are told by St. Vincent de Paul that the abandonment of children in his day was not an uncommon occurrence. And we know that in the decadence of Rome the same thing was true.

The recognition of children as individual souls, as the sons of God, as our brothers, begins for mankind with the words of Jesus: "Take heed that ye despise not one of these little ones. Whoso shall receive one such little child in My name, receiveth Me. It is not the will of your Father which is in heaven that one of those little ones should perish." None could disregard so plain a statement of the equal privilege of all men as the children of God, whatever their attainment be, and consequently of the duty which we owe to all as in the all-embracing human brotherhood. The sacrament of baptism recognises this sublime reality, and it utterly fails of its great meaning when it is employed by some sects as a rite confined to adults.

The teaching of Christ, however, adds an element of mystic purity to childhood which has been a great influence in making men look on them with reverence, as coming fresh into this world from the heart of God: "Except ye become as little children, ye shall not enter into the kingdom of heaven. Their angels do always behold the face of My Father which is in heaven." Plato, indeed, has a glimpse of this primal innocence of children in the *Laws*, where he says: "All our three choruses shall sing to the young and tender souls of children, reciting in their strains all the noble thoughts of which we have spoken or are about to speak; and the sum of them shall be, that the life which is by the gods deemed to be the happiest is the holiest, and we shall affirm this to be a most certain truth; and the minds of our young disciples will be more likely to receive those words of ours than any others which we might address to them."[1] But how different is the hopeful and inspiring view which Jesus takes of childhood, from the melancholy way in which Lucretius speaks of the opening of life: "Then, too, the baby, like to a sailor cast away by the cruel waves, lies naked on the ground, speechless, wanting every furtherance of life, soon as nature by the throes of birth has shed him forth from his mother's womb into the borders of light: he fills the room with a rueful wauling, as well he may whose destiny it is to go through in life so many ills."[2] No such dark thought enfolds the Christian heart. The babe is the child of God, a dear brother of His Son, and a sharer in all the great hopes of the human race.

The spirit of brotherhood derives its best impulses from the loving care of children; the water of baptism laves in its kindly beneficence, not the infant only, but all mankind.

Round the childhood of Jesus a legendary halo rested,

---

[1] *De Legg.* ii. 664 (Jowett's trans.).
[2] Lucretius, v. 222 (Munro's trans.).

and the apocryphal Gospels of pseudo-Matthew, of Thomas, and the Arabic Gospel of the Infancy, embodied narratives which found currency in the Golden Legend and the popular literature of the Middle Ages. We find them throughout all Europe, even as far north as Iceland; and they did more to form the belief of the people than the actual truth contained in the evangelists. The way the people thought of the child Jesus is an index of their general thought of childhood, although the veil of a strange ecclesiasticism may seem to modern eyes to rest over the legends. Not content with imagining the early years of Jesus, they pictured also the infancy of the Virgin Mary and of the saints. Of St. Catherine, of St. Elizabeth of Hungary, of St. Genevieve, marvellous tales of their childhood are told, which both gratified the sense of wonder, and created a pious feeling toward all children. To remember the Innocents on their festival, and the other child-martyrs in the Lives of the Saints, was to bring into the heart a tenderness for all the little ones. It is a touching part of the Roman ritual which entrusts some of the functions of worship to young boys; and a sweet reminder of childish innocence when we are told that the consecrated elements in the Eucharist which were not consumed were given to children. All such observances have had a marvellous power in bringing about a reverent and loving care for the young, who were so near to God.

It was the Church which first began the care of orphans, and first received foundlings into her sheltering arms. Monasteries and nunneries, where dwelt men and women who had renounced family joys, became the homes and schools of children; and to bring an infant to their care was in many cases to give them the best gift they could wish for.

This care of children was the best evidence the Church could give of its thorough belief in the brotherhood of man. It was enough that the child required its care to bring out all the charity of the religious. It mattered not what the past or possible future of the child might be, the babe was baptized into the love of God and the fellowship of men.

Childhood occupies but a little place in the literature of the Middle Ages outside the Service-books of the Church and the Legends of the Saints. How little there is in the mediæval romances which speaks of children; and how few are the references in the great poem of Dante to child-nature! When Chaucer tells us in his "Prioresses Tale" the story of little Hugh of Lincoln, he gilds the little boy with an ecclesiastical halo. It was the Church which threw her protection over the young, rather than the ordinary feeling of society. Chaucer makes Hugh

> "A litel clergeoun, that seve yer was of age,
> That day by day to scole was his wone,
> And eek also, wherso he saugh thymage,
> Of Cristes moder, had he in usage,
> As him was taught, to knele adoun, and say
> His Ave Maria, as he goth by the way."

This is an exact echo of the legends of the Breviary to which Chaucer indeed himself refers. The Church has preserved myths of the early piety of St. Chrysostom, of St. Nicholas, and others, in the same spirit as modern pietism loves to read its sickly books about unnaturally religious children who die early. But mediæval literature, outside the Church circle, speaks little of children. With the new world the Reformation opened, we come to a still broader sympathy and more universal human tenderness. Still, in the Middle Ages, the young were cared for, as the rise of schools and universities proves.

What work the monasteries did as centres of the higher learning is a disputed question, but they at least diffused elementary knowledge. At all times the pursuit of knowledge has been a great leveller, and there is nothing which gives a more vivid sense of the open and brotherly feeling of the Middle Ages, than the stories of the students begging as they travelled. Learning was not the exclusive possession of the rich, and it seemed to open a door for that obliteration of class distinction which, in our time, it has largely brought about. The monasteries, by their encouragement of steady labour and mutual service, gave a lesson of equal brotherhood, which their generous hospitality enforced. And this lesson was brought home to every corner of the land by the mendicant friars, who, in their earlier days, lived pure and humble lives. Such influences as these helped to mitigate that strong class feeling which was the natural birth of chivalry. Just and generous and noble-hearted as the ideal of chivalry was, it was an aristocratic movement, and limited itself to a privileged few. It produced an exclusive caste, and tended to widen the gulf between the classes of the people.

But monasteries, as a form of brotherly co-operation,

were inferior to the old Teutonic guilds. These were fraternities of men, who voluntarily combined to help each other in industry, to defend each other against injury, and to relieve each other in need. They had an essentially religious character in most cases, though it is unimportant to inquire what part the Church had in their origin, even were it possible to answer the question correctly. We seem to see in them a reflection of primitive Christianity in the common feast and the common purse. Necessity, perhaps, it was that drove men so to combine; for the power of nobles and princes had little limit, and an individual was powerless against them. It is at least certain that the ruling authorities regarded them with jealousy, as strong combinations of men. Their services to the cause of brotherhood have hardly yet been duly appreciated, though their merit as advancing the industrial arts is fully recognised. But the frank intercourse of members of the same guild was an education of the moral nature of the greatest value; and the whole freedom of modern life is in large measure due to the social feeling created by these guilds. Out of them arose the democratic government of cities, which still remains one of our best schools of universal brotherhood, notwithstanding the outrages perpetrated in its name by the Commune of Paris. As Hallam says: "From the private guild, possessing already the vital spirit of faithfulness and brotherly love, sprung the sworn community, the body of citizens, bound by a voluntary but perpetual obligation to guard each other's rights."[1] The

[1] Hallam's *Middle Ages*, i. p. 351. See Brentano's *History and Development of Guilds*.

guilds mark, as Lotze says, "an undoubted advance of the human race."[1] For they maintained brotherhood on Christian lines, and pointed to that combination in work and mutual aid and sympathy which must form the society of the future.

[1] *Microcosmus*, ii. 378, Clark's trans.

CHAPTER XVIII

BROTHERHOOD SINCE THE REFORMATION

IT is in modern times that the principle of human brotherhood has received its fullest exposition, and that most endeavours have been made to realise it in practice. In theology and philosophy it has found its interpreters and defenders, and in social and political life it has won its triumphs.

The theology of the Reformation was a great movement for freedom, which is the primary condition of brotherhood. To establish the truth of man's immediate relation to God, without the intervention of Church or priest, was to restore to men their sonship to God. The universal priesthood of the faithful, as taught by the Reformers, is an ideal presentation of the highest future of mankind. And yet the limited conceptions of theologians like Calvin were apt to mar the full beauty of the new truth. He was in part able to realise a city of God on earth, where all the dwellers should be His children, elect by His grace, and adopted into His family; yet he barred the gates too strictly by his extreme views on predestination.

The countervailing influence of Zwingli was only able to reach a few of the opener hearts of the times. The doctrine which Zwingli taught, of the natural illumination of all men by the one true Light, was the expansion of the Reformation idea of the immediate relation of the soul to God. To believe, as Zwingli did, that God manifests Himself in all men, of whatsoever creed, is to acknowledge the universal sonship of mankind, and the universal Fatherhood of God.

Socinianism, which in its later developments has loved to enlarge on these great truths, did not teach them at all in its early days. Its first teachers denied that universal light which was the keystone of Zwingli's system, and presented a hard legal form of religion which was less catholic than Judaism. And to this day there are some evidences of selfish concentration among professed Unitarians which are absent in more orthodox bodies. At the opposite pole from the Socinians stood the Mystics, who built the fabric of their theology on the doctrine of the universal Spirit; but few could receive their difficult creed. It moved out into the world, however, in such dreams of a new heaven and new earth as the Rosicrucians hoped for and strove after. But it was not till the theology of the nineteenth century had made plain the great truth of the universal Fatherhood, that Christendom fully realised the general brotherhood of man.

To enforce this truth, the open world, which the Renaissance revealed in art and letters and philosophy, brought all its powers. The social teaching of Plato and Aristotle, of Cicero and Seneca, received a new meaning in the reviving life of the modern world. The bondage of the feudal ages was passing away, and wider thoughts about mankind were becoming current. The "civitas generis humani," which the classical writers had spoken of, which Dante had before him in his treatise, *De Monarchia*, was becoming a part of Christian thought. Learning and commerce alike aided to bring the conception of a human race, bound together in brotherhood, into the realm of fact. The New World of the West, as well as the new world of Greek philosophy, were rediscovered together, and their ampler skies enlarged the horizon of men's thought.

The theological movement, though enforced by classical sympathies, went on its way but slowly; but its progress was ever to wider views. In the nineteenth century the influence of Goethe acted as an expansive force on German theology, and made a second Renaissance in thought.

The restricted views of the Reformed Church are seen in the attitude of Luther and Calvin toward missions. To such extensions of Christianity they were indifferent, Luther saying: "Let the Turks live and believe as they choose, just as the Pope and other false Christians are allowed to live." The Roman Church was truer to the ideal of a restored humanity when it sent missionaries in the track of the conquerors of the New World; and men like Las Casas showed truly apostolic zeal. But within the bounds of Protestantism the missionary movement was slow of growth. The conflicts of the seventeenth century occupied all the energies of Europe, and it was not till its close that missionary activity began to show itself. And even the early bloom of its enthusiasm was killed by the chilling individualism which was preached from the pulpits of almost all Protestantism till the nineteenth century dawned. The moral teaching, which was the type of pulpit instruction in the eighteenth century, was injurious, not so much by its absence of distinct Christian doctrine, as some think, but by its defective and narrow type of morality, which was destitute of altruistic enthusiasm. The discourses, which were sometimes compared to the teaching of Seneca or Cicero, lacked the generous breadth of the ancient sages. It was social and political movement which upset the easy contentment of the moralists of the eighteenth century. The upheaval brought about more than a mere doctrinal change; it gave birth to the widespread missionary effort of our times, which desires to give all mankind the highest knowledge and the best life possible. Recognising that all men have the same birthright in the gospel, it cements the human race together by its brotherhood of love.

The doctrinal changes which the French Revolution brought about were not comparable to its social and political force, but they are too important to be overlooked. It was with the thunder of the Revolution still pealing in his ears that Schleiermacher wrote his famous *Discourses on Religion*, in which he taught men that religion was in its essence social, and the Church the brotherhood of mankind. From his teaching have sprung many noble messages to men. It is his followers that have led men into those purer regions of theological thought, where they rejoice in the recovered truth of the universal Fatherhood of God. Such thinkers as Erskine and Maurice, not to name the many other men who belong to the "Broad Church," have set men's souls free from the limited views of God and man which were a heritage from the darker ages of men's thinking. To them is due the opening prospects of the future, and the great hopes which the unborn years are to realise. More especially, the teaching of Maurice as to Christ being the archetype of *all humanity*, has given an impulse to thoughts of the human race as a unity which is not yet spent, and which is showing itself in all schools of theology. The characteristic doctrine, indeed, of our time is the universal Fatherhood of God, which brings into view, parallel with it, the universal sonship of man. This dogma is in part based on the teaching of the Scriptures, but also takes shape from philosophical speculation.

Indeed, it may be said of our century especially, what is true to some extent of all ages, that theological thought takes its form and tendency from philosophy. In these latter days, both physical and metaphysical speculation have controlled religious thinking. Nevertheless, it is true that theology has in its own province travelled to the same goal as philosophy, and that they both seek the same lofty conclusion as to the unity and progress of humanity.

The general current of philosophic thought with reference to the social relations of mankind, takes its rise in the culture of the Renaissance. To this source are due the English Deism, the Age of Reason in France, and the Aufklärung in Germany. The stream of classical learning, as it flowed on, rested for awhile in these creeks, whence it gained volume for a fuller current.

The current swelled in France till it fell in the headlong torrent of the French Revolution, in which were seen the principles of brotherhood and equality drifting to strange conclusions. Such issue had come from the idyllic dreams of Rousseau, with his belief in the natural equality of man working itself into a "Social Contract." Whatever may be said of the awful portents of the Revolution, this much is clear, that it established as one of the axioms of life, that there is a natural brotherhood of mankind; and taught men that they dare not sin against that great and divine law without paying a heavy penalty. Accordingly, the philosophy of the Revolution had the theory of universal humanity for its central idea. Condorcet's *Sketch of the Progress of the Spirit of Man* is the first proclamation of the gospel of the Revolution. It clearly shows the lines on which all steps forward to human brotherhood must be made. With what a terrible voice did the Revolution proclaim that extinction of national and social inequality on which Condorcet founded his hopes of the future. The theory of the equality of man, steadfastly realising itself in a growing similarity of circumstances and knowledge, did not imply, with Condorcet, any lessening of the total contents of human knowledge and wealth. Far from that, the uniting force which such a social condition would bring, is in itself a guarantee of progress. The laggards in the race of life, for whom now we have to tarry, would no longer tax the energies of the pioneers. There would be no levelling down, but a gradual ascent upwards. And so men would advance to ever-increasing fulness of life, the better they approached the ideal of unity and equality. As Lessing taught, the path of the individual to perfection must be that of the whole race of mankind.

The ideas of Condorcet bore fruit in the teaching of Saint-Simon and Fourier, who are the parents of modern

Socialism, and they culminated in the great humanitarian scheme of Comte. Men have seen in Saint-Simon's views a too narrow thought of life, as a mere gratifying of the physical side of man. As Mazzini says: " It is only the kitchen of humanity they will succeed in organising." Pierre Leroux,[1] a disciple of Saint-Simon, with a singular attractiveness of his own, takes a higher view of the nature and destiny of mankind. Defining man as " an animal transformed by reason and united to mankind," he sees that the life of a man is in the true sense not individual, but a manifestation of the general life of mankind. The progress of mankind is not an advance of the individual, but of the whole human race. In a family, the wealthy brother enriches the others, if he lives the true family life. Leroux teaches the *solidarity* of mankind in a high and noble sense, though not without extravagances of his own. The same motive inspires Comte, and supplies the motive power for the unselfish and ever-progressive life.

An essential element in the doctrine of the unity of mankind, according to the French thinkers, is a belief in perpetual human progress. The closer the brotherhood, the purer will men's hearts become, and the stronger their mental powers. They will bring to the solution of the great questions of human life a united force, before which the darkest clouds of ignorance must vanish. The belief " in the progress of the species towards unattainable perfection " is, says Wordsworth, " a necessity of a good and greatly gifted nature." It may be said to be natural to a theist, but it elevates the creed of the

[1] *De l'Humanité.*

materialist, who holds it far above the narrow horizon of his system. And almost the whole range of French thought includes this ideal perfection within its scope.

The system of Comte is, however, the fullest exposition of the creed of humanity which the French Revolution gave birth to. With him the individual is lost in the species: one man is merely a member of the collective *Great-Being*, and exists solely for that *Great-Being*, as he calls the whole human race. For Comte, humanity is a real existence, not a mere general idea. Out of his lofty conception of human brotherhood arises a scheme of ethics which is in essence Christian. The duty of each man to the human race, and specially the subjection of the mere animal existence to the true humanity, develop a noble ideal of elevated altruism. We see but the earthly side of the divinely taught ethics of Christianity in the teaching of Comte. Does not he show, by his working out his theory on a naturalistic basis, that the only ethical system which is fundamentally *human* is the Christian life ? If, then, there be sanction for the whole practical sphere of Christianity outside of its distinctive doctrines, can we not see in this but an evidence of the unity of human life, which in all its manifestations proceeds from the same divine source ?

The German philosophers arrived at the same conclusions regarding mankind and the individual as the French, though their thought did not pass through the fiery alembic of the Revolution.

Lessing [1] and Herder [2] both saw that the human

[1] *On the Education of the Human Race*, trans. F. W. Robertson.
[2] *Ideen zur Philosophie der Geschichte der Menschheit.*

species is an end in itself; that man lives for mankind, and attains his goal in a general perfection of humanity. Both writers were inspired by a catholic feeling of sympathy with all mankind which has never been surpassed, which had great moral influence in their time, and from which we may still draw noble enthusiasms. It is Kant, however, who presents in a logical form the idea of united humanity. He brings before us the ultimate goal of human effort as realised in a perfect political union of all mankind. The great consummation towards which time is leading us is a complete brotherhood of man. "The rational powers of man can attain their perfect development in the species alone, and not in the individual." Kant, indeed, in his *Principles of Political Right*, purposely alters the French formula of Liberty, Equality, and Fraternity, to that of Liberty, Equality, and Self-dependency; but he does so only to show more clearly the method in which brotherhood is brought into the actual work of government. Still more fully does Kant endeavour to show the way to the federation of all nations in his "Essay on a Perpetual Peace." To him it was no dream, but an anticipation of a certain future, whose unveiling, he trusted, might help men to work towards that future. He felt the great law of being under which man lived had an irresistible tendency towards peace and unity, and he wished to make himself a co-worker with God. "It is to Providence," he says,[1] "that we must look for the realisation of the End of Humanity in the whole of the species, as furnishing the means for the attainment of

[1] Kant's *Principles of Politics*, trans. Hastie, p. 74.

the final destination of man." In the words of his translator, Dr. Hastie, "in its ultimate sense the purpose of Nature is only another name for the will of Providence, and the order of the State is none other than the growing organisation of the Kingdom of God."[1]

But Kant is only one of many mighty forces which revealed themselves in the eighteenth century, which all tended in the same direction—of the solidarity of mankind.

There is, of course, manifested in the progress of thought directed to the great problems of human destiny, the natural antagonism between the individualist school and the believers in universal humanity. But the general direction has been out of individualism into a conception of united mankind. This onward movement may even be traced in the gradual development of individual thinkers. How far does Fichte, for instance, go beyond his original idea of the rational freedom of the individual as the end of human existence in his deeply interesting lectures on "Politics," where he finds in the principle of love the basis of all human relations? In other writers, such as Schelling, a somewhat similar development may be traced.

The most perfect embodiment of the idea of universal humanity is, however, to be found in the writings of Hegel.[2] The actual gifts of knowledge which this thinker has bestowed on mankind in the appreciation of art and history are great, but the stimulus he has given to other minds is a still loftier boon. It is due to

[1] Kant's *Principles of Politics*, Translator's Introduction, xliii.
[2] See his *Philosophy of History*, trans. Sibree.

Hegel more than to any other philosopher, that men have come to regard as the primary postulate of their political thought that they should aim at the *social perfection of humanity*. The idea of freedom, which is the summit of human perfection, can be realised only in the community which gathers into one all the actual elements of human life.

But still further does he carry his thought of human development. It is not in mere outward communion that men realise their collective unity: their spirits must unite. To this divine end the history of mankind is moving, and to this it was specially guided and inspired by Christ. To this divine purpose all human activities lend their aid: the love of beauty, of justice, of truth, are expressions of the inward longings of men's mind for its attainment. The Church of mankind, the true universal Church, is thus being served through all the secular movements and all the political forms which mankind may develop.

But still more completely does Krause[1] give us the idea of a united humanity. He is one of the earliest writers to insist on the organic development of humanity, that history is, in fact, a form of biology. This enables him to take a firm grasp of the unity of mankind as ever realising itself more fully. All mankind is a

[1] Krause is a difficult writer, but the English reader has now the privilege of reading the admirable translation of Dr. Hastie. In that great storehouse of thought, Professor Flint's *Philosophy of History in Europe*, there will be found an admirable exposition of Krause's philosophy, which is summarised with a clearness even greater than usual by a thinker whose lucidity is preeminent.

Great-Being, such as appears in Comte's thought, and individual life is only perfected in that Being, and is, indeed, but a means towards the social perfection of humanity. To quote Professor Flint: "The humanity of the earth must become increasingly organised and increasingly conscious of its social unity. All the nations of the earth will ultimately be drawn closely together by association and confederation.[1] . . . The whole of mankind on earth will be united into one great peaceful and prosperous State. They will not only become conscious of their unity in God and humanity, but will realise it in every sphere of life. Science and art, religion and morals, law and policy, will all become, when they have reached their maturity, cosmopolitan, and will all contribute to bind together, to unify, our earthly race into a city and kingdom of God."

The thoughts of these philosophers have come to influence men mainly through the systems of theology and morals, which have been guided by them. Thence they have filtered into popular thought, and in some measure directed political action.

But there is an English school of thinkers, whose speculations are less remote from the ordinary currents of the popular mind, to whom the cause of brotherhood also owes a debt not easily estimated. The leaders of the utilitarian school which was long dominant in England, such as Mill and Bentham, were able to influence legislation, and bring into practice their theories. The inestimable service which Bentham did to law-makers in England, in showing them that the

[1] Menschheitbund.

good of the community must be their main object, cannot be valued too highly. And his influence travelled also to other lands. "The greatest happiness of the greatest number" was a happy formula which did good in its day, and is yet useful.

The whole course of philosophic thought has been an endeavour to put into form the great belief that man is marching forward to a united brotherhood, which is the end of his existence on earth. Such a theory is the only explanation of our activities, which we cannot regard as the mere effluence of our individual powers. We live and act for each other, and there can be no other explanation possible of our work. It may be, and doubtless is, true that we are not conscious of this end when we are active, but none the less we obey the great law of human solidarity. Still more, to regard the progress of history as the manifestation of the perfection of the individual, is to stultify all theories of life. "For," as Lotze says,[1] "no education of mankind is conceivable unless its final results are to be participated in by those whom this earthly course left in various stages of backwardness." To complete our idea, we must regard mankind as an organic whole, whose full life is not yet reached, but which is slowly marching toward it. That life is reached when a complete brotherhood or union of all humanity is attained.

Such has been the progress of theological and philosophical thought, and that progress is mirrored in the social and political development of the modern world.

[1] *Microcosmus*, ii. 175, Clark's trans.

The democratic principle had its origin in religion, and religion alone can be its true interpreter and guide. When the Reformers taught men that they were citizens of the kingdom of heaven by right of their new birth, and not by any gifts which men could bestow on them, or by any mercenary purchase, their thought saw in the things of earth an image of heavenly places. Deep down, too, in the Teutonic heart there lay the unconscious remembrance of the freedom of long-past days, when Tacitus told the Romans of the nobler German tribes. It needed no great effort of the Teutonic imagination to dream of a future equally free and brotherly. But the process of recovering their former liberty was a slow struggle.

The close connection of political freedom with religion is seen in the religious wars which devastated Europe during the sixteenth and seventeenth centuries. Throughout all Europe, for two centuries, men were making endeavours after individual liberty, which they only won by degrees at the point of their swords. And when the eighteenth century opened, the battle was but partly gained. Puritanism was the triumph of the religious element, and became the parent of the republican idea. To the Puritan spirit is due the founding of the American republic, with its extraordinary, though indirect, influence on European politics.

The triumph of the civil element in freedom was in part due to the establishment of that republic, which the French made the model of their own. The lofty sentiments in the Declaration of Independence might have come from an immediate follower of Rousseau. But the actual force which flooded European life with the democratic feeling was the terrific storm of the French Revolution. At all times a priest-ridden people, the French found that the priestly religion had played them false, and arrayed itself against the true law of human existence. Destitute of any sound guidance out of the darkness into which they had been led, they fell back on those instincts which had been developed in the soul of man by his social life, and declared their gospel of *Liberty, Equality, and Fraternity*. To a downtrodden people the draught of these strong natural principles was too intoxicating, and the marvellous portent of the Revolution burst on the horizon of the darkened sky.

It matters not that the theories of savage life on which these truths of human brotherhood were based were false and unnatural, the mere creatures of a sentimental imagination. Men can walk by a light whose origin they do not know; and the response which the principles of liberty awoke in men's hearts proved in large measure their authentic character. For it must be remembered that in the great democratic movements of almost all nations, no great leaders have summoned the people to their crusade; it has been the dumb pressure of the multitude which has forced on the cause of the people. Even the greatest leaders, such as Mazzini and Kossuth, seem to be little heeded in the progress of the movement, and still less at any of its resting-places, when there is contentment with what has been attained for a time.

The history of Europe since the French Revolution makes it clear enough that from its compelling power the growth of modern democracy took its strongest impulse, almost its origin. And even the later developments of the democratic spirit show evidence of their source. At first, men were content with efforts after individual liberty. Their religion, their ethics, their economics, were all conceived in an individualistic spirit. The dull morality of the eighteenth century had a fit companion in the selfish economics of the school of Smith; and Mill, in his "Essay on Liberty," expressed the corresponding political creed. But the great power which they liberated could not be confined within their narrow limits. The onward course of the stream, which they had seen gain new strength from their efforts, could not be turned by their entreaties. It was a great natural law which had been opened to mankind, and it must go on to its fulfilment. Hence it is that men are now thinking less of the individual than of the community; thinking less of personal freedom, and more of the general well-being.

To this great principle the growth of industry and commerce have contributed. Men who have to work together must consider each other, and their intercourse must be on equal terms. Nations learn the same lesson, and the common needs of mankind turn their thoughts and acts into brotherly forms. The vast increase of commercial activity in this century has not only given men many problems to solve with regard to the condition of the mass of the people, but has also inspired men with the principles on which to solve them — the principles of mutual aid and brotherly love.

The modern world has shown in all its varied activities a steady progress in, and a longing desire for, the united brotherhood of mankind, the realisation of which is the accomplishment of human destiny.

CHAPTER XIX

SOCIAL AND POLITICAL PROGRESS

THAT the condition of the labouring classes under the theories of individualism which prevailed before the French Revolution was wretched in the extreme, is a truism of history. In England and Scotland,[1] at the close of the eighteenth century, the lot of all rural workers was pitiable. Their misery was to some extent mitigated by the Poor Law, which was a child of the Reformation;[2] but the evils apparently are of such a character that they are still calling for an allotment system. The Parish Councils Acts mark a step forward towards the attainment of a measure of breadth in our country life. Our present state is but a disguised feudalism, which is the hardest of all enemies of brotherhood to destroy.

In France the great blessing of peasant proprietorship was conferred on the people by the Code Napoleon. Who can depict the miseries of the people before the Revolution? What a universal testimony there is to the degradation and poverty of the great mass of the population! And yet, notwithstanding all the political

[1] Young's *Eastern Tour*, etc.; *Scottish Review*, Jan. 1895.
[2] 1536 in England, and 1579 in Scotland, to take the earliest dates.

turmoils of the century, all the heavy wars which have burdened the peasantry, their present lot is one of toil, indeed, but also of security and comfort.[1]

Other nations, such as Germany and Switzerland, show the same features, and exemplify the same law.[2] In matters pertaining to *land*, the movement is towards an equal brotherhood in its possession. All the English legislation points to this end, and doubtless, as time goes on, this aim will be more and more kept in view. The Irish Land Acts and the Crofters Acts are instances of this prevailing tendency. And it may be added that the suggestion of such schemes of Land Nationalisation as Mr. Henry George's, futile as they are, is a sure indication of the signs of the times.

But in manufacturing industry the view that the good of the community must overrule the interest of an individual is equally manifest. It was in 1802 that the first Factory Act to regulate the conditions of labour was passed; and what a long series has there been of such legislation. Hardly a year passes but the law is amended in favour of the operative classes. Hours of labour are restricted, conditions of labour are improved, and employers are liable for injuries to their workmen. In these enactments the law only speaks the voice of the

---

[1] See Kay's *Social Condition and Education of the People*.

[2] Some writers, such as Lady Verney, persist, on very insufficient data, in taking a gloomy view of the condition of peasant proprietors. Doubtless instances exist of misery and destitution among this class, and on a large scale may be seen in the village communities of Russia; but in most instances some special economic injustice of a remediable kind will be found the true cause of the failure of such peasant proprietorship.

Golden Rule, only illustrates the practical application of the law of brotherhood.

The dwellings of the poor are the care of the municipalities, and their health is guarded by every possible sanitary restriction. It may be no more than common prudence that causes this interest in poor people's surroundings, for each may be the centre of a plague. As Carlyle says of the poor Irish widow who died of fever and infected others: "But she proves her sisterhood; her typhus fever kills them: they were actually her brothers, though denying it! Had human creature ever to go lower for a proof?" But the knowledge of remedies begets an interest in the subjects of them; and out of prudence for ourselves, or mere scientific curiosity in others, comes some faint spark of real brotherly feeling, which by and by becomes a real flame. The number of those who have a kindly interest in the poor was never greater, and their interest never more wisely shown.

It is unnecessary to enlarge on the amelioration of our criminal law; but while the changes which have made it milder show the growth of a humane spirit, a more important modification of the whole theory of the penal code is seen in the efforts men are making towards the reform of the criminal. While, as a whole, the view that punishment should have for its purpose the reformation of the offender is not generally accepted, the establishment of reformatory schools for young offenders, and prisoners' aid societies for others, indicate a marked tendency in this direction. Men who interest themselves in the question have the Howard Association and other societies for the promulgation of humanitarian views; and the success of the experiments in reform at Elmira have given encouragement to those who love their fellow-men to persevere in their efforts. The increase of orphanages, hospitals, and general charity has been very great in recent times; and the Vagrancy Acts are practically a dead letter. And even though the Poor Law is humanely administered, men have come to feel that the community must do more for its aged members than has yet been tried. Out of this feeling come injunctions from the Local Government Board to administer the Poor Law with tenderness, and proposals of various kinds for old-age pensions. Nay, in Prussia and Denmark these pensions are in operation, with happy results.

One of the great means which Condorcet relied on to bring about his future of happy brotherhood among men, was the advance of education. Every child was to have his fill from the fountain of knowledge. The best wisdom of the wisest was to be the common possession of all. In great measure the desire of the French thinker has been accomplished. The State has in the British Isles taken up the task which was before in the hands of voluntary societies, and educates the children of the nation. Throughout Europe this had already been carried out, and in all Christian countries the benefits of knowledge are being diffused. Still further does the State go, and the starving children are clothed and fed as well as taught; and doubtless we shall see yet further advances made in the methods which the State takes so as to rear her children strong in body and mind. Time was when it was regarded as undue interference with labour to prevent infants from toiling in factories, but what strides has the conception of the welfare of the community being the rule of legislation made since that day!

The whole aspect of government has changed during this century. Before the various Reform Bills were passed, it could not be said that there was any real recognition of the labouring classes as members of the family of mankind. Their life was mapped out for them like children, and they were slaves, not sons. Some have, indeed, said that they were and are but children, and must be led by wiser heads than their own. This is true of all mankind, but it is aside from the main issue. The franchise is not a mere arrangement by which property and interest shall be represented, but is one of the roots of human life. Without the franchise a man is not a true member of the community; for as long as his voice is not heard in the family councils, as long as he is excluded from them, he is deprived of part of his status as a brother in the brotherhood of men. Hence the desire in our country, and the practice in other lands, of manhood suffrage, and the agitation to extend to women the same status as men.

These objects will one day be attained, and soonest to come will be a franchise for women. For in our times a more perfect sense of the true unity of the community has admitted women to share in all the possessions of knowledge and activity which the community has at its disposal. Universities and professions are open to women, and their legal disabilities are largely removed. The removal of the remainder is a question of but few years.

The gradual abolition of absolute monarchy is one of the best features of modern history. Men seek for a constitution which will most fittingly embrace most men within the actual working and governing brotherhood. Men unite in governing themselves with a view to the highest good of all. A community which is not conscious of its real bond of union has a precarious existence; and an absolute monarchy cannot realise any permanent ideal of national union. Hence, when men have grown into better powers of associating with each other, they modify the absolutism by degrees till it is reduced to a mere puppet kingship, or do away with it altogether.

In the same line of growth is the unifying of nations. Italy and Germany have in recent times gathered up the fragments of their people and welded them into a homogeneous whole. In the task, what lofty ideas came in sight above the struggle! The views of Mazzini have eternal significance in the history of mankind, and are a prophecy of wider unions still. For although patriotism is a great thought, there is a still greater and nobler union than that which is limited by the bounds of any country. There was truth in the words of Schiller, who thought it but a preparation for better things in the progress of mankind. Out of national union springs a real fellowship of heart which must overleap the barriers of race. But doubtless Goethe, Schiller, and Lessing were less patriotic than German thinkers are nowadays, because of the division of their country. They belonged to mere fragments of the Teutonic nation, whose narrow governments largely repressed the national feeling. The rise of German patriotism is largely due to the union of the peoples in suffering, and their recent union in triumph.

But there are dark shadows on the landscape whose happier features we have been describing. Industrial wars paralyse labour, and international wars hinder the progress of mankind. But men are not content that these things should for ever block our way. In the sphere of industry, courts of conciliation are proposed, and it is hoped that by their means strikes will be averted. And in the wider conflicts of nations, arbitration has already prevented sanguinary strife. It was in France that first the idea of a universal peace was bruited, and it has been in France that it has found its most frequent advocates. Philosophers like Leibnitz and Kant, sovereigns like the two Napoleons, poets like Hugo, and communists like Fourier, have shown how a united Europe would put an end to international wars.[1] The Peace Society has its own methods of attaining the same end; and many men have each their separate plan for a universal peace. We need not call them impracticable, for the sentiment which such discussions must bring about will leaven the public mind, and help to hasten the day when war shall be no more. The mere fact that a wider brotherhood of nations is looked forward to, will help to prepare men for its accomplishment. In some measure

[1] Professor Seeley popularised the idea in his *United States of Europe*.

De Maistre's idea of uniting all the States of the world into a Federation of which the Pope was to be president, deserves a passing notice, as writers of the Roman Catholic Church since his day have developed it; but it has no actuality out of their dreams.

commerce and literature and art have already linked the civilised world together; and time will yet produce a closer union.

Plainly enough, all the social and political movements of our times are in obedience to the great law of human brotherhood. This principle underlies them all, and every new way of life and thought leads to the same great goal. All that has been said in this chapter is familiar to everyone; the most unobservant eye cannot have failed to read signs of the times which are so clear. But none the less the deeper law of onward movement must be acknowledged in all these facts. It is not from men who hold special theories on Socialism that we receive leadership in such attempts to unite more closely, to assimilate more perfectly, the whole body of the people; but from the ordinary thinker who lives according to the spirit of the times. He is obeying the unseen law which guides him; he is merely the interpreter of the unconscious instinct of humanity which urges him on. He is often borne on currents with which his desires do not go; but even then he bears most evidence that the community of which he forms a part is an organic whole, which thinks and acts, and uses him as its instrument. The community, however, is only imperfectly formed at present, and can only imperfectly shape its thoughts and imperfectly express them. But its life is ever becoming fuller and richer and freer.

The progress of society has been truly described as from *status to contract*. Among the earlier races a man's relations were made for him by birth, and his life was entirely conditioned by them. His first step is to feel himself free, and in the act he makes a contract of brotherhood with his fellow-man. He realises his individual life, but comes to know that he cannot be independent. There is a tacit contract in the free recognition of brotherhood; and the community therefore takes its form as a collection of individuals.

These individuals principally base their intercourse with one another on their "*rights.*" The doctrine of the " Rights of Man " is a companion of the " Social Contract "; but both are imperfect expressions of the facts of life. The next step which society takes after it recognises its existence as a community, cohering, not by some predetermined circumstances entirely, but partly by individual will, is to rise out of the conception of *rights* to that of *duties.*

It is this stage which most communities are now reaching. The stormy toils of past struggles have led the nations to this resting-place; and the peoples are beginning to consider all law and government from this standpoint. Although they at present regard their duty through the medium of their welfare, the result is the same, for the law of life has invariably joined them together. A man rises from the status of a slave to contract himself as a free workman. The State, not content any longer with leaving him free to pursue his activity, surrounds him with conditions which shall be to his own advantage and the general well-being. From a theory of rights, the community has advanced to an examination of duties.

But there is a still higher plane of social and political life. Our duty to a man may be carefully weighed and measured. We may keep strict accounts of what we owe to him, and our principle of action throughout be a regard to *justice*. Though in actual life we cannot get beyond *justice*, which includes in itself every virtue, yet the purer form of the idea is *love*. The highest progress in social life is from *justice* to *love*. This is the summit of the Christian teaching, and the perfection of the social life. A community bound together by ties of *love* to one another has reached the sum of attainment in principle; all that remains is to develop it more fully in practice.

There are indications in our modern life that men are ascending in part to this stage. The countless charities of life, the abundant pity which overflows the rim of our selfish luxury, and the earnest efforts to reclaim the erring, act like finger-posts pointing to the true secret of human life.

In the evolution of society the law of the struggle for existence applies only in a very modified form to its individual members. Family affection extends its protection to the weak, and the social instincts of mankind are developed so early, and act so strongly, that the individual life is hedged in by strong fences. The young and the old alike rest in the shelter of the community. It is civilisation, with its love of luxury, that creates individualism in some hearts, that teaches some men the lesson of selfishness. But such selfishness is an artificial growth in men's heart, and, like a fungus, flourishes only in corrupt and unnatural forms of life.

Some have thought that the religious sanction it is which alone operates to check the selfish desires of men's hearts, and prevent the struggle for existence being a fierce conflict. But there is no sufficient ground for believing this. The family love, the social friendship, the patriotic alliance, may indeed be forms of religion; and I do not object so to term them. They may be unconscious forms of the allegiance to the divine Father who is over us all. If we love His children we love Himself. "Inasmuch as ye have done it unto one of the least of these My brethren, ye have done it unto Me." But this, at all events, is certain, that the same law of development is found in the social instincts of mankind which is manifest in the tendencies of their purest religion put into practice. There is no conflict between the innate tendencies of men's heart and the better life which Christianity teaches us. They both come from the same Creator, and show the general unity of all His works. It is a harsh and external view of Christianity which regards it as at war with the general instincts of mankind and the general tendencies of his development. It only strengthens and confirms these tendencies, and makes them clearer to human understanding. By its help man walks intelligently and hopefully on ways where, before Christ came, he only blindly groped. This great law of unity is one of the most important in all considerations of human life and destiny.

But although the individual is only in a very imperfect form subject to the law of the struggle for existence, the same cannot be said of social organisms. They must conform to the general tendency of human development, and the fittest for carrying out the destiny of mankind alone can survive. Despotisms, oligarchies, aristocracies, have been all tried and found wanting, because they refused to aid the cause of human brotherhood. That form of government alone can abide which will aid this cause. Hence the progress of mankind is always toward a more broadly based State, with the largest liberty and most equal conditions of life. Our social and political development has been on these lines in the past, and it is manifest that on these lines its future course is still more to be guided. This is the lesson of history, and the open prophecy of the future.

CHAPTER XX

THE SERVICE OF LITERATURE AND ART

IF there is one feature more marked than any other in literature, it is its universal character: it speaks to man as man; and unites the human race, not only through space, but through the successive ages of time. Nothing makes one realise better that the human family is one, than the common possession we all have in the best writings of every age and country. We feel we belong to a brotherhood who hold the best gifts in common; we each sit down at the common feast.

The separation which language makes between different peoples prevents us enjoying the full blessing of the brotherly union which literature brings. But how closely a nation is welded by a common speech and national literature! Not institutions or interests or religion have the force to make the hearts of fellow-citizens warm to each other which their possession of a great poet has. "The tongue that Shakespeare spake" becomes a bond of union because Shakespeare spake it. The songs of Burns and the tales of Scott sum up Scottish nationality, and in remembrance of them social and religious differences are forgotten. Patriotism is created and nourished by the songs and stories of a people.

And in times when life was more disjointed than now it is, with our easy communication, the ballad-singer was the means of spreading through wide lands a common feeling of sympathy. Among the wandering minstrels of the Middle Ages every class was represented. Spendthrift nobles brought to sing for lack of gold, and workmen when their craft was idle, and monks, in weariness of their vows, took to this ballad-singing life. The very throng that heard him, in their common enjoyment of the song had a thrill of brotherhood through them. The whole world is made kin by their share in the heritage of poetry. What a uniting influence have the Calmuck bards who wander over the wide plains of Asia! The delight of the scattered tribes, their journey is a series of hospitable receptions, and their willing listeners hear their tales as if one mind and being animated them all.

The drama has immense force as a means of social union. All classes enjoy it, and meet together to share the pleasure. Large bodies of the people in other lands have little other means of mental culture, and the audience are children of a larger growth once more at school. To laugh together, to weep together, are bonds of common life; and though the fellowship be but brief, it is very genuine. To bring the monarch, the noble, the merchant, the artisan together, even for a time, in a common sympathy, is to realise in fact the brotherhood of man. Emerson [1] says that the best thing about the Church is

---

[1] Compare Carlyle's words: "I have strange glimpses of the power of association. Therein lies the true element of religion." "The action of mind on mind is infinite; religion can hardly support itself without this aid."

that it is a congregation of all sorts and conditions of men once a week, and has thus a healthy brotherly influence. This is still more true of the drama; and the nations that love it most have a keener social feeling than those that neglect it. The drama is destined to be a more powerful social bond in days to come. What it was in the days of the miracle plays, it is not easy for us to realise. But it is possible to form some idea from the intense joy it was to the Italians in the days of their oppression. At Naples and Milan the people flocked to the theatre as the one common platform they might stand on together. Forbidden other co-operation, they found it in the crowded seats of the auditorium of the opera or the playhouse.

What is true of the theatre is still more true of the unifying power of music. The extraordinary effect which the sounds of pipe and drum have had on people, savage and civilised, is not to be paralleled in the more rational appeals of literature. What mad excitement did the rippling flutes produce in the days of Nero and of Theodora! What frenzy wakes in the minds of the South Sea Islanders when their huge drums are set a-roaring! No one can fully account for these things, which are yet seen among us. A revival meeting of Negro Methodists will sing the same chorus time after time till they are half-frantic with the sounds; and the same feeling is shown in less enthusiastic gatherings over a familiar hymn. A wave of such sympathetic emotion sweeps over a vast audience. Less worthy, perhaps, but also moved by a joint fellow-feeling, are the crowd who sing some refrain over and over again in a concert hall.

The reasons for this sympathy are not easily stated, but we come within sight of the truth.

Music unveils for us part of the general harmony of nature, and we feel ourselves partakers of it. Men who hear together some sweet strains, are moved into an emotional communion which makes the heart tender. This ethical quality in Beethoven, specially marked in "Fidelio," is one of the marvellous instances of this power in music. The feeling of brotherhood, of harmonious affection, of serene union, is expressed by Beethoven as no other musician has ever done it; and brings the hearers' hearts into the same exalted regions. Plato puts among the principal results of music, that it begets love in the heart, a sympathy with one another and with what is good and true. It brings about that εὐήθεια, that willingness to believe the best of men, to enter into communion with them, to turn the sweetest side of our nature to them. How our hearts are moved by the memory even of sweet songs we have heard! Not a little of religious earnestness is brought into our life by the influence of sacred music. Our hearts become more gentle, and our beings more receptive, and love and brotherhood capture us before we know. Jean Paul thought that music was the suggestion to us of a world of perfect harmony to which our souls sent out their longings. And Schopenhauer develops the same thought: "The unspeakable inwardness of all music, by virtue of which it brings before us a heaven so near and yet so far, arises from the quickening of the inner nature which it produces." There is no more rapid link between the souls of men than music; none which wakes in them so warm a sympathy. And Shakespeare tells us how the opposite feeling of estrangement is the result of a lack of love for music—

> "Nought so stockish, hard, and full of rage,
> But music for the time doth change its nature.
> The man that hath no music in himself,
> Nor is not moved with concord of sweet sounds,
> Is fit for treasons, stratagems, and spoils :
> The motions of his spirit are dull as night,
> And his affections dark as Erebus."

Whatever there may be in psychological explanations of the sympathetic power of music, the fact cannot be doubted. How has patriotism been quickened by the familiar strains of "Scots wha hae," "Die Wacht am Rhein," or the "Marseillaise"! Such songs as these are the real emblems of national unity.

The joys of life as well as its duties arouse men's social feelings, and help on the cause of human brotherhood. The innocent pleasure which accompanies light and cheerful airs is a common feeling of humanity, and excites a friendly communion of spirit. The plantation songs of the Negroes were to them one of their few social bonds, and the common sympathy of their natures, repressed at all other points, found an outlet in the enthusiasm of their nearly meaningless singing. And they spread their uniting influence far beyond the bounds of the Slave States. They linked the pleasure of men in other lands to the darkened life of the Negroes, and prepared the way for their entrance into the equal brotherhood of man.

Amusements have their origin in this social feeling, which also they help to encourage. It is only an afterthought which regards amusements as a means of strengthening the body or refreshing the mind. They take their origin in a time when bodies were not weakened, nor minds overwrought, by civilisation. If it is to give skill of hand and eye that men play golf or cricket, there is an immense amount of labour for very little result. The real secret is, of course, the social element. Men come together, happy that no jarring element need intrude. And the development of the social sympathy which our age has shown, has also had its power manifested in the amusements of the common people. The crowd who come to look at a football or cricket match are but another evidence of the increase of the united life of brotherhood among us. The same law runs through all our life: "music" and "gymnastic," to use the words as Plato meant them, both serve the universal end of man.

The words of Schiller are probably the best statement of the social force of art. "Men are driven by necessity to associate with each other, and Reason gives them principles of association; but Beauty alone can bestow on them a social character.... A common share in the beautiful is a bond of society, for the beautiful has relation to what is the common possession of all men.... Beauty alone brings joy to the whole world, and every being forgets the narrow bounds of its existence while under the sway of its magic power."[1]

Of painting and sculpture, the same laws will be found generally true that apply to music. The general appeal

---

[1] *Ueber die ästhetische Erziehung des Menschen, in einer Reihe von Briefen.* Brief 27.

is calmer and less persuasive, but the sympathy aroused is as real. To the Greeks, the thrill of delight at seeing the unveiling of the great statue of Zeus, which was the masterpiece of Phidias, was as powerful and contagious as the raptures which follow a great singer's best song with an English audience.

And, apart from its power of uniting men's hearts, art can by its choice of themes deeply impress on men the claims of sorrow, or awake in them sympathy with labour or happiness. The painter can awake in our feelings a readier response to his rendering of scenes which are in their nature tender and touching. He can make us feel our common heritage with all mankind in the real elements of our human life. It is a truth as old as the *Memorabilia* of Socrates, that pictures have a moral influence. Who can doubt the magic power which the paintings of Millet possess, to wake within us a sympathetic union with the toiling peasants whom they reveal to us in the simplicity of their life? It is an initiation into human brotherhood to look on such representations. All art is permeated with this religion of humanity; this love of scenes and tales which inspire us with brotherly kindness.

Art degrades itself under a despot. It lends itself to the low ideas and narrow thoughts of its surroundings. It may live, for an artist has a freedom of a sort under every form of government; but it reflects only the thoughts of the class that is free, and keeps aloof from the great slave-mass of the people. Beautiful after their kind are Boucher and Watteau, but they do not call out the higher or better sympathies of mankind.

Art, to win its best rewards of beauty and truth, must breathe the air of true human brotherhood.

Still more does poetry aid the cause of brotherly union. What fresh human fellowship breathes in Chaucer; what sympathetic power in Piers Plowman! What a faith in human nature speaks in every one of Shakespeare's plays! And all the long roll of English poets is a record of men who were inspired by freedom, friendship, and love for mankind. Mr. Stopford Brooke shows how the idea of universal human sympathy grows from Pope to Wordsworth; but the artist need not have a perfect intellectual grasp of all the wide issues his work may lead to. The unconscious force of genius may lead him to express a deeper sympathy with a wider range than his intellect may intend. Wordsworth is a conscious labourer in the cause of universal humanity, but none the less has his work enduring power. His fellow-feeling for simple life, where the true humanity within men has a plainer voice, helped to bind together the English nation. And can his loftier services to freedom be forgotten? Can men ever forget the sonnet to Toussaint l'Ouverture, with the noble lines?—

> "Thy friends are exultations, agonies,
> And love, and man's unconquerable mind."

In Gray's "Elegy" there is a universal note which we hear sounding in

> "The short and simple annals of the poor."

And Crabbe paints these with a stern truthfulness which compels our entering into the actual facts of human life, and taking our part in its sorrows and hopes.

How many generous inspirations have been drawn from Burns' songs; how often have men been raised to a genuine feeling of true humanity by the simple words?—

> "For a' that, an' a' that,
> It's coming yet for a' that,
> That man to man the world o'er
> Shall brothers be for a' that."

And what heart so hard as not to be moved with his picture of—

> "Yonder poor, o'erlaboured wight,
> So abject, mean, and vile,
> Who begs a brother of the earth
> To give him leave to toil."

The healthy sympathy which we have in Sir Walter Scott is worth a thousand treatises on the social union of mankind. We rise refreshed with a draught of brotherly feeling after reading the pages of the Waverley Novels. More frothy, but not less genuine, is the human interest in Dickens. Though the great writers have it deepest, the feeling of human brotherhood is a common possession of our poets and novelists. It appears in different forms, from the mild landscape of Goethe's "Hermann and Dorothea," to the deeper shadows of Victor Hugo and George Sand. The enthusiasm of democracy inspired the two great French writers, and their association with Leroux, Lamennais, and the other leaders of revolutionary thought, has given some of their writings a set purpose of political reform which deprives them of true insight. But there is, as we have seen, a movement towards brotherhood in literature as well as in politics. It is partly conscious, as in writers like George Sand, and partly unconscious, as in the songs of Béranger, or the "Comédie Humaine" of Balzac. Of deeper import are the signs of progress toward brotherhood in the pure regions of art and emotion, than those which speak of political purpose. The fact that our poets and novelists give their inspiration in the homes and lives of the labouring classes, is both a great aid to a general sympathy and a proof of its existence. Literature, which under despotic rule confined itself mainly to the gilded idleness of life, has taken a wider flight, and brought back a richer burden of beauty and strength. As the heart has more joy in seeing the true life of men as set forth by the Dutch school, or English painters like Morland or Hunt or Wilkie, or French like Bastien Lepage, Frère, and Millet, than in any theatrical scenes from a false Arcadia; so books must now speak the truth or be silent. And the truth is fuller of refreshment to men than any fabric of dreams.

The movement towards the idea of humanity has, in modern times, three distinct stages. It existed in older days, and our English verse in the Middle Ages is full of it. The natural kinship between religious freedom and human brotherhood showed itself in the communism of the followers of Wiclif, and in the vision of secular empire which Dante as a Ghibelline brought before mankind in his *De Monarchia*. But, after the enthusiasm of the Reformation was over, there seems to have arisen in men's lives a great chasm between classes. Sectarian and political strife embittered life, and it was not till the close of the eighteenth century that the fresh feeling of true natural life began to return. It appeared in art as well as in letters first as a return to *naturalism*.

The first stage is represented by such writers as Fielding and Smollett in fiction, and Cowper and Burns in verse. With these writers it is the compelling power of genius which urges them to their view of human society as essentially one from highest to lowest, nature having made all men brothers. There is no set political purpose in their verse, except perhaps in Burns at times, and they move freely within the broad sphere of humanity.

Not long after these writers came Goethe and Schiller, who were inspired by the same thoughts. These poets frankly accepted human life, and enjoyed all its various forms; to them men were men, bare of the accidents of their mode of existence. It was this that inspired them with a love for liberty, as shown in Goethe's "Egmont" and Schiller's "William Tell"; but it is in their lyrics that their true human sympathy appears.

In France, the intensity of feeling which Rousseau put into his gospel of individualism carried the nation along on a torrent of sentiment. Both Saint-Pierre and Rousseau were by nature believers in mankind; and though the gay Sybarites of Paris thought it a strange gospel, as did also Frederick the Great,[1] it took root in men's hearts.

[1] His well-known reply to Sulzer, the writer on æsthetics, indicates his opinion of the "damned race."

The *second* stage in the mission of literature to unfold human brotherhood, is due to the influence of the French Revolution. Wordsworth, Campbell, Byron, and Shelley illumined with their genius the new love of humanity which had burst in on the torpid soul of the European States. The struggles of Greece inspired Byron and Delavigne to lift their voices for her liberty, as Campbell sung the woes of Poland. Shelley found at home motive enough for an ardour as great for the cause of humanity; but rather inspired other singers than found the people ready to hear his own song.

Chateaubriand was a connecting link between the new world and the world before the Revolution, and the great apostles of humanity were arrayed on different sides, but striving towards the same grand end. Paul-Louis Courier and Lamennais, Lamartine and Constant, Hugo and Beranger, did not see eye to eye in their mission of brotherhood, but their efforts joined to swell the rising tide.

The movements for national unity which this century has seen, had each their poets, to whom is due much of their triumphant success. It was the voice of Leopardi which awakened Italy, and the stern republicanism of Giusti was a strong force towards the triumph of the final unity. The hero of the conflict, Mazzini, was one of the noblest men in the history of mankind. His thoughts on the future of humanity are a gospel in themselves: but many of his writings were like flashes of his sword, seen but to vanish; and most of his literary work will soon be forgotten. It was by his acts, rather than by his speech, that Mazzini realised for Italy her true place in the federation of mankind.

To the songs of Petöfi, and the tales of Eötvös and Josika, Hungary [1] owes her freedom as much as to the indomitable courage of Kossuth, and the statesmanship of Deak.

To fanatics like Jahn, and poets like Arndt and Freiligrath, the Germans owe the strongest impulse to unity. The roll of their patriotic poets is a long one, from the fiery Körner and the gentler Uhland and Schenkendorf, to the songsters of our own day. And Heine is an apostle of freedom, whom no nation may claim, though all admire. "The great work of our age," he said, "is emancipation. Civil equality is one of the most pressing needs of mankind."

In Russia, that strange land which we gaze on with wonder in our Western eyes, there lay a dark blot on our modern world. Slowly was the wrong of serfdom righted. Karamsin did not see the darker side of the serf life of Russia, but his writings penetrated into the hut of the peasant, and enlarged their sense of being. Pushkin, in his late days, was untrue to the liberal creed of his youth; but his poems, which earned for him the name of the Russian Byron, were seeds of true humanity in the deep soil of Russian life. The gloomy pictures which Gogol drew of peasant life, with all its dull ignorance of the shame of its degraded slavery, had an almost maddening power; but they filled the heart with despair.

[1] The popular poetry of the Magyars, which kept alive the national spirit, is well described by Mme. Dora D'Istria in the *Revue des Deux Mondes* for August 1, 1870.

It is to Tourgenieff we owe the tender touch that opened the yearning heart of the vast millions of Russia to the sympathetic gaze of mankind. The writings of Tourgenieff are one of the most marvellous products of our century, and breathe the purest air of human brotherhood. Too heavy clouds still hang over the great empire of Russia; but when writers like Tourgenieff and Tolstoï can find their way to men's hearts, the future is not to be despaired of. The great principles of humanity will triumph there as they have done in the rest of Europe.

The poems of Whittier and Longfellow, and *Uncle Tom's Cabin* by Mrs. Beecher Stowe, rang the knell of Negro slavery, and helped to bring about the greatest revolution in history since the storm of 1789. And the less known struggles for freedom and unity have each their poet. The Panslavonic idea has been sung by Hanka and Palacky, and the Croats had Gaj and Jellachich, with their Illyrian scheme. Modern Greece has had a hundred bards who have emulated the lyre of Tyrtæus; but the strongest strains were heard from Rhigas, a man of heroic heart.

But the unnamed writers of the ballads of the nations have been greater powers than the authors whom the world rejoices to remember. What a fire there is in the ballads of modern Greece,[1] which tell us of the brave deeds of the Klephts; and the Servians [2] and Spaniards [3]

---

[1] Collected by M. Fauriel.

[2] Collected by Talvj.

[3] The Spanish ballads are familiar enough from Lockhart's translations; and of late years more attention has been paid by Spanish scholars to the ballads of their country. In Sweden, Arwidsson, not

have their popular songs with the same martial clang. The true poet has the spirit of freedom and brotherhood as part of his dower from nature, who teaches him to sing. Genius loses its inspiration when it turns aside from its nobler impulses, and prostitutes itself to the cause of tyranny, oppression, or the lust of empire. "To give to a party what was meant for mankind," is, after all, impossible, for the gift so narrowed loses its brilliance. The precious things of this world are only of value when they are made to serve the great and generous cause of humanity.

Alongside of these enthusiasms for national unity and freedom, there has sprung up a deep and strong sympathy with literature which depicts the life of the labouring masses of men. This sympathy has spread through all nations and animated all literatures. The writings of Dickens, whom the Hungarian poet Petöfi called "the benefactor of mankind," have marked an era in the history of literature. Perhaps he did not see very far into the reality of things, but he was animated by a spirit of kindly brotherhood which has helped to regenerate England. Scott's is a greater name, but his service to man has not been more weighty; and although others, such as Charles Lamb and Leigh Hunt, prepared the way for Dickens, yet his path was one he made for himself. Many other writers have walked in the way

to name earlier collectors; in Provence, Arbaud; in Italy, Ferraro,—have preserved for us these important illustrations of popular life and feeling. It is worth noting that in Professor F. J. Child's *English and Scottish Popular Ballads*, he is able to cull his illustrations from almost all the languages of Europe, and from well-nigh a hundred collections like his own.

of the people's life, from the strong flight of George Eliot to the more retired paths of our Scottish story-tellers.

In France, imitators of Dickens like Daudet, and unpretending writers like Souvestre, love the highway of our common life, though they come far behind their great fellow-travellers, George Sand and Balzac. Nor must we forget the burning page of the marvellous writer of *Les Misérables*, " the great epic and tragic poem of contemporary life and of eternal humanity."

The German Auerbach and the Flemish Conscience have opened to us the hamlets of their native land, and Miss Bremer has made us find close kindred in Swedish homes.

In America the people are even brought nearer to us. There is a wonderful reality of touch in the work of the Western writers, which makes us feel we are in the presence of deeper instincts of brotherhood than our old-world life commonly shows. Miss Murfree, Bret Harte, and Cable paint the New World with a pen dipped in some genial liquid of tender sympathy which flows deeply in these wide-watered lands. This love to read of simple people and their ways is a long step to dwelling in community with them. We journey in life together with them in thought, and our heart expands with the consciousness of a common humanity. Nothing so surely tells us how far a point we have reached in our way to a general brotherhood. Time was when the life of the noble alone presented any features of interest to the artist, when commerce was too mean, and labour too wretched, to give him a subject that would command interest. But that time is past: all that is human interests mankind; and the simpler the human element, the less trammelled by circumstances, the more do men love and admire. To bring this about, women have done good service. Their gentler hearts have seen the true pathos of life, and opened it to our view. And the more they enter the world of letters, the purer and sweeter will the air become, and more fragrant with universal charity.

But the poets have a vision beyond the present. To them it is given to unlock the gates of the future. "Poets," said Shelley, "are the mirrors of the gigantic shadows which futurity casts on the present."

> "'Tis still remembered that in days of old,
> The poets, ere Time's page was yet unrolled,
> Could to the eager world its fate unfold."

And still the far-seeing singer can open to us a long vista. While we have the sublime and hopeful strains of Shelley, Victor Hugo, Tennyson, and Browning, we need ask no clearer book of fate.

Shelley was inspired with the enthusiasm of humanity as few men have been. He lived and breathed in a world of his own making, where love was the universal element. He seemed to see

> "The world's great age begin anew,
> The golden years return,
> The earth, like to a snake, renew
> Her winter weeds outworn."

To him the spirit of love and harmony and beauty was

destined to conquer the estrangements of mankind, and give its unsetting light to earth.

> "They know that never joy illumed my brow,
> Unlinked with hope that thou wouldst free
> This world from its dark slavery."

The inequalities of life, and its sorrows and wrongs, were ever before his mind; but they passed out of sight in his prophetic vision of a world of love and peace. That vision, which to others was but a dream, but an airy cloud of unreality, was to him his refuge and strength. Men find it hard to follow him in his flight; and his attempts to turn into the plain prose of action his creed of the future, were but failures. His thought was in a world outside of this, and he was not at home with ordinary men. It is only those who love him that he becomes clear to; only to them become intelligible his "Epipsychidion," and his "Lines Written among the Euganean Hills." The one reconciling force among men was "love, which heals all strife," and his future of the world was a time when all the material elements which now make discords are removed, and our true selves are all in communion with each other. And yet Shelley had to be translated into other men's thoughts before he became intelligible to mankind. His message was to remind men of a higher ideal of their possible relations one to another; but he removed that ideal too far out of the ken of ordinary mortals. Tennyson's clearer song, with the same burden, was all the more welcome to the hopeful and aspiring hearts of his time. The new bard had a loftier mind and keener insight. Tennyson, by his wide eagle flight into the far regions of the future of mankind, is the greatest poet of our time. His name is imperishable, because it is allied with the great movement of mankind towards brotherhood. Swinburne is an ardent apostle of freedom, and his song is inspired by a deep sympathy with humanity: he is a noble poet; but the keen vision of Tennyson goes far beyond the gaze of Swinburne, occupied with the present and the past.

In his earlier poems he struck the chord which more and more is heard, though with different harmonies, through all his work. Is not the root of the whole tree of human brotherhood in the words?—

> "From yon blue heavens above us bent,
> The gardener Adam and his wife
> Smile at the claims of long descent.
> Howe'er it be, it seems to me
> 'Tis only noble to be good.
> Kind hearts are more than coronets,
> And simple faith than Norman blood."

And is not the accomplished goal brought before us in the vision of "The Parliament of Man, the Federation of the World"?

The perfect future is unfolded to us in "In Memoriam"; the ideal world which death opens for the individual, and eternal progress, shall we not say, for the human race—

> "And we shall sit at endless feast,
> Enjoying each the other's good:
> What vaster dream can hit the mood
> Of Love on earth?"

The poet's ears can discern the aeonian music of the universe; he can look forward to the

> "One far-off divine event,
> To which the whole creation moves."

Perhaps no poet has ever had such a deep sense of the eternal progress of things as Tennyson. Other singers have been moved by the sense of the shadowy character of life and all its teeming forms, that the world is an air-image, and

> "Shall dissolve,
> And, like an unsubstantial pageant faded,
> Leave not a rack behind."

To Shelley this is an almost paralysing thought: but Tennyson sees that if the world fades behind us, it grows and expands before us; and his firm grasp of the true reality of things in their unfolding progress makes him the poet of science and of the future of mankind. In such joyful hopes as are hymned in "In Memoriam," to the chime of the Christmas Bells, or are more doubtfully sung in "Locksley Hall,"—sixty years after, we open the book of time. True, it is with a trembling hand that the aged poet reads it—

> "When the schemes and all the systems, Kingdoms and Republics fall,
> Something kindlier, higher, holier, all for each, and each for all?
>
> All the full-brain, half-brain races, led by Justice, Love, and Truth;
> All the millions one at length with the visions of my youth?
>
> . . . .
>
> Forward then, but still remember how the course of Time will swerve,
> Crook and turn upon itself in many a backward streaming curve.
>
> . . . .
>
> Follow you the star that lights a desert pathway, yours or mine,
> Forward, till you see the highest, Human Nature is divine."

But notwithstanding the doubts and sorrow of his heart at the awful woes and wrongs of life, which blinded his sight at times, as they did the eyes of Shelley even more, the poet in his old age will not give up the

> "Golden dream
> Of Knowledge fusing class with class,
> Of civic Hate no more to be,
> Of Love to leaven all the mass,
> Till every Soul be free."

And amid his waning light he falls back on his faith—

> "Our Playwright may show
> In some fifth Act what this wild drama means."

After all, we must not reproach our great poet with his sad moods, when hope seemed to vanish from him. In the words of another poet, Arthur Hugh Clough, who had a baptism of a like spirit, but with little joy for himself—

> "'Tis not the calm and peaceful breast
> That sees or reads the problem true;
> They only know on whom't has prest
> Too hard to hope to solve it too."

How, too, was the undaunted spirit of Byron brought to a despair of the future! And Goethe, who in days before had sung his songs of hope, came to despair in his old age of mankind altogether, and think that God would grow weary of them too. Weakness and age isolate us from men; we commune with our own sad thoughts of the past, and our intercourse with men becomes laboured and painful. But if we can keep our hearts in contact with others, we will not lose the sight of the advancing progress of man, and the swelling tides of love that rise in mankind. After all, it is this love for some one dear to him that Tennyson falls back on to cheer his vision of the future. Victor Hugo has been called "the spiritual sovereign of the nineteenth century"; and though the words are strong, it is certain that no man has expressed the inner thought of the century more truly. Mr. Swinburne, who so speaks, tells us that Hugo is a redeemer and a prophet. We know, at least, that disappointments and evils could not shake his trust in the great future of his own people and of mankind. At the close of "Les Châtiments," how he rises to the height of his faith in the progress of the race!—

"The name of the future is Love."

Humanity, released from every fetter, shall come at last to his home in the perfect brotherhood of man and of Christ. The dawn and the day are before him, and he calls on men to see and believe in the future of love.

In "Sordello," Browning says—

> "God has conceded two sights to a man—
> One of men's whole work, time's completed plan;
> The other of the minute's work, man's first
> Step to the plan's completeness."

In both of these visions Browning had his part. It is in his earlier work that he thought more of the future of mankind; in later years the present absorbed him. But his universal sympathy is itself a lesson of hope. Michael Angelo's art was nothing but sorrow, if the love of beauty had not in it the promise of immortality. And our present love for men must be an earnest of closer and better relationship. As Tennyson learns this lesson from looking at the great process of time, the march of the whole universe of law, so Browning seems to read it in the soul of man. The one poet looks around at the vast harmony of all things, and feels that the jarring life of man must be brought also into order and beauty, into unity and love; the other anatomises the soul, and reads its inward testimony to the same great purpose. With less buoyancy of hope than his wife possessed, and a nearer knowledge of the actual world, Browning is yet a prophet of hope to mankind.

It is, after all, what we might look for,—that in the New World the hopes of the future should be highest. Life begins there a second childhood, but with the strength of a man, and rejoices at the long ages in front of us. It is Emerson who assures us that, though our earthly communions fade and vanish, they can only be supplanted by what is more beautiful, and so on for ever. There is an ascending scale of love and brotherhood which time cannot exhaust. And Walt Whitman takes up the theme with his deep and elemental tones. He sees as the root-idea of all religions and philosophies—

"The dear love of man for his comrade, the attraction of
    friend to friend,
Of the well-married husband and wife, of children and parents,
Of city for city, and land for land."

He summons us to hear his promise of the years to come—

"I will make divine magnetic lands,
    With the love of comrades,
    With the lifelong love of comrades."

Truly has it been said that such words as Whitman speaks are spoken to centuries far beyond us, to which our children will be travelling; but the inspiration of these hopes may shape our lives towards them—

"What whispers are these, O lands, running ahead of you, passing under the seas?
Are all nations communing? is there going to be but one heart to the globe?"

The future of brotherhood never had a bolder and more confident expounder; the rush of his thought carries with it the most sluggish mind of the Old World. What a vision of love and glory he gives us; our timid hearts refuse to believe it. But hear his own voice—

"Is it a dream?
Nay, but the lack of it the dream,
And failing it, life's love and wealth a dream,
And all the world a dream."

CHAPTER XXI

THE NATURAL GROWTH OF ALTRUISM

In Bishop Butler's sermon on the Social Nature of Man, he lays down as proved fact that "there is a natural principle of benevolence of man which is in some degree to society what self-love is to the individual." He points to the instincts of family affection and of natural compassion as evidence of the existence of this feeling; and looks on any who are destitute of it as exceptions to the general course of nature. From a consideration of the whole subject, he concludes that "it is as manifest we were made for society, and for the happiness of it, as that we were intended to take care of our own life and health and private good."

The writer of *Ecce Homo* similarly speaks of "natural kindness, which was not killed, but only partially paralysed, by ethical morality"; and enlarges on the "fellow-feeling, the yearning towards a human being as such, which is not dependent upon the character of the particular human being who excites it, but rises before that character displays itself, and does not at once or altogether subside when it exhibits itself as unamiable." This fellow-feeling, at once primitive and natural, as the writer calls it, does not fit in very well with what he says of "the earliest condition of mankind of which we have any knowledge," which is described as being "one of perpetual war," only tempered by the "imperative law of nature," which makes members of the same family live in perpetual alliance.

While admitting much of Bishop Butler's theory, the *growth* of man's moral nature is not taken enough account of in that common view which speaks of the natural altruism of mankind. It is because man is a social animal that he has developed social instincts; but these moral impulses show different stages of development. The utter lack of sympathy which some savages feel for each other may be on a par with their callousness to pain ; but it is proof enough that the altruistic instinct is by no means a strong one in great multitudes of mankind. Lotze is probably speaking scientific truth when he says that "absolutely naked egoism must be regarded as the only motive power of our activity, until a higher development has discovered better ideals of action." According to the extent of this development will be the nature and character of the altruistic feelings.

We may, with the evolutionists of Mr. Spencer's school, find the origin of altruism in the mere animal tendencies of man. M. Letourneau, in his *Sociology*, draws attention to instances of benevolence among the lower animals, such as birds; and our own naturalists record many corroborative incidents. In the lowest of mankind, these instincts have some form, though among the Australians and Fuegians they have not attained a permanent home in the savage breast.

The great school of altruism is the family life. Whether the family is a later development of human association, or the primitive form, is a disputed point; but this fact is certain, that when it does not exist, the social instincts are very low. It looks like a paradox to say that man, by isolating himself in his own family, develops more love to others; but it is certainly true. Even in our civilised life, the bachelor is regarded as the type of selfishness; and often with marked truth. It is found, moreover, that where polygamy exists, the altruistic feelings are less developed than where the marriages are between a husband and one wife. The reasons are not far to seek. A state of horde life, such as the early peoples are said to have dwelt in, must lead to perpetual strife; for there must be many claimants for anything that is regarded as worth possessing, and whose possession would only be decided by the right of the strongest. The fiercer passions of humanity, rather than the gentler affections, are naturally strengthened by such contests. A similar state of war is found in polygamous households. There is a clashing of interests; and although the husband may pronounce his judgments, he is powerless to check the feelings of rancour which rise in the hearts of those who are bound together by a chain which is their only bond of union. The Scriptures reveal to us the fatal discords which are an almost certain consequence of polygamy.

In monasteries, phalansteries, and other artificial associations, similar conditions are found; and neither the enthusiasm of fraternity, nor the principles of Christianity, have been found equal to keeping down the selfishness and strife of their members. The phalansteries have all naturally dissolved; and so would every monastery, had it not been for the perpetual vow which the Roman Church prudently exacted from monks, whose instincts would have soon scattered them as far as possible from each other.

Since the family life has been found to be the only true source of the social and altruistic feelings, anything which weakens the family bond is certain to develop egoism. The Nihilist movement, which some wrongfully identify with Socialism, but which is its extreme opposite and the acme of individualism, aims first at the abolition of all marriage relations. In America this is carried out to some extent by the Divorce Laws, and the fruit of these laws cannot do otherwise than hinder the progress of true social union. It is true this is in harmony with some currents of American life, which have tended towards a dangerous individualism. The weakest must go to the wall in the rush of a world not yet welded together. But if any relaxation of the marriage tie is advocated in the interests of purer relations in social life, the voice of history pronounces such an expectation a delusion. Nature tells us the first true step in the life for others is the family union. The family union carries its sympathies to all its kindred, and we have the patriotic fellow-feeling which induces all who belong to a nation to help and care for each other. This fellow-feeling becomes established in the heart, and at last rises into the general benevolence to all men which Bishop Butler speaks of. It becomes an involuntary instinct, and without any express reasoning, men (and more especially women) are ready to show kindness to the stranger, simply because they have been in the habit of doing the same to their own people.

Parallel with the extension of the family, there is the growth of law and practical ethics, to which the sanction of religion is given. These arose from the commands of the head of the family, and the reverence paid to him gave his precepts a solemn weight. Family tradition preserved the usages of the clans to which families grew, and out of which nations were born. Thus the laws of hospitality had mythological meanings attached to them, which by and by faded from the memory of the people as practical impulses, without rendering them less obedient to the customs. The children, however, were still educated in the traditions and mythology of the tribe, and habits of altruism were thus implanted in their thought and action. Such a tale as that of Baucis and Philemon would enforce the moral of kindness to strangers, who were, whoever they might be, under the protection of Zeus Xenios. The Arab custom of respecting him who had taken salt, had doubtless some far back reference to some sacred association with that necessity of life; and similar usages are found in other nations. In China, as in Athens, there are temples of Pity, where at least the women and children pray.

Thus the early religions, though in many ways narrow in their ideas of tribal worship, lent their aid to benevolent feelings and kindly actions.

The growth of altruism was fostered by the national unity, which led men to admire the hero who died for his fatherland; and the pious deed of a Curtius was for all time a noble example. The poets and philosophers aided the education of mankind, and the teaching of Plato and Aristotle marked a new stage in the history of mankind. Their conception of morals as conditioned by political life became the seed of the permanent social thinking of men. Though, in later ages, those who knew their teaching departed from them and thought more and more of the individual, yet their pervading power was never absent from the higher currents of social inquiry. Their influence was felt in the Christian Church through the great theologians and the education given at the universities; and moral life has been largely conditioned by the theories of Aristotle and Plato, which, though taking different forms, yet sprung from the same root-idea.

As we have seen, the spreading of the peoples of Europe among each other and in the other continents gave men a sense of the wider world; and with advancing knowledge, broader thoughts of social duty and international morality took root in the minds of men.

The two greatest forces which waged perpetual war against human brotherhood were the unequal condition of women and the possession of slaves. As long as woman is held inferior to man, as long as she is regarded as the servant of his pleasure, or kept for her usefulness, it is impossible that the true family life can be developed, and consequently a true human brotherhood be hoped for. We must not, however, accept the conclusions of writers on this subject who have generalised too freely. It is difficult to see a great difference between the position of the wife in classical times and that which she occupied during the most part of our English history. We must remember that the classical writers state facts where we shut our eyes to them, and that irregular and temporary relations between men and women are still both common and largely condoned. Too often the master of the house is as complete a monarch in his own territory as the ancient Greek or Roman or Arab, and looks on his wife in the same lordly way as a possession. A historian of modern Europe would not describe the wife's status in very different language from that which we find in the classical writers. Even in the East the influence and independence of woman is higher than what we think, as we may judge from the Scriptures, from the Arab tales, and the Hindoo poetry. But that the spread of knowledge has helped to raise woman is a certain fact; and although it is a circumstance on a lower plane, the dowry which women received and came in part to control has done much to vindicate her freedom and equality. The position of women in France is doubtless due to this custom of dowry.

The equal position of husband and wife, where both could confer obligations, has an important function in training the children in habits of altruism; and there has been in recent years a gradual advance towards removing the disabilities of women, and giving them their due place in the social fabric. The commercial growth of modern Europe is the chief factor in this change, which owes, however, not a little to the worship of the Virgin and the customs of chivalry.

The slavery of the ancient world came to be *in form* abolished, but it left a legacy in the social degradation of masses of the population which is still with us. "The Germans in their primitive settlements were accustomed to the notion of slavery, incurred not only by captivity, but by crime, by debt, and specially by loss in gaming. When they invaded the Roman Empire, they found the same condition established in all its provinces."[1] The feudal system carried this on, though with many modifications which the growing activity of commerce brought about. The Reformation saw the end of serfdom in the countries which it took hold of, but in France the worst evils which accompanied feudalism—for villenage had no necessary connection with the feudal tenure—remained till the Revolution of 1789. From France, accordingly, came the impulse to the new movement of social altruism.

The diffusion of Christianity had infused into the earlier ages habits of kindness for others, but the political circumstances of the development of Europe had largely limited their exercise. Had it not been for the charities of the Church, the condition of the peasant would have been a hopeless one. And when faith declined, and the Church became little but a part of the governing power of the State, a new influence was born which was to form an epoch in the history of mankind.

What was the condition of the poor at the time of the Revolution? "They are sent for to do statute labour, to pay statute taxes, to fatten battlefields—named

[1] Hallam, *Middle Ages*, i. 198.

"beds of honour"—with their bodies, in quarrels which are not theirs, their hand and toil is in every possession of man; but for themselves they have little or no possession, untaught, uncomforted, unfed; to pine stagnant in thick obscuration, in squalid destitution and obstruction: this is the lot of the millions; *peuple taillable et corvéable à merci et miséricorde.*"[1]

In sight of this wretchedness there arose the dreams of Rousseau and the other philosophers of the time,—dreams of equality and fraternity, which were not without rays of hope, but which were a cruel mockery of the existing facts of life. Different standpoints were taken by the writers who helped in the work of liberty. Rousseau held that "the public welfare is nothing unless all the individuals who make up society are safe and protected," and that liberty would be too dearly bought with the blood of a single man. On the other hand, Helvetius put the well-being of the State first, and maintained that "any action becomes lawful and virtuous in the furtherance of the common weal."

The democratic movement, which was born of such thoughts, and baptized in blood at the French Revolution, is regarded by many as the germ of the social sympathy which the more hopeful among us think is increasing in our civilisation. As Mazzini says: "What is the movement but an attempt at the practical realisation of the prayer (Thy kingdom come, Thy will be done on earth as it is in heaven)? We are labouring that the development of human society may be as far as possible in the likeness of the divine society, in the likeness of the

[1] Carlyle, *French Revolution*, i. 2.

heavenly country, where all are equal, where there exists but one law, one happiness for all."[1]

The Revolution did not vindicate the principle of liberty and fraternity, but it at least avenged the wrongs of centuries of oppression, and made impossible a return to such a hell on earth as the poor lived in under the *ancien régime*. Men came to see that their own safety lay in obeying to some extent the law of brotherhood; that if they did not care for the poor, social disaster and epidemic disease would result. The spread of plague has been in all times a reminder to the rich, that if they do not regard the kinship of their poorer brethren by giving them healthy surroundings, the levelling hand of nature will show them that they too are mortal, and liable to contagion from their unacknowledged brother. The events of the Revolution cast a horror over Europe which made men reflect, and the gradual amelioration of the lot of the labouring classes became a theory of politicians, if but poorly put in practice. Further, the recognition that freedom was a necessary forerunner of true social welfare led to the progressive movement of liberalism, which in England and other countries was of real service to the working classes and to the cause of human brotherhood.

The Revolution in France and the growth of the United States mark the new epoch in the progress towards social altruism.

The next period in the development of fraternal sympathy is marked by the Saint-Simonian movement and its connection with the Revolution of 1830. The funda-

[1] *Thoughts on Democracy in Europe.*

mental error of the old Revolution was its principle of the *rights* of man, which is practically a declaration of war; but the new movement rather inclined to that gospel of the *duties* of man of which Mazzini became the great apostle. To labour for the people as a unity became a maxim of the new movement, which desired to associate men on an equal platform. Men must resign their dreams of individual happiness with a view to the general welfare; and they could best do this by a co-operation in labour. Associations of their disciples were formed, soon to break up; but an experiment on a large scale was tried by the French Government in 1848, at the entreaty of Louis Blanc, in the national workshops. With the commercial aspects of the movement we do not concern ourselves, but it is clear that it makes a new ethical standpoint for the modern world. The recognition of the State's interest in the poor, and duty towards them, as well as the sentiment of fraternity that pervaded the whole movement, render it of great interest to the student of the developing thought of mankind.

As important a result as any that flowed from Saint-Simon's work, was the philosophy of Comte, who was his follower for the time.

His whole theory based itself on the unity of man, and the social duties which that unity implied. Men were under the sway of two powers, a strong egoist influence, and a less prevailing altruist or social feeling. The latter must be victorious if man is to realise his existence. To carry out more perfectly his life, man must regard himself as a part of the great being of humanity, to whom he is bound by feelings of gratitude and reverence which reach a religious fulness. He directs attention to the union of co-operation of men in labour and progress, and shows how all the facts of life lead us up to a true sociability. The idea of the unity and solidarity of the human race was by no means a new one, yet Comte seems to have given it its widest currency; nor was his thought of the natural altruism of man's nature essentially different from that of Bishop Butler, but it struck deeper into the soil which was prepared for the seed. His intellectual contradictions and his repudiation of Christianity have but little to do with the message of Comte to his age. Those who believed him had already attained to that stage of his teaching before they came under his influence; but the altruistic spirit of his philosophy was a revelation to them. It may be nothing more than a shadow of Christianity, but it wins men to Christian kindness who repudiate the great founder of the Christian religion. And its influence has been felt in Christian circles. Light has been borrowed even from the lamps of Comtism and Socialism for the temple of divine worship; and men have been moved to recall the teaching of Jesus with regard to their brethren. It may be true, as Quinet says, that "the spirit of the gospel of Christ has only just begun to be applied in the civil and political world"; but it cannot be doubted that the Church has been led to examine her ways and rouse herself out of her individualistic teaching by the wind which has blown from the strange lands of Comtism and the socialistic theories of Saint-Simon and his followers.

It was the condition of the poor in France that caused

the terrible upheaval in 1789; and the rise of Socialism in Germany was due to a like state of things. The hard lot of the German peasant is one of the best-known facts of modern life. Writers of all schools, with many different lessons to teach us, from officials like Von Goltz to socialists like Liebknecht and believers in happy England like Lady Verney, have told us how dark an existence is that of the peasant homes of Germany. The wages earned by a peasant family is generally little more than a half of what is necessary to sustain healthy life;[1] while the labourers who have no allotment of land are still worse off. The whole family must toil, and that for a long day of twelve hours at least, and the house is cared for by the school children when they come home.

Meanwhile the peasant sees around him luxury which is indifferent to his sorrows, and a Church which is too busy with dogmatic speculation to attend to such trivial concerns as material welfare. Out of these fermenting elements arose the sympathetic study of Rodbertus, Lassalle, Marx, Liebknecht, and Bebel. They saw how the surroundings of the labourer failed to realise any approach to a real brotherly condition; that the poor were worse off than the slaves of the ancient world; and held that free competition and the monopoly of land helped to increase the misery of the working classes. The social democrats enlisted in their number a host of people of all classes anxious to put these things right. Professors and clergymen, merchants and artisans, frater-

[1] Von Goltz calculated that to keep a peasant family a sum of not less than £45 per annum was necessary, whereas the total earnings (three workers) never exceeded £35.

nised freely, and whatever their hope of success through political action might be, the kindly intercourse of men of different ranks and pursuits had a healing influence. Whether Socialism may ever be able to realise its dream, and whether it would be well could it do so, we do not discuss; but it has done much to develop the mutual interest of men in each other, and help on the cause of true brotherhood. One of the ablest of socialistic writers, Dr. Schäffle, does not expect to reach his goal till every man will work as hard for society as at present he does for his own gain;[1] but meanwhile the very possibility of such a future helps to create feelings of social unity.

In England the movement has been almost entirely dependent on German and French influences. Englishmen do not take kindly to theories, and in Scotland they may be said to have taken no hold whatever. Hard times in Ireland have compelled State interference in socialistic directions, but it cannot be said that it has in any way inaugurated a reign of brotherhood. On the contrary, class feeling has grown more bitter, till the social unity is in danger of being entirely broken up.

The rural labourer of the southern counties of England, and the "sweated" factory hand of the East of London, as well as the underpaid nail-maker and the stunted operative of the manufacturing towns, have made men think what their duty was to these people. Carlyle was the strongest force to set men thinking about the problem, and the socialistic writers of the Continent got a band of followers in our own country. The movement to regulate labour and rearrange life so as to give all workers a fairer

[1] *Die Quintessenz des Socialismus*, Eng. trans.

share than they have now, has enlisted in its service the religious teachers of our country, and a considerable amount of talk about the matter is current, but little fruit has been realised. It may have helped to induce men to study the condition of others, but it is very doubtful whether it does not spend in dreams of the future the practical energy which would be useful in the present. Our social chasms are wide, thousands of our people are in abject poverty, and they are suffering and dying while all this dilettante talk is going on. Sentiment is apt to expend itself in words, and the robuster charity, which would have sacrificed some luxuries in days gone by for the poor, is now too often satisfied with lamenting their case. It still remains largely true that the Church is the great source of charity, notwithstanding all the new methods proposed and never carried out. But that there is a daily advance in sympathy is undoubted, and its increase must lead, not only to the profession, but the practice, of human brotherhood. The life of Mr. Edward Denison[1] in Stepney was an example to others which has borne fruit. Mr. Denison's thoughts were far-reaching, but it is his acts which have done most good; and the university settlements in East London in memory of Mr. Toynbee, and their imitators, have a vision of future possibilities within them as well as a present practical good. The time will come when rich and poor will be closely associated together, and love regulate their relations one to another.

[1] *See Letters and other Writings of E. Denison*, by Sir B. Leighton.

CHAPTER XXII

CHRISTIANITY AND PATRIOTISM

As the family is the first training school for human sympathy, the wider affection for the fatherland is also a condition of progress in human brotherhood. There may be a patriotism which is narrow and selfish, which is built up of interest and prejudice, but there is also a generous and heroic feeling which is one of the noblest elements of human nature.

Love of fatherland was in classical times the most religious of passions, for it took the place of that Christian enthusiasm which in later days led men on to martyrdom. The memory of captivity and struggles for liberty begot similar feelings in the Jewish heart, and the story of the Maccabees reads like a page of Greek history. Nor was the patriotic spirit extinguished in the breast of the Christians, for St. Paul is willing to give his life for his fellow-countrymen. But the surroundings of the early Christians were not favourable to a close attachment to the empire of Rome. The heathen rites, which were mingled with public duty, prevented them taking any share in the life of the State, and they became a class apart, not unlike the Jews of our own time. Nor did the Christianising of the Roman Empire much affect the attitude of the Church towards it. The fatherland the devout looked to was, as St. Augustine taught them, the "paradise above"; and although life and its circumstances were more stable than when the writer of the Hebrews wrote, amid the great tides of change that were engulfing the world, "Here we have no continuing city, but we seek one to come," the Christians still held to the same creed. It is true that St. Augustine occasionally gives us some such echo of Cicero, as when he says that "the good man knows no limit to his zeal for his fatherland";[1] but the leading thought of men in connection with national life and public duty was taken from the pagan and not the Christian writers. There was a slumbering consciousness of the unity of mankind, but it had more regard to their future union in heaven than to their actual present condition.

This condition of things lasted till the dissolving of the empire and the gradual formation of the European monarchies. Some stronger feudal lord, with the help of some large city, gained to himself power over his neighbours, and by force of arms founded a State. Europe, which before had been broken up in small baronies, began to concentrate itself in these absolute despotisms, and the birth of the new feeling of patriotism took place. At first it was the attachment of soldiers to their chief, of vassals to their lord; but a settled possession of land brought into being a deeper form of loyalty of the whole body politic, corresponding closely to the teaching of Cicero and Aristotle. Along with national life in secular matters, there grew up a national *religious*

[1] Epist. 202.

consciousness, which indeed was the real formative influence in the building up of the nation. Usages of worship and independence of government began to mark out each individual nation; and with the rising tide of national independence these became more and more distinctive. But it was the policy of Rome to fight against any such defiance of her universal authority and uniformity of ritual, and one by one the national Churches gave up their own flags for that of the chair of St. Peter. The history of the Gallican Church is an instance. It had its origin independently of the Roman See, and was finally unified and strengthened by Charlemagne, who created a patriotic and religious empire. It struggled for centuries against Rome, but its final extinction came when it forsook the cause of the people for that of the court and its own ecclesiastical privileges; and when it yielded to Ultramontanism it became unpatriotic.

It was the Reformation which gave the national Churches a real hold on the people, and true patriotism in the European countries may be said to date from that era. In Roman Catholic countries to this day the baleful influence of the Papal See is felt, and the most steadfast foes of the unity and progress of Italy, Germany, Austria, Ireland, and the United States, are the priests who have given their allegiance to the foreign power of the Papacy.

De Tocqueville said that patriotism and religion are the only forces which can permanently direct the whole of a body politic to one end. The history of mankind testifies to the truth of this; and it is equally certain that there is no guarantee for sound patriotic feeling unless it is inspired by religion. Men will not be easily moved from their luxurious enjoyment of life, which now may reach such a height, unless some strong power urge them. If we indulge self, we lose our power of serving others; our altruistic feelings become atrophied for lack of use. But it is easy for the Christian, whose whole life is moved by love, to give himself for his fatherland. Indeed, the true love for country cannot be taught by direct instruction, or take the form of a wholly rational judgment of gain or loss by serving it. Is it not a passion which thinks not of reckoning with danger or death? A writer says "that it exists in a child from the beginning: we breathe it in as we do nature. Our institutions have in them the spirit of our fatherland, and through them that spirit takes possession of our minds involuntarily."[1]

But not only does religion prepare the soul for true patriotism; all national unity comes from a common faith. It is not by chance that men come together as a people; they do not form a "social contract" of partnership; they are united by influences which they do not control. The nation is a real unity formed by the providence of God, and men are born into the life of the nation, with its benefits and responsibilities. Neither common advantage nor common necessity can consolidate a people; there must be a deeper source of union. That deeper union is found alone in religion. From the earliest times, when the tribe held the same totem sacred, down to the wars of religion in modern Europe, the common faith of men in some divine truth has been the

[1] Passow. Cf. Mazzini: "The true country is the idea to which it gives birth. It is the thought of love, which unites in one all the sons of the territory."

centre of their national life. In Greece the national life centred in its religion; art, literature, politics were but expressions of the piety of the people. The temples and statues of the gods, the poems of Aeschylus and the other great writers of Greece, the appeal to the Delphic oracle, are all proofs of that deep religious feeling which St. Paul spoke of in his address to the Athenians. In Rome the same spirit is found, and the Arcadian Polybius, who always loves to philosophise what he sees, is struck with the reverence paid to the gods in that city. If we go still further back to the earlier empires of the valleys of the Nile and the Euphrates, we find still more evidence of the power of religion to associate men; and when we stretch our glance back to primitive man, we see all life finding its centre in religion, which was the atmosphere in which it lived. The decay of Greek and Roman piety heralded the decline of patriotism and the fall of their States. *It is by religion that the peoples are formed; and the State organisation is a result, not a cause, of religious unity.*[1] Thus patriotism is but a form of the practical action of Christianity. It is but an endeavour of men to realise the human brotherhood within the limits which are practicable for them. Wider and wider their boundaries grow as the common faith extends, and the tribe becomes a nation, and the nation an empire. Such is the history of the greater peoples, and such is the future of mankind.

The nation is a divine organism for the development

[1] "The English Revolution has succeeded because it has the sanction and authority of religion. This gives it a security which we have not in France."—Quinet's *La Révolution*.

of the individual with a view to his fuller membership in the whole human family. The wider sphere of duty which a man has as a citizen of a great State, the more complicated relations which he has with other men, train him for his perfect duty to all mankind.[1] It is only in the training school of the national life that a man can grow to a stature sufficient to enable him to take his part as a citizen of the world. "Our country is the fulcrum of the lever we have to wield for the common good. If we abandon that fulcrum, we run the risk of rendering ourselves useless, not only to humanity, but to our country itself."[2] Whether the nation, like the family, is a permanent institution on earth, has been doubted; but the diversity of men's ways of thinking and acting make us think that it will ever abide with us as a factor of human life. Although men have different speech and customs, they may have the same inner faith, and manifest the same brotherly kindness.

And yet the nation is but a shadow of the universal citizenship into which St. Paul said he had entered, but to which certainly the brotherhood of men must one day lead us. In the far future such dreams must lie; but their brightness may come into our hearts, and quicken our sense of universal humanity.

There are certain forms of thought and action which prevent the nation from fulfilling its mission with regard to the brotherhood of man.

That feeling, which would maintain the interests of

[1] M. Renan doubts this, and thinks that any people which seeks the well-being of mankind must perish.
[2] Mazzini.

the native country in spite of justice and honour, did not die with the decline of barbarism. It is still present in our thought, and nations are moved by its madness to their own ruin. What was the cause of the unhappy Franco-German War, but this folly of unreasoning self-assertion? Bitter was the price that then was paid for the wrong; but often it happens, as in dealings with savage peoples, that the anger of Heaven sleeps long ere the poor barbarians are avenged. No civilised power has been free from the stain of such crimes against God and man; and the national life which is appointed for such noble ends is basely prostituted in the cause of oppression. We may read on a monument to a naval hero:[1] "A man who always maintained the cause of his country, right or wrong." Such a sentiment is only to be expected from half-civilised peoples, like the Chinese; but it is doubtful if many Christians would repudiate it. It has been said that no nation can act from the same motive of love as an individual can. M. Challemel-Lacour said, in a speech made while he was ambassador to England: "We must not ask a people to sacrifice its interests. The spirit of self-sacrifice is a great individual virtue, but it is not one which is possible for a nation or a government." Hegel holds the same opinion, which is essentially Macchiavellian: "The history of the world is outside the standpoint of righteousness and virtue." And in Professor Mozley's *University Sermons* we read, not without astonishment: "It may be said, why may not a nation give up its rights on a principle of humility and generosity, as the individual does? But to impose such

---

[1] Commodore Decatur.

humility on a nation would be to impose on it something quite different in ethical constitution from the same humility in an individual. An individual's abandonment of his rights is what the words grammatically mean, the individual sacrificing himself; but a nation's abandonment of its rights means the individual sacrificing the nation; for the nation only acts through individuals. The individual is humble, not for himself, but for another, which is a very different thing."

There is an extraordinary confusion of thought in this passage; and the writer has not the remotest idea of either the unity of national sentiment, or the fact that free peoples can express that sentiment. The basis of the opposition to Christian principle here is a form of the love of glory which we are so fond of attributing to the French. The fact is that the whole of national life implies such sacrifices on the part of individuals as are spoken of here, and these sacrifices are often offered on the altar of strife by an unwilling people at the bidding of ministers, who have the power to act till they are removed from office by an indignant people. Certain it is that, if we disregard justice, not to say mercy, in our dealings with foreign peoples, it is vain to offer them a share in that religion which our own acts blaspheme.

There has occasionally appeared at different stages of the world's history a cosmopolitan spirit, which regards patriotism as a narrow absurdity. Frederick the Great shared this opinion; and Schiller thought patriotism a weakness.

One of the objects of the Society of the Illuminati, under Weishaupt, was to promote this cosmopolitan feeling, as against the low and selfish idea, as they styled it, of patriotism. Priests, kings, nobles, as well as separate languages and customs, were to vanish before this dream of a united humanity. The part which Anacharsis Clootz took in this movement in its French phase is best told in Carlyle's picture of it graved with his savage burin: "One scene the hastiest reader will momentarily pause on, that of Anacharsis Clootz and the collective sinful posterity of Adam. It occurred to the mind of Anacharsis that, while so much was embodying itself into club or committee, and perorating applauded, there yet remained a greater and greatest; of which, if it also took body and perorated, what might not the effect be! Humankind, namely: in what rapt creative moment the thought arose in Anacharsis' soul; all his throes while he went about giving shape and birth to it, . . . of all this the spiritual biographies of that period say nothing. Enough that, on the 19th eve of June 1790, the sun's slant rays lighted a spectacle such as our foolish little planet has not often had to show, Anacharsis Clootz entering the august salle de ménage, with the human species at his heels—Swedes, Spaniards, Polacks, Turks, Chaldeans, Greeks, and dwellers in Mesopotamia: behold them all; they have come to claim place in the grand federation, having an undoubted interest in it." [1]

Poor Clootz came to the guillotine as his share of universal fraternity, and doubtless some of his companions too. Since his day the cosmopolitan idea has been advocated by sceptics and revolutionaries, but has

[1] *French Revolution*, vol. ii. p. 43.

obtained few followers among thinking men. Cosmopolitanism is but another name for selfish individualism, and is a certain foe to human progress and union. The words of Mazzini are true: "To desire to efface the sentiment of country from the heart of the peoples, to suppress at once all nationalities, to confound the special destinies of countries, to bring down to the level of, I do not know what cosmopolitanism, all the beings that God has classed in races, as a ladder by which humanity must mount to Him,—that cannot be done; and all labour directed to such an end will be labour in vain."

There are men who are in practice cosmopolitan, or who are at least denationalised. The selfish Englishman or American, who lives abroad in luxurious indifference to the progress of his native land, is a contemptible being, whom the forces of time will soon extinguish; but meanwhile he is not without elements of danger to the true realisation of peace and brotherhood. His wealth becomes the object of envy, and his luxury demoralises the poor around him. However, he is so useless and unworthy a being, that his power even to do harm is hardly worth reckoning.

A more dangerous form of antipatriotism is found in pessimistic views of life, which lead men to abandon faith in humanity, and to think of nothing but seizing what poor consolation the passing pleasure of the day may yield. But life is too real, and men are too busy, to be much troubled with pessimistic thought. Were it not that there is a tendency to throw government into the hands of literary doctrinaires, who are apt to be infected with the passing malady of the age, the danger from this source would not be serious. But when men whose culture has been in the idle dreams of philosophy turn their hands to governing men, their powers of evil are augmented. We cannot believe that free peoples, who desire to serve God and man, will allow themselves to be sneered out of one of their best possessions—which Heaven has bestowed on them in the love of fatherland—by a few men who think themselves superior to the great laws and generous emotions which govern our human nature. There is every hope, on the contrary, with the increase of the people's share in the government, that their patriotism will grow, and will rise out of the narrower forms of race-jealousies into the nobler desire for the welfare of humanity.

CHAPTER XXIII

THE OPPOSITION OF SCEPTICISM

THE movement towards human brotherhood is essentially a Christian one. It may appear in secular life and take secular form, but has essentially a religious foundation. That great and noble man, Mazzini, recognised this central principle; in his own words: " When the arms of Christ, even yet stretched out on the cross, shall be loosened to clasp the whole human race in one embrace, —when there shall be no more pariahs nor brahmins, nor servants, nor masters, but only men,—we shall adore the great name of God with much more love and faith than we do now."

It is in the faith of Christ that true social progress finds its loftiest impulse, though we only may see indirectly the working of that faith in the minds of men. Silently it transforms the heart, influencing even those who openly deny it. It brings about an atmosphere of consideration for each other which no man can disregard. The *Ethos* of the modern world, the spirit of the age, is steeped in Christian altruism, which the sceptic himself is born into. The mighty hand of God shapes the thoughts of men, not only in the so-called religious duties and reflections of mankind, but also in secular affairs. As Rothe says: "That Christ in our day takes a much more lively interest in the development of our political circumstances and conditions, than in our so-called Church movements and current questions, I cannot for a moment doubt. He knows full well on what things really depend, and on what they do not."[1]

The spirit of brotherhood, then, even though taking form and impulse chiefly in secular life, has a religious origin. Sceptics have not been slow to discern this, and from them no little opposition to all brotherly movements has come. On the other hand, it has been an accusation against Christianity by its foes, that it has weakened the forces of altruism. Professor Clifford thought that it "lowered men's reverence for the marriage bond"; and Mr. Frederic Harrison sees in Christianity a great influence in favour of selfishness. These opinions have little ground, and the interpretations they give of Christianity are repudiated by its adherents. It is otherwise with the opposition to hopes and purposes of brotherhood which are found in sceptical writers. They speak plainly enough, and have no wish to disown their individualist sentiments.

Sir James Stephen in his treatise, *Liberty, Equality, and Fraternity*, utterly opposes the doctrine of the brotherhood of man, and disclaims any obligation which such a belief might possibly enjoin on him. His view of life is that for people who are moderately fortunate, and take a just view of their position, life may be still extremely pleasant; although he does not shut his eyes to the fact that if Christian theology went, Christian

[1] *Stille Stunden*, p. 274.

charity would go too. Everyone for himself; and this world for men of hard hearts and good digestions may then be bearable, perhaps even enjoyable. Such are the selfish thoughts of some of the new evolutionist sceptical school. A man is the creature of his environment, and must make the best of it. As for rights, they resolve themselves into mights. If a man can obtain wealth and power, he is lucky; but if not, he must learn philosophic contentment as the next best thing.

M. Renan said cheerfully that the millions must toil for the few, must give their lives and their happiness that a select class should enjoy all manner of pleasures without caring for the men and women who made the enjoyment possible for them. Should a vision of the injustice rise before the dull brain of the oppressed labourer, who reaps so few fruits, and those mostly bitter, of his toil, stern repression must be tried. The brute mob must yield their lives, lest they soil the garment of culture and refinement. The cruel cynicism of such acquiescence in the worst facts of life is possible only for a sceptic, not only in God, but in man's capacity of progress. To think that there are minds which can accept the dismal actualities of modern life, with its daily sacrifices of blood and tears, more awful than the altars of the Aztecs were wont to witness, makes one doubt if such culture be not a snare of the power of evil rather than a gift of Heaven. Yet such is the gloomy view which scepticism takes of human prospects, and all the time refuses to improve them.

The views of Strauss[1] on human brotherhood are worth

[1] *The Old Faith and the New*, trans. Blind.

hearing. Having done his best to take from men their religion, he desires to steal their freedom also. With him only the rich have a right to govern, and the masses have already got more in the way of privilege than they ought to possess. He does not give a cheering picture of futurity, but tells us that there will always abide as the enduring scourges of the human race, bloody wars, social estrangements, and the scaffold. Alas for the new faith! The old was at least a sweeter element in human life, if it were but a smiling rainbow which we follow and never reach.

M. Lefèvre, in his *Philosophy, Historical and Critical*, written from a materialist point of view, says in criticising Comte: " *To love our neighbours as ourselves*, and still more *to live for others*, are exaggerated formulas, whose application is as undesirable and useless as it is impossible. Why? Because such maxims are opposed to nature, which, though he may modify, man cannot suppress. What a dull and commonplace society that would be in which everybody loved and lived for everybody else! What value would love, friendship, generosity possess in such a state of things? Nor is this all. A moral system based exclusively on duty and sacrifice becomes arbitrary, the instrument of tyranny, as despots are well aware. If merely inaccurate in point of thought, it becomes dangerous in its practical application to the social order." The lofty contempt for the *proletariat* which fills the French philosopher, is born of a scepticism in the possibility or usefulness of elevating the masses.

The curse of modern life is the desire for luxury, for

an increase of sensual enjoyment. In France this has become a passion which absorbs the soul of the successful man, ay, and rouses the cupidity and anger of the unsuccessful. Anarchism is but a protest of the desperate wild beast which lurks in the nature of the oppressed and struggling man. But anarchism is but the prelude to a more bitter warfare, if views like M. Renan's still maintain themselves in sceptical thought. The memories of the Commune are not yet extinct, and the way in which those who emerged from the *proletariat* glutted themselves on the remains of Imperial luxury, should be a lesson to men that the citadel of their selfishness is not impregnable. If the conflict come, with whom will the victory lie? Suppose it is not M. Renan's friends who repress, and that they find themselves among the repressed.

The materialist view of life, however, need not take account of anyone but the individual himself. Professor Moleschott says: "The moral rule for each man is given by his own nature only, and is different, therefore, for each individual. What are excesses and passions by themselves? Nothing but a larger or smaller overflowing of a perfectly legitimate impulse." And the voice of another modern prophet speaks thus: "Enjoyment is good, and frenzy and love are good; but hatred also! Hatred answers well when we cannot have love. Wealth is good, because it can be changed into enjoyment. Power is good, because it satisfies our pride. Fraud is good, theft, robbery, murder, if they lead to wealth and enjoyment."[1] To Max Stirner there is no significance

[1] Translated by Max Müller from Carrière's *Die sittliche Weltordnung*.

in such expressions as a general thought of morality or of united humanity. "Of all men, he whom I know and love best is myself. The ego is my whole catechism. I do what I wish, and what pleases me." Laas follows in the same lines: "The primary right of man is that of self. My rights are my needs, without regard to my duties."[1]

The career of Garibaldi supplied an interesting commentary on the effect of atheism on the sentiment of human brotherhood. In early days, Garibaldi was a believer in God and man. He had abandoned the Roman Church, but he avowed himself a devout believer in God. He said he was "of the religion of Christ." In his first romance, *Clelia*, which he began during his imprisonment in Varignano, we see evidence that scepticism had taken some hold of his mind, and at the same time his trust in humanity and its destiny was waning. The man who in his youth was filled with thoughts of free human brotherhood, who cherished the same ideals as Mazzini, whom he called his master, turned his back on all these great ideals in his later years. In his romance, *Cantoni, the Volunteer*, written before his French campaign, he describes the whole race of mankind as a "family of apes," and said he "covered his face with shame at belonging to this race of asses." He spoke of himself as an "atheist"; said that "man created God, and not God, man"; and at the same time rejoiced in the attempts to assassinate the various crowned heads of Europe which were made some years since. To such utter forgetfulness of the great principle of love and

[1] Quoted in Lichtenberger's *History of German Theology*.

unity and sympathetic fraternity did scepticism bring that heroic heart. " Oh, what a noble mind is here o'erthrown ! "

The pursuit of science seems in some men to fill the heart with a contempt for the ignorant, who are for little use except as hewers of wood and drawers of water, with the wages of slaves, and to lead the life of slaves. Their lives are of little value, and a famine may be regarded as nature's way of ridding the world of surplus population. Still more, if they are dead, they are at peace ; their life was not happy, and there is nothing beyond. So speaks the atheistic materialist, as he philosophises on the wreck of other men's lives. Men are so manifestly unequal to the scientific observer, that such an idea as that of brotherhood is impossible between them. The old theory was that they had souls, and were alike children of the divine Father ; but evolution scorns such a view. They have developed in various degrees out of lower existences, and it is the fate of the inferior development to perish and the higher to abide. But will the inferior men believe this ? They have the majority on their side, and will they not awake to see it if the materialist theory of life be true ?

It is undoubted that the love of luxury and refinement renders the soul selfish, and may exist with the most utter indifference to other people, nay, may even base itself on the misery of other people. A sceptical life which is self-seeking, and which has means to gratify its desires, has in it a great power of social estrangement. Most men will sympathise with Mr. William Morris when he says : " I do not want art for a few, any more than education for a few or freedom for a few. No, rather than that art should live this poor, thin life among a few exceptional men, despising those beneath them for an ignorance for which they themselves are responsible, for a brutality which they will not struggle with,—rather than this, I would rather that the world should sweep away all art for awhile." But the sceptic does not generally sympathise with such a view, although we cannot leave out of our consideration the fact that a great deal of socialist thought seems to have taken an irreligious attitude. In this country, as well as in France and Germany, socialists are opposed to religion, as in their view it is on the side of their antagonists. To what extent they are right, and to what extent Socialism would really act in furtherance of human brotherhood, we have already considered. Meanwhile we may say that there are many ways in which scepticism assaults the faith and practice of human brotherhood. To loosen the ties of marriage, which has not only found advocates among the extreme Nihilists of Russia, but in other free-thinkers, cannot but be a prelude to social anarchy of the worst kind.

The spurious cosmopolitanism which scepticism is inclined to put in the place of patriotism, is another precursor of the war of individualism, when every man will be an Ishmael. *Ubi bene, ibi patria*, is an infamous maxim in the lips of men who have been well treated by fate in their early life; but we cannot judge hardly a man who has known nothing but poverty and misery and wrong as the only gifts his fatherland has yielded him. It is a blind instinct which leads the oppressed man to abuse the national feeling; he seems to see in centralisation the terrible force which has held him down, and gives his hatred to that unity which he imagines has been the cause of his wrongs. The artificial consolidation of society by the Roman Church, which represses the individual instincts in their noblest form, has led to a violent reaction, when the religious allegiance is thrown over. Men learn to think for themselves, and decline to recognise any duty to care for others. The Roman Church treated men in the mass, and took charge of their conscience. Society under its discipline became more compact, and the wheels of life rolled more smoothly on. Even yet, in countries under papal direction, there is a unity and similarity of the people which is not found in Protestant lands, and a harmony of life which is easy enough, but perhaps monotonous. There is less individuality of action, less marked character of thought, and a stronger social bond, than is seen in the nations which have thrown off the yoke of Rome. The long list of religious sects in Whitaker's *Almanac* would be an impossibility in France. There is much that is admirable in this, but we must not forget that it is the result of discipline, not of free choice; that it is not a voluntary surrender of the individuality, but a primary privation of it. Thus it happens that when a reaction does come in such countries as France, it is a violent storm, and breaks asunder, not only the bonds of religious creed, but the social unity. The scepticism which succeeds unquestioning and mechanical faith is also hostile to the compact social organism which was bound up with that faith. When we turn to

Russia, we see an equally impulsive reaction from the dull uniformity of the life which despotic tyranny inflicts on the people,—a life as flat and cheerless as the vast steppes of that empire. In these facts we may find some of the origin of the opposition of scepticism to the brotherhood of man.

But the real root lies in the nature of atheism itself. To doubt God is to doubt man. The world is a hopeless place if it is not governed by a wise and good Power who is on the side of love and truth. Throw overboard that essential belief, and there is no reason why we should live for any interests but our own. Have we not returned to the old worship of strength, which was a characteristic of pagan times? Power and self-assertion, these are the qualities which must make man's success, if life is a struggle for existence where the fittest survive. Where is the room for that self-denial and gentle yielding to others which have been the glory of the Christian ages? If life is best when its good things are most plentiful, what is to prevent a contest for them? And will not he win who fights the battle least encumbered by care for others or regrets for the fallen and the vanquished? If our career on earth is the mere manifestation of blind forces, and there is no future, why not give ourselves over to the old maxim, "Let us eat and drink, for to-morrow we die"? In France they have had the courage to face this problem, and the utterly egoistic and unscrupulous tendency of atheism is painted with a master hand by M. Octave Feuillet in *La Morte*, and in deeper tones by M. Paul Bourget in *Le Disciple*.

It is but natural, after all, that scepticism should decline to believe in human brotherhood. Self-sacrifice without motive of love for man, or hope of reward in their progress, is an impossible factor in human life. The mere sentimental love of doing good, which reaps its recompense in the gratitude of the receiver, is not a lasting feeling in man's heart. It soon gives way to other forms of emotion, which take its place in the ranks of pleasurable sensations. The man who is a pleasure-seeker finds most of them pall on his palate, and, like Nero, he turns from his music or other fine art to lust and cruelty to excite his jaded sensibilities. M. Renan [1] said he did not know that the chaste man had the best of it after all; that perhaps the libertine was right, and practised the true philosophy of life; this is sure, at least, that the unchaste man is regardless of his victim. Cruelty is but the other side of the base animal passion, as the experience of mankind tells us in those dark pages of history which we turn our eyes from. To seek one's own pleasure is in the very act to heed not for other people; and the vulgar Epicurean view of life which our rich men often show, is a steadfast foe of true brotherhood, even where the denial of the human kinship may not be heard.

But to cull our pleasures carefully and selfishly, from the pessimist point of view, is even more hostile to humanity. To hold that this life is so bad that we can but endure it, is a doctrine which does not make one love one's fellow-men. The awful cynicism of contempt for

[1] *Souvenirs d'Enfance et de Jeunesse,* p. 149. " I saw clearly the vanity of this virtue," p. 359.

his fellow-mortals which Swift showed, proceeded from a
heart sick of life, and doubtful as to the future. What
a description of man he gives under various masks in his
Gulliver, where hardly a kindly sentiment escapes him;
and what rancour breathes in the oft-quoted lines—

> "Offending race of humankind,
> By nature, reason, learning, blind;
> You who through frailty stepped aside,
> And you who never fell from pride;
> You who in different sects were shammed,
> And come to see each other damned."

Nothing keeps men more closely wrapped in their
selfish thoughts and ways than the thought that selfishness will do most for them in life. An enlightened
selfishness the new scepticism preaches: obey the laws
which lead to earthly ease and comfort and pleasure, and
you will pass a more cheerful life than if you occupied
yourself with other people's needs and sorrows. Science
teaches us that this world will all come to an ignoble
end; and a day will come when the sun itself will roll
a cold black ball through infinite space. Man will have
long perished from the earth, and the page of his
history closed for ever. Such is our destiny; and if
there is no more before us, why should we grieve over
the sorrows of anyone but ourselves? Let us keep
health and a cheerful spirit, says the pessimist, and we
may manage to live. And if life goes fairly well with
men, why should they darken it by the shadow of
self-sacrifice, or anticipate the day of their death?

Atheism must, in its very nature, cut men off from
their fellows, seeing there is no God to serve but one's

own desires, and must in the nature of things be a foe to human sympathy. The picture of love which the Cross presents, and which for ever has consecrated meekness and martyrdom, will only give to the atheist an instance of a man who was weak enough to perish, and who was not *fit* enough to survive. The brotherhood of man which He taught will be regarded as the delusion of sentiment; and while the ignorant remain in their ignorance, the poor in their poverty, the wise and well-to-do will felicitate themselves on the evolution which has made them not as other men. As the Pharisaism of the atheistic heart, which reckons up its treasures of existence, will not imperil its happiness by sharing a jot with the poorer neighbour; so the prospect of the future of an atheistic world is a vision of selfish greed, disturbed at times by anarchic war.

CHAPTER XXIV

OTHER FORCES WHICH ARE AGAINST BROTHERHOOD

The opposition of scepticism is not the only foe with which the spirit of brotherhood has to fight. There are in our modern life tendencies which are hostile to its growth, and which are commanding in their power. In part they are legacies of a darker past which ever casts its shadow over the progress of man, and in part they are the creation of our own time and its apparent needs.

When men have a hard fight for life, they have little time to think of others. It is only when despair has numbed the energy of the mind, and made it hopeless of life, that most men are willing that others should take their share of the necessaries of existence. In our own crowded cities this stage is often enough reached, and the trembling hand of exhaustion gives the cup of sustenance, with its few drops, to the lips of youth, which still has dreams of a future. The struggle for existence in the centres of population palsies the feelings of brotherhood. Mazzini tells the poor peasant " that he injures his brother by accepting a remuneration below the value of his labour "; that he owes a duty to his fellow-workmen: but his words are in vain. When there is but the day's pittance between the labourer and starvation, when his little wages is the frail plank on which his life rests, there is no time for him to pause till the world goes right. The Roman matron looked callously on at the horrors of the struggles for life in the great amphitheatres; and her British successor loathes her for her cruelty. Yet the wealthy classes are indifferent spectators of a greater arena and a more bitter contest, where more blood and tears are shed. In the crowded lanes of our metropolis the circumstances of our time have enclosed a famishing host, who cannot be blamed if they trample each other down in the awful fight for life itself.

It is folly to talk of brotherhood till this unnatural state of things is remedied; and it is the duty of the Church to care for the poor in the truest sense, not by doles of charity, but by removing conditions which tend to obliterate all the better human instincts. It is time to cease the mockery of telling men to love one another, when they are placed on a battlefield where some must slay the other, and where they have no possession but a common misery. Religious teaching to such people, especially coming from the rich or well-to-do, is a blasphemy against Christ.

The struggle for existence is a powerful force against brotherhood; but even its darkness is illumined by rays of affection and kindness. The poor, we are told in the Report of the Parliamentary Commission, have some of the evils of their existence mitigated by the social feeling which leads them to share each other's sorrows and help each other's poverty. I believe, after all, more is done for the very poor by their own neighbours than by the condescending charity of the rich. *Haud ignarus mali*, the poor man tries to come to the rescue of his still poorer brother.

It is this struggle, which is fostered by unnatural conditions, that is the parent of anarchism and pessimism, which are dangerous foes of humanity, and which spread rapidly in disguised forms through life and literature.

Another great obstacle to brotherhood is the separation between the life of employers and employed which the great factory system begets. In field and farm labour the master and labourer live near each other, and join more or less in the same toil. There is a human union in all their operations, and the farmer is not hedged in from his men by a great band of underlings. The same is even truer of small shops, such as those of the blacksmith, where the same work is done by master and man. The kindliest feelings prevail in most of these cases of joint labour, and a healthy and manly acknowledgment of guidance by the master and aid by the servant. There is a wholesome air of brotherhood in the co-operation in useful work, which makes the farm or the smithy an actual aid in the furtherance of true human communion. It is far otherwise with a great factory: the owner dwells in isolation, and often in luxury; the factory hands have a sense of working for some unknown power which fate has doomed them to serve. Doubtless some men know their many workpeople, and take an interest in them; but the whole system is unnatural, and contrary to the general interests of mankind. It reverses the truth which Rousseau states in *Émile*: "It is the common people who constitute the bulk of mankind; the rest above that order are so few in number that they are not worth our consideration." The utilitarian formula of "The greatest happiness for the greatest number" is a good rule-of-thumb for working life; and the concentration of wealth in the hands of a few, for whom the many toil, is a violation of it so gross as to lead to a reversal of all the conditions of life, and a blasting of the hopes of progress.

The true remedy for this unhappy cause of social disunion is in profit-sharing. This has been tried in various instances, with general success. It may be that its commercial aspects would not turn out entirely prosperous, though there is every reason to anticipate the contrary; but even if wealth were not so rapidly accumulated, the better result of a store of brotherly love would be garnered. "A man's life consisteth not in the abundance of things which he possesseth." The natural state of things would be restored by such a co-operation of labour as the farm or smithy will show. There need be no equal partnerships; it is enough to make men feel that they are sharers in the common fortunes of the factory, to remove from them the sense of a social chasm. Some tell us that we should miss the successful men; that their force of character and power of riches are a valuable element in our life. But are the rich manufacturers so useful men? Are they not used as the type of vulgar ostentation and selfish vanity? Is it not the case that the lowest forms of talent—such as the skill of overreaching by cunning, lawful enough perhaps, but contrary to the best altruism—are the road to riches? We may be assured that the world would lose nothing by reducing the overgrown proportions of some of those so-called captains of industry.

Joint-stock companies have been regarded by some as an approach to the social unity as shown in a common activity; and at first sight it seems right so to class them. But unless the members of the company are themselves sharers in its work, it is at least doubtful if it in any way realises the hopes or beliefs of such thinkers. Is it not by joint-stock companies that we often see the pound of flesh exacted from the labourer? Heedless of all save the dividend, the Christians who form them are sometimes found indifferent as to the poor housing of their employees, to their protracted labours, to the loss of their Sunday rest, to the arbitrary rule of their superintending officials. They are probably a dangerous feature of our social system, constituting as they do small and almost irresponsible oligarchies. The agitators of this country and of the United States have some justification in seeing in them forms of organised tyranny of an ominous kind. If the citizens who are members of such companies realised their responsibility, they would lose their worst features; and they would become valuable aids to the great cause of human brotherhood if the workers were all partners in the concern, and were sharers in the profits of the association. What has been done in this direction has been of great promise for the future, and goes far to lead us to hope for a time when capital and labour shall be one in sympathy.

The greed of gain and love of luxury is in all its forms

the most deadly foe of brotherhood. It shows itself in many forms, and begets many hideous products. But one which is common enough to be lightly esteemed is the heedlessness which employers manifest to the feelings of those under them. As an American workman said : " We working people don't envy you your pie or your pictures, if we can have bread. It is the deeper thing that makes us indignant: it is being called fools and simpletons by our employers, and bearing it, because we must have the dollar. Labour is owned, and women are owned more than men, and will be until they can dare to combine and dare to refuse offers of ill-paid work, larded with harsh words."

The fierce complaints which many people make of imperfect work, such as Carlyle seems to have often been unfortunate enough to meet with, are a form of the same feeling of tyranny. We do not find fault with our equals in like manner for their faults.

The root of the whole matter is in the unconscious feeling of caste, which governs the hearts of men. Thackeray did not dislike Colonel Newcome for showing it; but none the less it is a dangerous possession. Our Saviour should have taught us by this time to rise above it; but inherited instincts are too strong; and even though the better part of mankind should forget it, the great mass of men have in their blood the memory of the slavery of bygone centuries, and calmly acquiesce in a state of injustice.

It cannot be said that the co-operative store system is altogether a wholesome movement. True brotherly feeling does not always dictate it, but often a love of petty gain.

Among well-to-do people it is especially selfish. A sound social life is best promoted by the increase in the number of those who are not in servitude to other persons, but who, as tradesmen, merchants, and the like, serve the community. The store system is simply a means of changing men who might think for themselves in business, into servants of others. Such a loss of real individual character is not compensated by the gain to other people of some small sums of money. Speaking generally, where the co-operative store system does not arise from the actual poverty of the members through scanty wages, it is a system which has many of the faults of the joint-stock system, and it masquerades all the while as a promoter of social union.

But on a wider field we see greater obstacles to the brotherhood of man. The antipathies which certain races feel to others is a very real fact in human life, however it may be accounted for. It leads to a Chauvinist patriotism which cannot but end in war, which is engaged in without much consideration as to success or cost. Without doubt its presence in Europe, not to speak of the other continents, constitutes a real danger, which is augmented when there is a religious difference as well as a racial. The hatred which the Irish Celt seems to have to the English Saxon is found even in the prejudice which the more intellectual Scot has to the ways of England, which returns to both people a still greater feeling of aversion. It apparently is also found in the mutual dislike of French and German, and another race antipathy is observable between Germans and Hungarians. History may tell us the reason of these feelings. People at war with each other for centuries cannot be expected to love each other much; but it is also possible that unrecorded history may have the secret. Men of diverse character are antipathetic as individuals; and the same seems true of nations. The lower forms of literature strengthen this unreasoning prejudice between peoples; and the theatre, often in recent times the mouthpiece of low views of life and vulgar thought, or rather unthinkingness, has helped in the unhappy cause of race separation. Even Communism has its prophet of race-antagonism; for Felix Pyat proposed in 1870 a coalition of the Latin against the Teutonic race.

This fact appears in its most aggravated forms in the contact of white races and the black or yellow. The aversion which Americans feel to Chinamen, and their treatment of the Negroes, are explicable by a sense of the marked difference between the various races. A foreigner who settles in an English village is soon made to learn very forcibly the strength of this prejudice against strangers among the uneducated classes.

Other examples are seen in the treatment which Hindoo and other natives of India receive from the English there; and the relations between the Dutch and the South African tribes. English feeling is hardened beyond belief on this subject, as the language of travellers and correspondents proves; and if such is the sentiment of the better taught among nominally Christian people, what is to be expected of those of less education? It springs from an antipathy which has as little reason to guide it as the mad rush of a bull at a wayfarer; it is a mere animal impulse, unworthy of civilised man, and ought sternly to be repressed. It is not difficult to check, for missionaries tell us they soon come to love those whom they give their lives for; and I suppose even an Englishman would master his dislike to them, and endeavour to save a drowning Zulu or Hindoo. It would be easy to collect a number of instances of this disregard of our common humanity in dealing with savage races. The case of Governor Eyre is not forgotten; and although the Governor's own action is quite defensible, it is not so with the language of some of his supporters, who spoke of Negroes as if they were noxious animals. There were instances in the late Burmese war, as in every war we have had with uncivilised, or less civilised, races, of the same contempt for human brotherhood, which, after all, is an equal insult to our common Father in heaven.

Soldiering is a trade which is carried on amid surroundings which cannot help to humanise men; yet the excesses of cruelty in its operations have not solely been found among savage peoples. The "century of dishonour" which records the history of the dealings of the United States with the Red Indians, still more enforces this practical disbelief in the real kinship of man.

It is a formidable portent for the future to find men apparently unable to rid themselves of race-antipathy, nay, to find these antipathies growing even stronger. Till man can subdue the mere animal impulse of hatred to the man who does not look like himself, and can master his brute lust of conquest, the final realisation of human brotherhood is yet far off. But surely these antipathies should not be fostered by the religion of peace, which should enlist all its professors in an army of reconciliation.

And pity it is that a most powerful enemy to the communion of men with each other in friendly intercourse and aid is connected with religion itself, though it is by no means a part of it. The spirit of religious intolerance is the refined form of the hatred which savage tribes have to their neighbours. It no longer uses the same weapons of murder and torture which it formerly shared with the barbarian warriors; but its feelings of hatred are little less bitter. No sect has a monopoly of it, though perhaps in the great national Church of Russia may be found its present triumphs, while England is not free from it. Clergy who still find occasion of bitter strife over the burial of the dead, have a good deal to learn, even from the great heathen moralists, not to say the ordinary everyday feelings of the ancient world. Church and Dissent, with their mutual prejudices, poison the life of many a village, and estrange people from each other who ought to be united in love and service. England is rent in twain because some theologians have differed from others. Mr. Mill deplores this in the interests of truth and freedom; but its worst result is the fact of the separation itself. No possible dogmatic disagreement could justify a social separation so great; and it is mere irrational prejudice, a survival of the Stone age, which keeps apart men of the same nation, and with the same great purposes in life. This intolerance is found in sceptics as well as in orthodox thinkers, and the sceptics rise with ease to the height of the *odium theologicum* in argument at least. A recognition of the great truth that God is the Father of all men, and that His Spirit guides them, will teach men to believe in the sincerity of those who differ from them, and enable them to preserve both respect and affection for the worthy of all forms of creed. If they cannot rise to that height, and still must hold to the belief that they alone have received the divine teaching, and obeyed it, a knowledge of human infirmity will surely moderate the bitterness of their intolerance. We are all mortal, and liable to error; let us not think worse of our fellow-men because we find them fallible, as we know we are ourselves.

These elements of opposition to human brotherhood which we have spoken of, are strong powers deeply rooted in our modern life; but they all may be made to yield to the influence of Christianity. If only men come to recognise how hostile they are to the progress of true religion, they will bend their efforts to remove such obstacles. It will be long till men see that the poor have not to struggle desperately for bare existence, till employers and employed have the bond of common sympathy and interests, till race prejudices disappear, and religious intolerance be forgotten in the brotherhood of the true love of God and man; but the world is marching on to that goal, and the divine purpose will be accomplished.

CHAPTER XXV

THE KINGDOM OF GOD AND THE CHURCH

It is clear that a phrase such as "the kingdom of God," which is used often by Christ and His apostles, deserves our close attention. It cannot be said that "the kingdom of God" was an idea whose interpretation was much developed in this country until recently. The loose way of thinking, which ran into one mould all the expressions which Jesus or His disciples used in order to describe their mission, has even yet too many followers among us. But the more thoughtful mind of the present-day theologian looks with earnest attention at the exact force of any words which are so often used as to be a characteristic utterance of Jesus.

The words "kingdom of God" are manifestly in their first use calculated to direct the Jewish mind to the Messianic hopes which the nation cherished. They have their backward gaze to the old theocracy, and a forward prospect of some future kingdom which would be in some way like the former. Hase believed, and apparently the author of *Ecce Homo* followed him in thinking, that Jesus had an idea in His early teaching of an outward and temporal monarchy, which He afterwards laid aside for a more spiritual view of His mission as the Founder of the divine society. It is not easy to establish any such opinion, for the spiritual character of the new dispensation is proclaimed from the first. But it is manifest that the attention of the people was meant to be fixed on this view of the mission of Jesus as the beginning of a new kingdom, a kingdom of God.

Although the words Jesus used were not dwelt on by the older Christian writers, the idea of the extension of the kingdom of God is a root of their theology. In the Nicene Creed, indeed, we find the words, speaking of Christ, "whose kingdom shall have no end." St. Augustine, in his *City of God*, develops his conception of the divine life in mankind, subject to the perpetual growth and eternal triumph of the work of Christ. And in times before St. Augustine we find in the apologists of Christianity a grasp of the growing power of Christianity which has had much effect in later days. Justin Martyr and Clement of Alexandria, each in his own way, show an appreciation of the universal character of Christianity, which Christ Himself unfolds over and over again in His explanation of the kingdom of God. Justin speaks of the Word as seed in the souls of men of old; and Clement regards the Word as the instructor of all, because all men are His children. It is, however, Origen who, in his treatise *De Principiis*, first puts into distinct form those thoughts of the universal kingdom which have become current among men. The Alexandrian theology has had little influence on Western thought, which has been a long shadow of St. Augustine, and the wide views of Origen were almost forgotten.

The newer German theology has many affinities to the Alexandrian mind, and the kingdom of God has been much thought about in many aspects. It has come to be regarded as a centre from which to view the complete Christian scheme of moral regeneration for man. The result of this examination has always led to that wider idea of the historical development of Christianity which embraces its total influence on mankind.

The older Protestant view had its limitations. It identified the kingdom of God with the personal acceptance of the offer of salvation. The kingdoms of grace and glory were looked at in an individual light, and their boundaries too narrowly defined. The Church and the gospel were presented in a personal aspect, which may have been a natural reaction against the too exclusively corporate idea of Catholicism, but which has maimed Lutheran and Calvinist Christianity for centuries.

Out of this the Churches are slowly ascending to a higher view of the Church and its mission in the general progress and improvement of mankind. The idea of the kingdom of God has been a great stimulus to right thinking in this direction. There seems, indeed, still a tendency to narrow thoughts of the Church, and a desire to escape from these shows itself, not by enlarging the conception of the Church, but by substituting for it as a new centre of Christian influence the kingdom of God; as Mr. Matthew Arnold contrasts his ideal infallible Church Catholic with the concrete papal Catholicism.

But the theory of the invisible Church which came into prominence with the Reformation, and whose ablest expounder in recent times is Neander, has lost practical force, though it still underlies much of Protestant dogmatics. It is extending its meaning, however, in the direction which Zwingli pointed out, to embrace all good men of all creeds; and begins to correspond almost exactly to what the Roman theologians call the *soul* of the Church. Still, such a conception is too far removed from actual life to be of much real service to men; and most thinkers see the need for making objective the results of Christianity. The view of the kingdom of God which the Lutheran theology has in recent times developed, comes very near to the Roman idea, in its best form, of the Catholic Church.

The natural rebound from the crude modern form of the Roman view, as taught in the Vatican theories of Catholicism, is seen in Stahl[1] and his opponent Bunsen. Both agree in making the State the kingdom of God, though Stahl approaches from the side of authority, and Bunsen from that of freedom. The real organic unity of the State, and its duty to the individuals composing it, are clearly recognised in both theories. But a principle which says that the welfare of all may be wrought out in this human sphere by one man, is an absurdity which history has exposed.[2]

Dean Fremantle[3] is a follower of the free State theory, and points out that those who now govern nations are waking up gradually to the fact that they, and not the clergy only, are the ministers of religion. But the

---

[1] For an account of Stahl's views, see Lichtenberger's *History of German Theology*, Hastie's trans.

[2] See Mazzini's essay on *Cæsarism*.

[3] *Gospel of the Secular Life.*

chief source of the movement which leads men to identify Church and State, the great expounder of this view of the kingdom of God, was Dr. Arnold of Rugby. With a lack of practical clearness as well as of theoretic symmetry, his scheme was one of the formative conceptions of modern theology, and well entitles him to be placed in the first rank of English theologians. True though it be, that since his death other theological forms have occupied the English mind, yet these differ rather in expression than in inward essence. The Oxford Movement had many points of difference with the theology of Dr. Arnold, which differences neither school made little of; but its practical issue has come to be the same—a desire to permeate all activity with religion. There is evidence to show that the Oxford theology is freeing itself from its exclusive occupation with dogma, and finding a new avatar in the practical world. Its foundations are no longer the object of its ceaseless study; it has arrived past the apologetic stage; and, after all, it is going to turn out very like the school which opposed it most. Such movements as Christian Socialism now nestle under its wing, and it breathes the spirit of freedom, not of hierarchical domination.

In Stahl there is a bitter distrust of all movements towards freedom, which Stahl identifies with individualism. Bunsen showed how far wrong all Stahl's premisses were, when the latter pointed out the evil effects of tolerant charity, and how impossible it was to be Christian and yet autocratic. There is an absolute discrepancy between the principles of personal government and the freedom of the gospel of Christ. The direction of the affairs of life involves a thousand interests which are too grave to be at the hazard of any man's will. It is hard to see how the principle of brotherhod can work, when one man must, by the nature of things, hold himself aloof from all the rest. Carlyle thought such a government the best; but the days of hero worship are no longer possible. The State has ends to serve which are within the ken of every man, and which it is every man's duty to forward. It is true that Stöcker and other State socialists attempt to reconcile this general welfare with a warm belief in an autocratic system; but the State hardly can be said to live at all in such a system. It becomes the apotheosis of an individual will working outside the members of the community. Such a community as Stahl imagined is an impossibility in our day. The whole tendency of Christianity is to move away from autocratic government in Church or State, and to tend to brotherhood.

A different view of the same theory is brought before us by Rothe.[1] The mission of Christianity is to form an ideal State, which is the kingdom of God. Christianity will so regenerate the whole world of human activity, that the Church, as a separate institution, will cease to exist, being no longer necessary. All aspects of human life will be then religious, and the kingdom of God be established on earth.

The opposite side of the same view has been taken by Kliefoth,[2] who sees that the leaven to which Christianity is compared is meant to leaven the whole lump. It is from the possession of the truth by a nation that an

[1] *Anfänge der Christlichen Kirche.* [2] *Von der Kirche.*

individual grasps it. The divine Spirit animates the Church, which is the fountain of grace to those who dwell within its fold, and which extends itself till it embraces all humanity. The Church will then come to be identical with mankind. By a different route we come to Rothe's conclusion.

The kingdom of God, according to Martensen,[1] is the highest good, which, apart from eschatology, is that influence which penetrates the natural life of man, so as to elevate his nature and form the divine unity blending together all his earthly existence. To this all other things are but as means to an end. The family, the State, the Church, art and science, are but servants of this ideal. All are but temporary vestures which will become time-worn. Some other and greater thing is before us; but we must not expect it on earth. To dream of a harmony of existence here would be but to set ourselves a vain task and to cherish for ourselves an impossible hope.

The impression that the Lutheran theologians rather make an interpretation of their own than follow humbly the guidance of the Master and His disciples, and the lessons of His Church's life and history, is deepened when we come to the views of Ritschl and his followers. There is a depth of insight in these writers which makes them even more stimulating than the always interesting speculations of Rothe. They examine into the subjective principle, which is the spiritual essence of the kingdom, which gives it life, which binds it together. They truly expound this as love. And while the heart is filled

[1] *Ethics*, i., trans. Clark's Theol. Library.

with this uniting spirit, there is an objective manifestation of the kingdom which includes every kind of moral and æsthetic activity of man. By this love working in the hearts of men, and showing itself in their outward energies, the complete moral regeneration of mankind will be accomplished.

There is in the Ritschlians that confusion which is natural to the mind of man in contemplating his future destiny. Is the kingdom of God to be accomplished upon earth? Or must we look forward to a new heavens and a new earth? There is a manifest development in the later followers of Ritschl towards a view which looks to a solution of the hopes of men beyond the sphere of mortality, to an accomplishment of the kingdom of God in heaven, not in earth. It is not within our present purpose to point out how difficult it is to reconcile the central principle of Ritschl with such theories as his followers Kaftan and Weiss express.[1] It is enough to show how large and comprehensive a view they all take of the aim of Christianity and the future destiny of man. There is, indeed, in all these writers too light an estimate of the actual facts of history, too narrow a conception of the great unfolding of the providential government of God. But that the Church is indebted to the theology of the writers who are more or less allied to the views of Ritschl for an entrance into a wide atmosphere of thought, no one would deny.

The Ritschlian ideas take their place among the many noble thoughts and great conceptions of Christianity which our century has brought forth. The theories

[1] Herrmann does not go far from Ritschl's own views.

which we have noticed are in themselves interesting as meditations on the future of mankind, founded on the teaching of Christ; but they also mark the tendency of theological thought to rise out of the individual to the general salvation, and in this they are related to the views of theologians like Maurice, Flint, Bruce, and Mulford. Some of the Germans, such as Hase, insist more on this consecration of all human life: they desire not to call anything common which God hath cleansed. The root of this principle, as far as the Germans are concerned, is found in Schleiermacher's *Discourses on Religion*; but the practical English mind had long appropriated it. In our literature, if not always in our theology, it has made itself seen; and it is the fundamental spiritual truth which underlies the Arthurian legends and the poems of Chaucer. From these golden fountains it has flowed through English life and thought.

The narrow view which German Protestantism has taken of the Church as a mere system of public worship and individual concern for another world than this earth of ours, has made them welcome the wider idea of the kingdom of God. But the Church, as thought of by St. Paul, has in itself none of these limitations: it is sectarianism which has made them. Surely a consideration of the long history of the Church, and its countless activities in all the elements of human life, might teach men to form a nobler ideal of its reason for existing. If it is the Reformation which has given man so narrow thoughts of the mission of the Church, it is a great loss to have been deprived of a catholic idea, notwithstanding many compensating gains. The separation from the historical Western Church which Luther effected, had perhaps too dogmatic a ground; the subsequent course of the German Protestantism has certainly occupied itself too much with doctrinal discussion. The extraordinary idea that the basis of union in a Church is dogma has often been shown, both in theory and practice, in Scotland; but it is perhaps more prevalent on the Continent. So able a man as Julius Müller elaborately developed in different forms this conception, first in a broader and simpler form, and afterwards in a narrow and restricted sense.[1]

The first great truth to establish is that the unity of the Church is a part of its essence. The Church is a brotherhood of men who acknowledge they are brothers. They may do so from different reasons, but the fact of their brotherly union makes them members of the Church. To keep alive in their hearts this feeling, the sacraments have been appointed. The early history of the Church proves this, for St. Paul over and over again insists that unity and charity are supreme; that difference in doctrine forms no reason for separation, or likeness of doctrine no sufficient basis for union. The Church is therefore a visible body, a social communion, whose unchangeable element is the feeling and fact of brotherhood. Changeable elements are forms of doctrine, of worship, of government, of outward activity or of inward thought; but the great fact of the unity remains as the *raison d'être* of the Church. Rothe said that Christianity was of all things the most subject to change; and in doing so he did no more than echo the words of St.

[1] *Die Evangelische Union*, etc.

Paul, who told us that prophecies shall fail, and tongues shall cease, and knowledge shall vanish away. But there is one element which is permanent, which ever abides; and that is love and unity.

Sects which keep fast to the social bond, such as Methodists and Moravians, have supreme power over morals; while those who neglect this form of Christian life lose their most powerful means of edification. Though such social union be only imperfect while it is sectarian, it yet is an effort after and longing for a fuller communion. The most worthless form of religious life is that which centres itself round a special preacher, who is, for some reason, the focus of admiration. Nothing is more fatal to the true ideal of the Church, and the soul of the preacher is often itself darkened by the surroundings. He forgets the universal mission of the Christian religion, and becomes a self-seeking man, believing chiefly in himself. Such men are mostly found indifferent to the wider ideas of the Church, where they do not oppose them; and their influence, while seeming extended, is really nothing. The career of Edward Irving gives a good example of the results of such individual action. The giddy crowd who followed him, heard his message only to forget it; and his unconscious vanity was hurt. Himself an egoist in religion, his training had not led him to think of the universal Church as a real existence. But circumstances taught him that the voice of a single man was nothing, that the organic life of the Church was great. "How little," said Neander, " it is in the power of anyone to create anything! How little one can achieve in a conflict with Providence, which leads and forms according to its own eternal decree the spirit of all the periods of history." Though Edward Irving got to see this truth, his excessive personality again led him astray; and although his sect have got hold of a real truth, they make a poor use of it.

The unity of the Church has, as its correlative, the universal priesthood. The community is, in a sense, wrapped up in every member of it. Every man who has the feeling of Christian brotherhood within him is a priest of Christ. The priestly office is exercised by many who are not conscious of their calling, "for he that is not against us is for us."

The Church, therefore, is outward and visible, and unity is the breath of its life. Whence, then, come our divisions? It is because we forget the principle of union. We drug our hearts by an easy belief in an invisible unity. What kind of unity is it which never manifests itself, which is a mere article of faith contradicted by our daily experience? It is a vain imagination to think that the ideal of the Christian Church can be satisfied by an invisible unity, whose proofs are too hard to seek for. We are assured that in the strife of sects there is a real unity, which they believe in and seek after. It is hard to credit this, and harder to see the advantage of such a union. We need a unity which men can see and know, and whose fruits are daily reaped in our life; mere empty verbiage cannot satisfy our hearts.

What advantage is there to any thinker in dissociating the Church from the kingdom of God? It is, we are assured, a return to a consideration of Jesus' own words, apart from the interpretation time has put on them. But we cannot disregard the events of history and the development of human life. The Church is the permanent element in our being, and is destined to be the expression of universal mankind. The words "kingdom of God" do indeed bring before us the divine sovereignty, which none can deny, and which exists independent of man altogether. But the Church, the gathering of men, has a nearer human meaning. It may be but a part of God's kingdom, but it embraces all mankind.

The kingdom of God is but the divine aspect of the visible Church of mankind, of which Christ is the Head. Its life principle is love and unity, of which the Church is the outward and real manifestation.

The poor have the kingdom for theirs, because of their mutual help and aid; the rich, because of their selfish isolation, find it hard to enter. The kingdom spreads like a leaven because love begets love, and knits men to men. It is within us, because it is an inner principle which God kindles in our hearts, and cometh not with observation. It is righteousness and peace and joy in the Holy Ghost, who is the Spirit of unity. It comes with power when the Church fully realises its divine end.

Briefly speaking, therefore, the kingdom of God is realised on earth by the visible Church, which is ever marching on to a perfect unity, until at last it mirrors the unity of God. "*That they may be one, even as we are one.*"

But this unity of the Church does not mean any hierarchical or dogmatic unity. It cannot be confined within these narrow bounds, but must embrace everyone who "in every nation feareth God and worketh righteousness." It is a unity in "faith which worketh by love."

But what practical plan shall we take to realise it? The basis of dogma will never suffice. There is no evidence that such agreement will exist among men within any conceivable time. Is there any mind so formed that it can grasp all the truth? Yet such a supposition really underlies the theory that a doctrinal basis will be found on which to unite the Christian world.

Another plan is suggested and more and more put into practice, and that is the union of those who hold the same system of Church government. Pan-Anglicanism, Pan-Presbyterianism, Pan-Wesleyanism, are schemes to which more or less of an actual shape has been given. Now, though this seems a less dignified basis than doctrinal unity, though it seems less permanent to take the outward organisation, which after all may be temporary, as the uniting element, it is nearer the heart of the truth. For the outward organisation is in itself a testimony to the social and brotherly unity of Christians; it is in itself, with its agencies of mutual intercourse, friendship, and help, a mirror of what the whole Church should be; and is in itself a promise of better things, of a wider and deeper union.

But it is not enough. We cannot be content to divide Christendom into sections, however large they be. The unity of the Church can only be realised on the principle of the unity in the Christian life of brotherhood. This is its basis, and on this alone will it reach its divine ideal. Still more, that form of Church life and government, which best serves the cause of unity and brotherhood, alone possesses elements of permanence, and eventually must absorb all other systems.

The Church can never fulfil its complete duty with reference to human brotherhood till it is itself united. A spectacle of jarring sects, such as Christendom now presents,—and must always present if disunited, notwithstanding people shutting their eyes and talking of spiritual union,—is a permanent obstacle to the growth of human brotherhood. It may be that the union of the Church will come from the union of mankind; that ecclesiastics, as in days gone by, will not interpret the signs of the times till they are made clear by secular events: but the unity of the Church must come, for it is a necessity of humanity. We must strive for it with all the might we can; for it is not a mere matter of worldly convenience, as sometimes people think, it is the divine life of the Church coming to perfection. I do not hope for it soon, but the purer our hearts become, the nearer we shall come to it. We must keep in view the commandment—"Be ye therefore perfect, even as your Father which is in heaven is perfect."

CHAPTER XXVI

THE FUTURE

WHAT, then, have we ascertained as to the progress of mankind which would lead us to hope for the future?

We have seen the gradual formation of nations into united societies; and we have seen these nations longing for wider federations. Men's thoughts have risen to a conception of united humanity, not as a mere idea of the imagination, but as a practical possibility. Influenced by this conception, they have striven for equal freedom and social brotherhood. They are beginning to look at life from the standpoint of duty to all mankind, for all are sharers in the common life.

Religion has, equally with secular life, lent its aid to the great cause of human unity. The doctrines which have divided mankind into sects, with their shibboleths, are being relegated to their true place. The Church is now being regarded as a vast society of helpers and lovers of mankind, whose uniting principle is brotherhood. With this living force in their hearts, men are being impelled to seek such a unity in the Church as will make it include all the children of the divine Father.

Both in Church and in State the tendencies of men

are towards union. What is to be the outcome of it all?

We believe that these tendencies show the divine purpose towards man; that they point the goal to which the race is tending. They reveal the secret of man's existence, and explain all the course of his history. Man came into the world to train himself, by a long course of action and thought, to a perfect association in love with all his kind. Mankind is destined to attain to a complete unity in itself.

Mankind must be regarded as *a thing which has its end in itself*, i.e. apart from the other works of God. A theory of life which is sufficient to explain human life in the relations of men to each other, is a complete theory of humanity. Such a theory, indeed, could not escape accounting for more than the mere existence of man, present and future; but it could, nevertheless, be self-contained as regards mankind. It is almost certain that any explanation which we are able to arrive at regarding the purpose of human life and the destiny of the human race, would also have something to say on the relation of man to the universe. All creation is a harmony, and to discover the secret of any one sphere, must necessarily bring us over the border into other regions. Human duty and human hopes may be unfolded in their entireness without a true theory of astronomy. Some men say that they cannot be so explained; others think they have found an entrance in the secret of all things. Carlyle despairs of a solution that will bring all into harmony; the Hegelian and the Positivist are confident that they have found a universal key. Time will bring us nearer a complete solution of all things; though eternity will be needed to attain it. Meanwhile let us inquire within the region at our command, and try to make a theory of man.

The first character of that theory will be its unity. We must have no chasms in our explanation, no contradictions. The progress of man in material things and in moral, must tend in the same direction. The animal nature of man, and his inner soul of reason and conscience, must serve the same great end. It is a favourite way of looking at life with some writers, to deepen the contrasts of existence; to multiply the oppositions that appear in our earthly life. They revel in discord, and are incredulous of unity. We are told that the animal instincts of man would lead him to utter selfishness, to that natural condition of war which Hobbes believed in, and that these instincts still fight against love and brotherhood. Another power,—too often conceived as external to man,—the power of religion, will, however, overmaster these separating tendencies, and teach man to love and serve and live at peace with his neighbour. But may we not ask if it was not the same God who gave man his physical instincts as well as his nobler powers? Is it not a dark relic of Manichæanism to believe in this conflict within the life of man? It needs not a deep observer to see how the physical passion of love is made to serve the highest ends; how it runs alongside the spiritual steed which draws the chariot of man's soul. Still more, does it not bring about man's first form of unity—that family life which is the promise and potency of his perfect future? These ordinary affections, which are the conditions of our earthly existence, are unconscious longings for the divine Father: it is through these ethical purities that we learn to love the Supreme.

And in less deep matters of life, does not the fact that men have to league themselves for self-defence against the powers of nature, lead them to a close association for mutual aid and comfort? Religion acts on the lines of man's nature; and that nature is a harmony of tendencies, physical, animal, and spiritual, which lead all in the same direction. Not that there are not desires and weaknesses, physical, mental, and moral, which take us from the true way; but the general tendency of human nature in all its activities is towards the same goal.

We believe that that goal for humanity is a perfect association of men in brotherly love. This union of mankind implies as its correlative an absolute recognition of, and enjoyment of, God as the universal Father. The one cannot exist without the other; a complete recognition of man's brotherhood is only possible when God is recognised as the Father of all; a complete recognition of the divine Fatherhood is only possible when all mankind are acknowledged as brothers. The course of God's ways with man is to assure men of the sublime truth of His Fatherhood; the course of man's life on the earth is to bring him into this universal brotherhood. The ideal of this brotherhood is the Church, which has Christ for its Head. The Church is the image of the future projected on the present. But by the Church we do not mean any present embodiment of it in hierarchical form; but rather that outward and inward unity of which all such embodiments are but shadows. A free State at present offers such benefits as it can confer to all. There is no question as to the religion or philosophy of the citizen; he is a member of the civic community simply because he is a human being dwelling within the bounds of the country. A similar catholic view must some day be taken by the Church: it must be universal as humanity itself.

The complete union of mankind could not have been accomplished without Christ. Though age after age might contribute, and did contribute, some aid to the bringing about the union of mankind, yet the task would have been infinitely far off without the mission of Jesus to direct and complete it.

Such a society of mankind implies *ethical purity*. If men live in love with their neighbours, seeking at all times their neighbour's welfare, they will not do him any wrong. The commandments, which are all summed up in *love*, will all be observed. An altruism which is perfect leaves no loophole for offence. The life of brotherhood is the perfect life for man.

The *happiness* of mankind will be secured. It is vain for any system of morals to exclude happiness from its sphere; for men will seek it. Those who preach stern duty cannot fail to see that in an ideal state of existence, happiness must always accompany duty; and that the two will tend by degrees to become invariably companions. The main source of happiness in this world is in the intercourse we have with one another in our family and in our social life. Our love, our friendship, are the summits of human joy. Perfect love among men will bring perfect happiness.

But what of the physical conditions of life? Will pain and disease not visit men with their dark shadows, and chill the glow of being within us? As long as man is imperfect, he must bear the consequences of that condition; so these elements of life cannot be overcome. But we shall come nearer to conquering them as time goes on. Life must free itself more and more from their bondage, and the travailing of the creature come to an end. After all, when we speak of perfect things in connection with man, we only mean a growing approach to perfection. Nearer and nearer we come, till an infinitely small distance severs us from the absolute consummation.

And if pain and sorrow dwell with us, will they not be soothed almost to stinglessness by the happy thought of perfect love surrounding us? If our present service to each other can so lighten the burdens of life, we may be sure that, as life becomes more loving, its loads will almost disappear. For the greater part of the sorrow of life comes from unkindness, from unbrotherly acts; and if these sources are dried up, the river of misery will cease to flow. Sin is nothing but selfishness; and if we conquer selfishness by a perfect love for others, sin will vanish from our hearts.

Happiness is but one side of the principle of love. It is one harmony of our souls, and love is the complete unity of our being which causes that harmony.

The view of the end of man's life on earth, as being a perfect society of love, satisfies, then, the ethical needs of purity and happiness. How does it stand related to knowledge?

Clearly an advance in knowledge is a condition of

our life here. Our minds cannot rest in the attainments of the past. We must advance, though advance be toilsome and slow. But it is evident that a general sympathy of being implies a mental ease of communication, which will make discovery more ready and progress more rapid. The whole mental energy of the race will be given to solving any problem; the mind of man will move, not in scattered skirmishers, but as a solid phalanx. Of this mental sympathy we have examples in the ready understanding which people who love each other have of the working of each other's minds. Sometimes, even when such are far apart from each other, they can each know the other's thoughts. There is evidence enough of this possibility to make us see that men's minds have a capacity for sympathetic intercourse in ways we do not entirely discern.

But still more proof of this sympathy is found in the fact that discoveries are made often at the same time by separate observers; that scientific men who come much into each other's company develop similar methods of reasoning. The great examples of this universal sympathy are found in the wider movements of human thought, which work like leaven, and are spread from mind to mind with inconceivable quickness. What power does man gain from this combined emotion and intelligence? It is this alone which can accomplish anything great in deed or thought. And it seems nowadays that this is to be the general character of human thought. History used to be largely the biography of the men who made their names famous in the age when they lived. Carlyle and Macaulay give us a series of epics, more or less stately, but we do not arrive at any close understanding of how the world moved in the days they write of. Modern historians like Stubbs and Maine, and Freeman and Coulanges, pay little heed to individual careers, but the whole march of events is brought before us. Democracy does not in our time choose great leaders; it does not follow some trumpet call of a hero; but speaks through some average man, who is the child of his age, and the product of its combined mental activity is seen in his acts.

Outstanding men are less common; it may be because the whole race whose life we know is being elevated. But it is certain that the perpetual intercourse of men, and the common enjoyment of the intellectual facilities of our life must lead, and do lead, to a sameness of mental structure. Men work much together, and play much together; they take their ideas from the same sources, and express their opinions much in the same words. This is a natural result of political organisation, which demands so much surrender of the individual will, if that individual will should exist. Eccentricity is almost a memory of the past; and decided individuality is rarer than ever. The association of men must tend to this; but while it lessens the prominence of such features, it strengthens the total mental capacity of humanity, and gives it a stronger impulsive force. For though one man may be weary and baffled, the race ever renews its youth, and goes forward with unabated vigour.

Does such an association of mankind as we seem to see in the future as the goal of mankind, imply equality? Condorcet said that what we must look for is an *equality of fact*, as well as what men were supplied with in his day, an equality of right.

There must be a tendency towards equalisation of possessions, by the mere operations of the law of love; and as there will be equal facilities for acquiring knowledge, there will be a tendency to equal attainments. But the individual soul will not therefore be extinguished in its freedom. The process of the spread of knowledge and happiness will find its fittest analogy in the doctrine of the dissipation of energy. Energy overflows when it can, and tends to bring all its manifestations to one level; and a time will, in the nature of things, come when everything will possess an equal amount of energy, and the universe be quiescent. But this dissipation of energy depends on the fact (or theory) that atoms have a certain physical size. If they are infinitely divisible, no dissipation is possible; for an equal level never could be reached.

If mental processes have any likeness to physical, it is clear that any equalisation which would take place would still leave the individual soul with its own mental dimensions. But we know that physical analogies cannot hold in the sphere of mind. The dissipation of energy is a fact which depends on the conservation of energy,[1]

[1] Dr. Macquorn Rankine supposed that the conservation of energy must be believed in, subject to a belief in its absolute renewal on dissipation; for the margin at the bounds of our universe between the atoms adjacent to the void beyond, must be the difference between nothing and the general diffused energy of this universe. A belief in the immediate action of the divine Spirit on the souls of men presents an analogy to this speculation of Dr. Rankine's. A Christian may, at least, always point to the divine Life as renewing and invigorating the collective soul of man.

which cannot apply to the intellectual progress of the race. Higher and still higher will the race rise, and the mere fact, therefore, of its progress implies the preservation of inequalities in intellectual endowment, and probably also of actual possessions.

The goal of humanity is far removed from the Utopia of the socialist. In the first place, it is arrived at by the action of free will, not of compulsion. Its principle is the welfare of the body, while its advocates leave the soul to take care of itself. Love cannot be commanded; it must rise spontaneous in the heart; and an association of men based on any other principle than love is a tyranny, not a brotherhood. Such a tyranny contains within itself its own elements of dissolution. It has within the idea of caste, of inequality, of the surrender of freedom, the unwilling surrender of some to the power of others. Such a state of life, however its form may be attractive, is but a makeshift to be overturned in the progress of man.

Again, the true ideal of life is a harmony of various activities and levels of intelligence; not a dull unison of minds that are cast in the same mould. As St. Paul says: "For as we have many members in one body, and all members have not the same office; so we being many are one body in Christ, and members one of another." The socialist plan represses individuality, so that man has nothing to offer as a sacrifice to humanity. A slave cannot offer a freedom he does not possess, and under Socialism men would be slaves. The human will repressed would cease to exist, and love and intelligence perish of atrophy. But it is an impossible theory which we combat, and a complete Socialism would only lead to an arrogant opposition of Nihilism.

How different is the free association in love for which God has been preparing the human race during all the ages of humanity! As Mr. Ruskin says: "The love of the human race is increased by their individual differences, and the unity of the creature made perfect by each having something to bestow and to receive, bound to the rest by a thousand various necessities and various gratitudes; humility in each rejoicing to admire in his fellow that which he finds not in himself, and each being in some respect the complement of his race."

There is no need to suppose that even the extremest democracy would lead to a dull level of life, where existence would be little more than automatic. A deep thinker, who spent his whole life in the most republican State of modern times,—the author of the *Journal Intime*,—does not anticipate any such gloomy future to our hopes of universal brotherhood. "Is equality," he asks, "which in the dawn of existence is mere inertia, torpor, and death, to become at last the natural form of life? Or rather, above the economic and political equality to which the socialist and non-socialist democracy aspires, taking it too often for the term of its efforts, will there not arise a new kingdom of the mind, a church of refuge, a republic of souls, in which, far beyond the region of mere right and sordid utility, beauty, devotion, holiness, heroism, enthusiasm, the extraordinary, the infinite, shall have a worship and an abiding city?"

The universal principle of love and brotherhood, which we regard as the end for which man came into being, satisfies the intellectual conditions of such an end. It is a universal principle, and is also an abstract principle. No material end whatever can be regarded as the goal of man's life. We are not born to achieve mechanical progress, however great, or scientific acquirement, however high. For mechanical and scientific advances have for their end the quickening and enriching the social life of man. The real end in all man's labour and effort is man himself,—not the individual, but the race. In this view our systems of education should be carefully considered, and should be based on the foundation idea of completing the social perfection of man. The newer methods largely lack this central thought, though their deficiency is supplied by the other conditions of modern life, which develop the social instincts.

The principle of brotherhood is equally applicable to all men, and forms a solution of every life. No other kind of progress can be said to have this general applicability.

But further, this principle in man is a reflection of the character of God, as far as our knowledge extends of Him. "God is love," we are told by St. John; "and he that dwelleth in love dwelleth in God, and God in him." If man is ever to see God, this is the impulsive force which will lead him to the true vision. If the divine nature is to be communicated to mankind, it must be because man makes himself receptive of and kindred to the essential principle of that nature. "We shall be like Him; for we shall see Him as He is."

Our labour and knowledge, and our life itself, are fundamentally different from the knowledge, activity, and self-existence of God. The limitations of our being so condition us, that we cannot say we resemble the Absolute in these attributes. But the union which subsists between the hearts of men may be like that which unites God to all His children. Love is one, wherever it is found throughout the universe. St. John tells us that our intellectual efforts must fail to grasp the Eternal; for "no man hath seen God at any time." There is one way by which the soul can rise to communion with the divine existence, and only one. If we yield ourselves to the great tide of divine goodness which brings us day by day nearer our fellow-men, we enter into God's purpose and commune with Him. "If we love one another," says St. John, "God dwelleth in us, and His love is perfected in us." His purpose of love towards men is completed, their destiny is accomplished, when they all love one another.

But the universal character of the destiny of mankind in a social union of love is further illustrated by the intellectual analogy of love, which is, indeed, its other aspect. It is almost beyond the power of human speech to give form to the thought, but in his best moments man is conscious that the harmony of the universe is akin to love. Shelley was sure of his vision here. He had glimpses of

> "That sustaining Love
> Which, through the web of being blindly wove
> By man and beast, and earth and air and sea,
> Burns bright or dim, as each are mirrors of
> The fire for which all thirst."

Whitman, too, is aglow with the same feeling. " Smile," he says, " O voluptuous, cool-breath'd earth ! Smile, for your lover comes ! "

That " cosmic emotion," as Professor Clifford called it, is one of the highest joys of man ; but it is felt most deeply by a soul which is tuned to the love of mankind. We cannot but feel that when the world seems fairest to us, on some summer day at noontide, that there is a deep chord of love vibrating through the whole earth before us, to which our souls respond. And it is a fuller joy to the open and loving heart. As men have loved mankind more, they have felt the beauty of the universe more strongly. The poets of nature are the poets of man. Mr. Ruskin says truly : " Instead of supposing the love of nature necessarily connected with the faithlessness of the age, I believe it is connected properly with the benevolence and liberty of the age."

We often speak of faith as the link between man and man, and between man and God. It would better express our meaning did we follow Plato, who generally calls the sympathy between mind and mind by the name of *love*. It is from Him who is Love that this uniting power descends, and fills our hearts. It is this Love which is destined to be the common possession of united and regenerated humanity.

To this by slow steps we are advancing. I do not say that the progress is steadfast, although its general movement is onward. There are times when the spirit of mankind grows weary, and his energies droop, and he falls back in his march upwards. But the infinite Power above us cannot be stayed in His divine purpose, nor ever slacken His efforts. We do not despair of the returning tide because here and there a wave does not reach the height of its forerunner.

> "For while the tired waves, vainly breaking,
> Seem here no painful inch to gain,
> Far back, through creeks and inlets making,
> Comes silent, flooding in, the main."

Nor do we despair of the return of summer because the spring is checked by some bitter frosts. The seasons will fulfil their course, and the year reach its destined height. And the cause of love and brotherhood, notwithstanding some hours of sorrow and darkness, must one day prevail, and men abide for ever in the peace of God, which passeth all understanding.

INDEX

ABORIGINES, extinction of, 63.
About, Edmond, on human unity, 61.
Adam, descent from, 139.
Adler, Dr., on Jews, 40, 71.
Agape, 174.
Altruism, natural growth of, 295.
Ambrose, St., 169, 215.
American literature and freedom, 284, 286.
Amiel, H. F., 105, 370.
Amusements aid social unity, 275.
Antipathies between races, 340.
Apostolic Fathers, their teaching social, 142.
Apostolic succession, 26.
Aristophanes, 72.
Aristotle, 72, 155, 300.
Arnold, Dr., 349.
Arnold, Sir Edwin, 30.
Arnold, Matthew, 10, 126, 347.
Art, its social influence, 273, 276.
Asceticism, pagan, 144; opposed to labour, 147.
Augustine, St., on the immaculate conception, 65; on conversion, 188; quoted, 25, 51, 89, 145, 151, 188, 191, 215, 224, 311.
Aurelius, Marcus, 208.
Avestan creed, 45.

BALLADS, influence on national life of, 284.
Balzac, his human sympathy, 70, 280.
Baptism, of heretics, 22, 172; of infants, 171, 190; its meaning, 173; baptismal regeneration, 177.
Béranger, service to brotherhood, 280.
Bernard, St., 189, 190.

Boarding out of pauper children, 165.
Bradley, F. H., 11.
Brahmo Somaj, 47.
Brotherhood, before Christ, 39; taught by Christ, 96; in the Epistles, 128; in the early Church, 206; in mediæval Church, 224; since Reformation, 242; forces against, 321, 334; its future, 360.
Browning, 292.
Buddhism, its ethics, 46, 197.
Bunsen, 348.
Butler, Bishop, on social instinct, 295.
Burns, 279.
Byron, 282, 291.

CALVINISM, 89, 144.
Canon of Scripture, 2.
Carlyle, 77, 112, 120.
Chantal, Mme., 105.
Charity in early Church, 216.
Chateaubriand, 282.
Chiarini, Abbé, 40.
Children, religious training, 191; in Middle Ages, 234.
Chinese ethics, 47.
Chivalry, 232.
Christianity, social, 101; relation to patriotism, 310.
Chrysostom, 149, 215, 225.
Church, Catholic idea, 225; Neander's view, 226, 347; disunion, 343; unity the essence of, 354.
Cicero, 41, 43.
Clemens, Alexandrinus, 12, 142.
Clemens, Romanus, 169.
Clifford, W. K., 13, 322.
Clough, A. H., 77, 291.
Coleridge, 20.

INDEX

Communion, Holy. *See* Eucharist.
Communities, life in, 203.
Community of goods, 214.
Comte, 16, 32, 124, 140, 249, 305.
Condorcet, 247.
Confession, Scots, 7; Augsburg, 181; Westminster, 181.
Conscience, the Christian, 108, 177.
Co-operative stores, 339.
Cosmopolitanism, 317, 328.
Councils, Carthage, 22; Nicæa, 23; Lateran, 84.
Crabbe, 278.
Creed, Apostles', 17.
Cyprian, St., 144, 152, 188, 217.

DANTE, Purgatory, 9; Hell, 51; *De Monarchia*, 229, 280.
Darwin on aboriginal life, 157.
Delitzsch, 181.
Democracy, 240, 255, 303.
Denison, Edward, 309.
Development of Christianity, Roman and Protestant views, 4; its ethical purpose, 27.
Dickens, 112, 279, 285.
Didaché, 218.
Divorce, in United States, 160; dangerous, 161.
Doctrine, its end in morals, 10; how efficacious, 14; not made by priesthoods, 30.
Donatists, 224.
Duties of man, political theory of, 268, 305.

EDDA, hospitality in, 45.
Education, advance of, 262.
Egoism in Christian life, 182.
Egypt, slavery in, 48.
Eliot, George, 11, 286.
Emerson, 74, 176, 293.
Employers, relation to employed, 336.
Epictetus, 41, 209.
Epistles, brotherhood in, 128.
Eranians, 45.
Essenes, 141.
Ethical principle of Jesus, 96.
Ethics, relation of systems to Christianity, 113; relation of brotherhood to, 364.

Eucharist, administration, 153; communion in material things, 174; sacrificial doctrine, 178.
Evil, nature of, 196.

FACTORY Acts, 260.
Fall of man, 58.
Family, its past and future, 154; primary social union, 151; school of altruism, 297.
Fénélon on love of God, 99.
Fichte, 127, 251.
Fiske, J., 28.
Flint, Professor R., 43, 252, 353.
Fourier, 247.
Franchise, the, 263.
Freedom, condition of morality, 202; struggles for, 282.
Fremantle, Dean, 348.
Future of mankind, 360.

GALLICAN Church, 312.
Garibaldi, 326.
Giusti, 282.
God, conception of, in sacrifice, 81; fatherhood of, 80, 184; Aryan and Semitic views of, 186.
Goethe, 11, 76, 106, 175, 196, 279.
Gogol, 283.
Gospels, agreement, 80; Synoptists compared with St. John, 210.
Greece, national exclusiveness, 40 modern, 282, 284.
Greek Church, 65.
Green, T. H., 125, 204.
Guilds, social influence of, 73, 240.
Guyon, Mme., 105.

HAMANN, 11, 15.
Happiness through union of mankind, 364.
Harrison, F., 50, 85, 322.
Hegel, ethics, 113; future of mankind, 251.
Heine, 283.
Helvetius, 303.
Herbert of Cherbury, 9.
Herder, 8, 249.
Hermas, "the heavenly Church," 12.
Hilary, St., on conversion, 188.
Hindu castes, 46; attitude to labour, 72.

History an unfolding of divine purpose, 18.
Hordes, did man dwell in? 55, 156.
Hospitality, 44, 299.
Hugo, V., 279, 292.
Humiliation of Christ, 65.

IMMACULATE conception, 65.
Incarnation, 66, 246.
Individual character, decline of, 367.
Individualism, Vinet and Channing, 103; in life of Church, 139; in politics, 257.
Infanticide, 234.
Inquisition, 225.
Interest on loans, 219.
Intolerance, religious, 343.
Intuitionalism, 113.
Irving, Edward, 355.

JAMES, St., brotherhood in Epistle of, 129.
Jerome, St., 145.
Jesus, why He chose calling of workman, 67; centre of His theology, 81; Son of God, 90; ethics of, 96; authority of, 115.
John, St., Gospel narrower than Synoptists, 210; view of new birth, 189; brotherhood in Epistles, 130; in Apocalypse, 130.
Joint-stock companies, 338.
Jovinian, 145.
Judaism, exclusiveness, 40; teaching on labour, 71.
Justice, progress from, to love, 268.
Justification, by faith, 184; by works, 193.
Justin Martyr, 51, 83.

KANT, categorical imperative, 11; on passive love, 98; on religion, 115; on morals, 123; on united mankind, 250.
Karamsin, 283.
Kempis, à, 107; *Imitation* defective, 110.
Kingdom of God, views of Fathers, Reformers, German and English theologians, 345.
Kingsley on marriage, 168.
Kliefoth, 181, 350.

Knowledge through union of mankind, 365.
Kompert on Jewish dislike to labour, 71.
Krause, 252.

LABOUR, attitude of Jesus to, 66; blessing to community, 73; social influence, 77; future of, 79; end of, 371.
Labouring classes, 231, 258, 261, 302.
Lamennais, 279.
Lecky, W. E. H., 43, 226.
Leopardi, 282.
Leroux, 248, 279.
Lessing, 9, 249.
Letourneau, 159, 296.
Lilly, W. S., 226.
Limitations of earthly life of Jesus, 91.
Literature, its service to freedom, 278; and sympathy, 285.
Lotze, 241, 254, 296.
Love, motive of love to God, 99; principle of action, 101; progress from justice to, 268; of nature and man, 373.
Luther, on justification, 24, 35, 117; on missions, 244.
Lutheran doctrine of sacraments, 179.

MACAULAY on theological progress, 6.
Magyar poetry, 283.
Maine, Sir H., 156, 266.
Maistre, De, 91, 265.
Man, unity of, 52; fall of, 58.
Marriage, 154, 300.
Martensen, 181, 351.
Mary, Virgin, worship of, 23; its origin, 33; in Middle Ages, 233.
Maurice, F. D., 246, 353.
Mazzini, 68, 282, 303, 305, 315.
Method in theology, 18.
Mishna, 40.
Möhler, 4.
Moleschott, 325.
Monarchy, absolute, 264; formation of, 311.
Monasticism, 145, 239, 297.
Montanists, 142.
Mozley on national self-sacrifice, 316.
Music aids social unity, 273.

Mysticism, its nature, 98, 105; its selfishness, 148; in St. John, 212; mediæval, 228.

NAPOLEON on social influence of Christianity, 89.
Naturalism in art, 280.
Neander, view of Church, 226, 347.
Negro incapacity for co-operation, 60.
Neo-Platonism, 142, 215.
Newman, F. W., 220.
Newman, J. H., 4.
Nihilists, 159, 298.
Novalis, 151, 171.
Novatianism, 144, 151.

OBEDIENCE, means of knowledge, 117; unconscious to Christ, 127.
Origen, 3, 65, 346.

PASCAL, 8, 84, 114.
Patriarchal life, 156.
Patriotism, 264: relation to Christianity, 310; false forms of, 315.
Paul, St., brotherhood in Epistles, 132; conception of united humanity, 132.
Peace, universal, 265.
Peasant proprietors, 258.
Personality, the Christian, 198.
Pessimism, an anti-social force, 319, 331.
Peter, St., brotherhood in First Epistle, 128.
Petöfi, 283, 285.
Philemon, Epistle to, 221.
Plato, 72, 75, 84, 155, 198, 236; Republic, 107, 159, 163, 168, 191.
Pliny, 209.
Polygamy, 297.
Poor laws, 259.
Positivism. See Comte.
Priest, opposition of prophet and, 30, 187.
Profit-sharing, 337.
Progress, social and political, 259.
Purgatory, belief in, 32.
Purity through union of mankind, 363.
Pushkin, 283.

QUESNEL, 65.

RACE, peculiarities, 54; antipathies, 340.
Real presence, 178.
Reformation, its importance, 35; its theology, 242; social influence, 312.
Religion, the distinction of man, 56; the formative influence in nations, 314.
Renaissance, 21, 243.
Renan on St. Paul, 107; on social inequality, 323, 331.
Revolution, French, 303; of 1848, 305.
Richter, J. P. F., 56, 185, 274.
Rights of man, 267, 305; progress to *duties*, 268.
Ritschl, school of, 351.
Roman Church, 65, 112, 226; sacraments, 174; missions, 244.
Roman law of nations, 43.
Rothe, 19, 322, 350.
Rousseau, 281, 303.
Roux, Abbé, 149.
Ruskin, 71, 370, 373.

SACRAMENTS, witnesses to brotherhood, 171; their number, 175; views of, 179.
Sacrifice, conception of God implied in, 81, 185.
Saint-Pierre, 281.
Saint-Simon, 247, 304.
Sainte-Beuve, 106.
Sanctification, 193.
Sand, George, 11, 279.
Savages, free will in, 201.
Scepticism opposed to brotherhood, 322.
Schelling on primitive revelation, 58.
Schiller on art, 276.
Schleiermacher, 35, 56, 245, 353.
Scholasticism, 84, 230.
Schools, English public, 164.
Schopenhauer, 124, 199, 274.
Scott, Sir Walter, 279.
Semites, early life, 158; conception of God, 186.
Senancour, 105.
Separatists, 152.
Sermon on the Mount, 81.
Shelley, his view of the future, 287.
Sidgwick, H., 123.

INDEX

Slavery, in ancient world, 48, 221, 300; decline of, 231.
Smith, Robertson, 158.
Social contract, 267.
Socialism, may be opposed to brotherhood, 60; rise of, 267.
Society in Roman Catholic and Protestant countries, 328.
Socinianism, 242.
Socrates, 41, 198.
Spencer, H., *Data of Ethics*, 123.
Spirit, Holy, doctrine of, 94.
Stahl, 348.
Stanley, Dean, 30, 187.
Stirner, 325.
Stoics, 41, 67.
Strauss, 74; opposed to brotherhood, 323.
Swinburne, 289.
Synoptic Gospels, their central thought, 210.
Synthesis of knowledge, 85.

TACITUS, 45, 74.
Temple, Bishop, 9.
Tennyson, his vision of the future, 289.
Tertullian, 51, 174, 175.
Theatre, a social force, 272.
Theology, its scope, 49; development, 1; of Jesus, 80.
Tolstoï, 71, 284.
Totemism, 53.
Tourgenieff, 284.
Trinity, Mahomet's view of doctrine, 24; victory of orthodoxy, 29.

Truth, scholastic theory of a double, 84.

UNIFICATION, of nations, 264; of Churches, 358.
Uniformity not implied in human unity, 370.
Unitarians, 180.
United States, 255, 304; of Europe, 265.
Unity of man, 52.
Utilitarianism, 113, 123, 253.

VILMAR on sacraments, 175.
Vinet, his individualism, 103.
Vogüé, E. M. de, 69.

WEALTH, its relation to life, 68.
Whichcote, 10.
Whitman, Walt, his vision of the future, 293.
Whittier, J. G., 284.
Will, bondage of the, 198.
William of Auvergne, 9.
Women, position of, 232, 300; franchise for, 263.
Wordsworth, 77, 189, 248, 278.

XAVIER, 99.
Xenophon, 41.

ZINZENDORF, 109.
Zoroaster, 45.
Zwingli, 51, 242, 348.

THE FIRST THREE VOLUMES NOW READY,

PRICE 12S. EACH.

[See pp. 2 and 3 of this Prospectus.]

The
International Critical Commentary

on the Holy Scriptures of the Old and

New Testaments.

UNDER THE EDITORSHIP OF

THE REV. SAMUEL ROLLES DRIVER, D.D.,
Regius Professor of Hebrew, Oxford;

THE REV. ALFRED PLUMMER, M.A., D.D.,
Master of University College, Durham;

AND

THE REV. CHARLES AUGUSTUS BRIGGS, D.D.,
*Edward Robinson Professor of Biblical Theology,
Union Theological Seminary, New York.*

EDINBURGH
T. & T. CLARK, 38 GEORGE STREET.

LONDON AGENTS:

SIMPKIN, MARSHALL, HAMILTON, KENT, & CO. LTD.

To be had of all Booksellers.

THE INTERNATIONAL CRITICAL COMMENTARY

Just published, in post 8vo, price 12s.,

A

CRITICAL AND EXEGETICAL COMMENTARY

ON

DEUTERONOMY

BY THE REV. S. R. DRIVER, D.D.,

REGIUS PROFESSOR OF HEBREW, AND CANON OF CHRIST CHURCH,
OXFORD;
FORMERLY FELLOW OF NEW COLLEGE, OXFORD.

'There is plenty of room for such a comprehensive commentary as that which we are now promised, and if the subsequent volumes of the series come up to the standard of excellence set in the work that now lies before us, the series will supply a real want in our literature. . . . The Introduction is a masterly piece of work, and here the Oxford Professor of Hebrew is at his best. It gives by far the best and fairest discussion that we have ever seen of the critical problems connected with the book.'—*Guardian*.

'A most lucid and scholarly treatment of Deuteronomy, "one of the most attractive, as it is also one of the most important books of the Old Testament." . . . Professor Driver's Commentary will be found extremely interesting, not only to students and ministers, for whom its assistance will be invaluable, but also to every conscientious reader of the Scriptures.'—*Daily Chronicle*.

'The publication of this series marks an epoch in English exegesis of the Old Testament. It is the first attempt to provide the English student of the Hebrew Bible with a critical and exegetical commentary on the whole of the Old Testament which shall fully and frankly accept and utilise the results of modern criticism. . . . It is a handsome volume, clearly and beautifully printed, . . . even a slight examination shows that this book will materially increase Dr. Driver's reputation for exact and exhaustive scholarship.'—*British Weekly*.

'The series seems likely to surpass all previous enterprises of the kind in Great Britain and America.'—*Methodist Times*.

'The text of Deuteronomy is treated throughout with the scholarly thoroughness which marks the Introduction. The work altogether will be not less a treasure to the English student than a credit to English scholarship.'—*Christian World*.

'We have said enough, we hope, to send the student to this Commentary. . . . To the diligent miner there is a wealth of gold and precious stones awaiting his toil and industry.'—*Church Bells*.

'The Commentary on the text of Deuteronomy is characterised by the highest learning and fulness of research, and will be of great value, not only to the ordinary student, but to the mature scholar.'—*Record*.

'The work will be not less a treasure to the English student than a credit to English scholarship.'—*Christian World*.

EDINBURGH: T. & T. CLARK, 38 GEORGE STREET.
LONDON: SIMPKIN, MARSHALL, HAMILTON, KENT, & CO. LTD.

THE INTERNATIONAL CRITICAL COMMENTARY

Now ready, in post 8vo, price 12s.,

A
CRITICAL AND EXEGETICAL COMMENTARY

ON THE

EPISTLE TO THE ROMANS

BY THE

Rev. WILLIAM SANDAY, D.D., LL.D.,
LADY MARGARET PROFESSOR OF DIVINITY, AND
CANON OF CHRIST CHURCH, OXFORD;

AND THE

Rev. ARTHUR C. HEADLAM, B.D.,
FELLOW OF ALL SOULS COLLEGE, OXFORD.

Now ready, in post 8vo, price 12s.,

A
CRITICAL AND EXEGETICAL COMMENTARY

ON

JUDGES

BY THE

Rev. GEORGE F. MOORE, D.D.,
PROFESSOR OF HEBREW IN ANDOVER THEOLOGICAL SEMINARY.

EDINBURGH: T. & T. CLARK, 38 GEORGE STREET
LONDON: SIMPKIN, MARSHALL, HAMILTON, KENT, & CO. LTD.

The International Critical Commentary
on the Holy Scriptures of the Old and New Testaments.

EDITORS' PREFACE.

THERE are now before the public many Commentaries, written by British and American divines, of a popular or homiletical character. *The Cambridge Bible for Schools*, the *Handbooks for Bible Classes and Private Students*, *The Speaker's Commentary*, *The Popular Commentary* (Schaff), *The Expositor's Bible*, and other similar series, have their special place and importance. But they do not enter into the field of Critical Biblical scholarship occupied by such series of Commentaries as the *Kurzgefasstes exegetisches Handbuch zum A. T.*; De Wette's *Kurzgefasstes exegetisches Handbuch zum N. T.*; * Meyer's *Kritisch-exegetischer Kommentar*; * Keil and Delitzsch's *Biblischer Commentar über das A. T.*; * Lange's *Theologisch-homiletisches Bibelwerk*; Nowack's *Handkommentar zum A. T.*; Holtzmann's *Handkommentar zum N. T.* Several of these have been translated, edited, and in some cases enlarged and adapted, for the English-speaking public; others are in process of translation. But no corresponding series by British or American divines has hitherto been produced. The way has been prepared by special Commentaries by Cheyne, Ellicott, Kalisch, Lightfoot, Perowne, Westcott, and others; and the time has come, in the judgment of the projectors of this enterprise, when it is practicable to combine British and American scholars in the production of a critical, comprehensive Commentary that will be abreast of modern biblical scholarship, and in a measure lead its van.

* Authorised Translations published by Messrs. Clark.

EDITORS' PREFACE.

Messrs. T. & T. Clark of Edinburgh, Scotland, and Messrs. Charles Scribner's Sons of New York, U.S.A., propose to publish such a series of Commentaries on the Old and New Testaments, under the editorship of Prof. S. R. DRIVER, D.D., for the Old Testament, and the Rev. ALFRED PLUMMER, D.D., for the New Testament, in Great Britain; and of Prof. C. A. BRIGGS, D.D., in America.

The Commentaries will be international and inter-confessional, and will be free from polemical and ecclesiastical bias. They will be based upon a thorough critical study of the original texts of the Bible, and upon critical methods of interpretation. They are designed chiefly for students and clergymen, and will be written in a compact style. Each book will be preceded by an Introduction, stating the results of criticism upon it, and discussing impartially the questions still remaining open. The details of criticism will appear in their proper place in the body of the Commentary. Each section of the Text will be introduced with a paraphrase, or summary of contents. Technical details of textual and philological criticism will, as a rule, be kept distinct from matter of a more general character; and in the Old Testament the exegetical notes will be arranged, as far as possible, so as to be serviceable to students not acquainted with Hebrew. The History of Interpretation of the Books will be dealt with, when necessary, in the Introductions, with critical notices of the most important literature of the subject. Historical and Archæological questions, as well as questions of Biblical Theology, are included in the plan of the Commentaries, but not Practical or Homiletical Exegesis. The Volumes will constitute a uniform series.

President W. R. HARPER of Chicago University, announcing the Series in "The Biblical World," writes: "It is hardly necessary to say that this Series will stand first among all English serial commentaries upon the Bible. It stands with and admirably supplements the 'International Theological Library,' to which we have already learned to look for the best and most recent in the historical, literary, and linguistic study of the Bible. We are greatly in need of just what this Series promises to give."

The International Critical Commentary

on the Holy Scriptures of the Old and New Testaments.

UNDER THE EDITORSHIP OF

THE REV. SAMUEL ROLLES DRIVER, D.D.,
Regius Professor of Hebrew, Oxford;

THE REV. ALFRED PLUMMER, M.A., D.D.,
Master of University College, Durham;

AND

THE REV. CHARLES AUGUSTUS BRIGGS, D.D.,
*Edward Robinson Professor of Biblical Theology,
Union Theological Seminary, New York.*

THE following eminent Scholars are engaged upon the Volumes named below :—

THE OLD TESTAMENT.

Genesis. The Rev. T. K. CHEYNE, D.D., Oriel Professor of the Interpretation of Holy Scripture, Oxford.

Exodus. The Rev. A. R. S. KENNEDY, D.D., Professor of Hebrew, University of Edinburgh.

Leviticus. The Rev. H. A. WHITE, M.A., Fellow of New College, Oxford.

Numbers. G. BUCHANAN GRAY, B.A., Lecturer in Hebrew, Mansfield College, Oxford.

Deuteronomy. The Rev. S. R. DRIVER, D.D., Regius Professor of Hebrew, Oxford. [*Ready*, 12s.

Joshua. The Rev. GEORGE ADAM SMITH, D.D., Professor of Hebrew, Free Church College, Glasgow.

Judges. The Rev. GEORGE MOORE, D.D., Professor of Hebrew, Andover Theological Seminary, Andover, Mass. [*Ready*, 12s.

Samuel. The Rev. H. P. SMITH, D.D., late Professor of Hebrew, Lane Theological Seminary, Cincinnati, Ohio.

Kings. The Rev. FRANCIS BROWN, D.D., Professor of Hebrew and Cognate Languages, Union Theological Seminary, New York City.

Isaiah. The Rev. A. B. DAVIDSON, D.D., LL.D., Professor of Hebrew, Free Church College, Edinburgh.

Jeremiah. The Rev. A. F. KIRKPATRICK, D.D., Regius Professor of Hebrew, and Fellow of Trinity College, Cambridge.

Minor Prophets. W. R. HARPER, Ph.D., President of the University of Chicago, Illinois.

THE INTERNATIONAL CRITICAL COMMENTARY—continued.

THE OLD TESTAMENT—*continued.*

Psalms. The Rev. CHARLES A. BRIGGS, D.D., Edward Robinson Professor of Biblical Theology, Union Theological Seminary, New York.

Proverbs. The Rev. C. H. TOY, D.D., Professor of Hebrew, Harvard University, Cambridge, Massachusetts.

Job. The Rev. S. R. DRIVER, D.D., Regius Professor of Hebrew, Oxford.

Daniel. The Rev. JOHN P. PETERS, Ph.D., late Professor of Hebrew, P. E. Divinity School, Philadelphia, now Rector of St. Michael's Church, New York City.

Ezra and Nehemiah. The Rev. L. W. BATTEN, Ph.D., Professor of Hebrew, P. E. Divinity School, Philadelphia.

Chronicles. The Rev. EDWARD L. CURTIS, D.D., Professor of Hebrew, Yale University, New Haven, Conn.

THE NEW TESTAMENT.

Mark. The Rev. E. P. GOULD, D.D., Professor of New Testament Exegesis, P. E. Divinity School, Philadelphia.
[*In the Press.*]

Luke. The Rev. ALFRED PLUMMER, D.D., Master of University College, Durham.

Acts. The Rev. FREDERICK H. CHASE, D.D., Fellow of Christ's College, Cambridge.

Romans. The Rev. WILLIAM SANDAY, D.D., Lady Margaret Professor of Divinity, and Canon of Christ Church, Oxford; and the Rev. A. C. HEADLAM, M.A., Fellow of All Souls College, Oxford. [*Ready, 12s.*]

Corinthians. The Rev. ARCH. ROBERTSON, D.D., Principal of Bishop Hatfield's Hall, Durham.

Galatians. The Rev. ERNEST D. BURTON, A.B., Professor of New Testament Literature, University of Chicago.

Ephesians. The Rev. T. K. ABBOTT, B.D., D.Lit., formerly Professor of Biblical Greek, Trinity College, Dublin.

Philippians. The Rev. MARVIN R. VINCENT, D.D., Professor of Biblical Literature, Union Theological Seminary, New York City.

The Pastoral Epistles. The Rev. WALTER LOCK, M.A., Fellow of Magdalen College, and Tutor of Keble College, Oxford.

Hebrews. The Rev. T. C. EDWARDS, D.D., Principal of the Theological College, Bala; late Principal of University College of Wales, Aberystwyth.

Revelation. The Rev. ROBERT H. CHARLES, M.A., Trinity College, Dublin, and Exeter College, Oxford.

Other engagements will be announced shortly.

EDINBURGH: T. & T. CLARK, 38 GEORGE STREET.
NEW YORK: CHARLES SCRIBNER'S SONS, 153, 155, & 157 FIFTH AVENUE.

The International Theological Library.

EDITED BY

PROFESSORS S. D. F. SALMOND, D.D., AND C. A. BRIGGS, D.D.

No. I. of the Series. Fifth Edition. Post 8vo, price 12s.,

AN INTRODUCTION TO THE LITERATURE OF THE OLD TESTAMENT.

BY PROFESSOR S. R. DRIVER, D.D., OXFORD.

'By far the best account of the great critical problems connected with the Old Testament that has yet been written. . . . It is a perfect marvel of compression and lucidity combined. A monument of learning and well-balanced judgment.'—*The Guardian.*

No. II. of the Series. Third Edition. Post 8vo, 10s. 6d.,

CHRISTIAN ETHICS.

BY NEWMAN SMYTH, D.D.,

AUTHOR OF
'OLD FAITHS IN NEW LIGHT,' 'THE REALITY OF FAITH,' ETC. ETC.

'There is not a dead, dull, conventional line in the volume. It is the work of a wise, well-informed, independent, and thoroughly competent writer. It removes a reproach from our indigenous theology, fills a glaring blank in our literature, and is sure to become the text-book in Christian Ethics.'—Professor MARCUS DODS, D.D., in *The Bookman.*

'It is so beautifully clear, devoid of dulness, and has so many "bursts of eloquence," that it will take the reader who considers Christian Ethics for the first time under his tuition literally by storm.'—*Methodist Times.*

No. III. of the Series. Now ready, Second Edition, post 8vo, 10s. 6d.,

APOLOGETICS;

OR, CHRISTIANITY DEFENSIVELY STATED.

BY PROFESSOR A. B. BRUCE, D.D.,

AUTHOR OF
'THE TRAINING OF THE TWELVE,' 'THE HUMILIATION OF CHRIST,'
'THE KINGDOM OF GOD,' ETC.

'In this noble work of Dr. Bruce, the reader feels on every page that he is in contact with a mind and spirit in which all the conditions for a genuine apologetic are fulfilled. . . . At the end of Dr. Bruce's work the reader is uplifted with a great and steady confidence in the truth of the gospel; the evangel has been pleading its cause with him, and he has felt its power.'—*British Weekly.*

Detailed Prospectuses of the 'International Theological Library' free on application.

EDINBURGH: T. & T. CLARK, 38 GEORGE STREET.

www.ingramcontent.com/pod-product-compliance
Lightning Source LLC
Chambersburg PA
CBHW020105020526
44112CB00033B/920